STEPHEN ADAMS is an associate professor in the Department of English at the University of Western Ontario.

Murray Schafer is one of Canada's few composers to have achieved an international reputation. His innovative and often controversial work extends beyond music into the areas of education, literary scholarship, journalism, theatre, and graphics, as well as a new field of his own making – environmental sound research. This comprehensive critical survey of his life and works reveals the unifying pattern within an amazingly productive and varied career.

Adams examines Schafer's extensive writings, which form the intellectual context of his music. Though Schafer is both avant-gardist and self-confessed romantic, his writings solve this apparent paradox and show, as well, the central position of the 'soundscape' in his thought. Adams traces the development of Schafer's music from his early works in a mild neo-classical vein to his experimentation with various modernist procedures – serialism, electronic sound, stereophony, graphic notations, and elements of chance – all of which he fused together in his first stage work or 'audio-visual poem,' Loving, in 1965.

This volume includes a full bibliography, discography, and catalogue of works.

R. Murray Schafer, 1975

STEPHEN ADAMS

R. Murray Schafer

UNIVERSITY OF TORONTO PRESS
Toronto   Buffalo   London

© University of Toronto Press 1983
Toronto   Buffalo   London
Printed in Canada

ISBN 0-8020-5571-0

Canadian Composers/Compositeurs Canadiens 4

Canadian Cataloguing in Publication Data

Adams, Stephen, 1945–
   R. Murray Schafer

   (Canadian composers, ISSN 0316-1293; no. 4 – Compositeurs
   canadiens, ISSN 0316-1293; no 4)
   Bibliography: p.
   Includes index.
   ISBN 0-8020-5571-0

   1. Schafer, R. Murray (Raymond Murray), 1933–   . Works.
   I. Title.   II. Series: Canadian composers; no. 4.

   ML410.S32A32   780'.92'4   C82-094923-X

31,493

ok has been published with the help of a grant from the Canadian Federation for
_umanities, using funds provided by the Social Sciences and Humanities Research
Council of Canada, and a grant from the Publications Fund of the University of Toronto
Press.

Excerpts from *Divan i Shams i Tabriz, Son of Heldenleben, String Quartet No. 1,
East, Gita, Arcana,* and *Hymn to Night* used by permission of European American
Music Distributors Corporation, sole agent in Canada for Universal Edition.
   Excerpts from *Minnelieder, Loving, Train, Requiems for the Party-Girl, Threnody,* and
Epitaph for Moonlight used by permission of Berandol Music Limited.

Contents

Preface

This is a book about Murray Schafer in mid-career. The primary function of such a book is to bring together the most relevant information about that career in one place, because even for earnest devotees of contemporary music, experience of a prolific, currently active composer like Schafer is fragmentary – hearing a piece here, reading an article there. This book offers an opportunity to see the complete pattern, even while it is emerging. The pattern, of course, is still open-ended, and one of my worries while writing has been to keep up with my rapidly developing subject. But the lines are clearly in place, at least to date, and in his lifetime of less than fifty years, Schafer has already produced material enough for a much larger book than this one.

Not all this material is music. In his amazingly diverse career, Schafer has been composer, graphic artist, dramatist, creative writer, educator, social critic, literary scholar, and journalist. But I have given most of my attention to the compositions. The first chapter is biographical. The second uses the prose writings (not all of them, or they would have taken over the book) as a means of sketching Schafer's intellectual loyalties. All the remaining chapters are given to the music: first Schafer's acquisition of a contemporary technique is traced, and then, after the turning point of *Loving* (1965), the works are surveyed by genre, for after 1965 the lines of development become too difficult to disentangle. Activities since 1979 are summarized in an epilogue.

Schafer's development curiously epitomizes the growth of Canadian music over the middle decades of this century. A reading of George A. Proctor's invaluable *Canadian Music of the Twentieth Century* makes this quite clear. Proctor details how Canada, a musical backwoods in 1940, caught up with developments elsewhere in the world in the space of about thirty years, turning from a Stravinskian neo-classicism in the 1940s and 1950s to a more romantically expressionistic serialism in the 1960s, until finally (with the centennial year, 1967, as a convenient marker), it has become fully modernized. Schafer – a few years younger than the generation of Somers, Beckwith, and Papineau-Couture – has followed this pattern exactly. Thus, for all his apparent idiosyncrasy, he is not only a dominating personality in our music but one who truly typifies the musical experience of the nation.

Throughout his career, Schafer has consistently displayed two general qualities. The first is a seemingly inexhaustible capacity for surprise. There are recurrent preoccupations and mannerisms of style, of course, but, wholly apart from the qualities of the music itself, Schafer's strength as a composer has been his unique ability to invent a reason for writing yet another piece. His pieces as a result tend to be much unlike each other, none of them wholly 'representative.' A second quality of his music is its audience-appeal. Despite Schafer's mature idiom, which must be called (for lack of a better word) *avant-garde*, and despite the posture of indifference or antagonism to the audience that he sometimes strikes, Schafer's best pieces almost always make some kind of sense to a concert audience on first hearing – whether through programmatic subject matter, lyrical expression, or theatricality.

Many people have made contributions to the writing of this book, but my thanks must go above all to Murray Schafer himself. My personal gratitude dates back to 1970 (see page 19), and since then not only has he suggested me as the author of this book for the Canadian Composers series, but his behaviour as its subject has remained exemplary. He has co-operated in every way, answering questions and opening to me private files of tapes, papers, and correspondence; and his factual comments on initial drafts have been incorporated wherever appropriate. Beyond this he has refused to interfere: he declines to analyse his own music, and he has not questioned my pronouncements upon it. So if he has been an immediate presence, he has at the same time allowed me to feel that this book is my own.

'Every great man nowadays has his disciples,' said Oscar Wilde. 'And it is always Judas who writes the biography.' To write a dull book about Murray Schafer would be betrayal indeed, but if I have accomplished it, the feat is mine alone.

Acknowledgments

Chief among those who have contributed to this volume is John Beckwith, most patient and meticulous of editors. Special thanks are also due to Alan Gillmor, who made his bibliographic work available to me, and to John Fodi, for his expert musical copy. I owe particular debts as well to Jack Behrens, Peter Racine Fricker, Richard Johnston, Allen Noon, Marcus Reinkeluers, Jean Schafer, Robert Skelton, and Gordon Tracy. At the University of Toronto Press I must thank Margaret Parker, who could always spot the error where I saw only perfection, and Will Rueter and Ron Schoeffel. I must also thank Berandol Music Limited and European American Music Distributors Corporation for providing me with many necessary materials, as well as for permission to print musical examples.

Anyone concerned with Canadian music realizes how indispensable is the Canadian Music Centre. This book, like others in the Canadian Composers Series, was initiated and commissioned by the Canadian Music Centre. There I must also thank two former directors, John Roberts and Keith MacMillan, as well as Henry Mutsaers, Norma Dickson, Chris Wilson, and Karen Kieser. Of many typists, the greatest burden has fallen to Launa Fuller at the University of Western Ontario. And of many librarians, the others will forgive me if I single out my wife, Ruth, whose help and support are beyond acknowledgment.

I wish to express my gratitude to several other individuals whose presence in my life made writing this book possible: at the University of Toronto, to Maria Rika Maniates, to Douglas LePan, and to the late Marshall McLuhan; at the University of Minnesota, to Domenick Argento, who did his best to fend off my failure as a composer, and to Charles McHugh, for hours of conversation that are not forgotten.

Lastly, to my father, Merle Adams – a violinist with the Minneapolis Symphony under Verbrugghen, Ormandy, Mitropoulos, and Dorati, and later head of music for the Minneapolis Public Library. Through all those years he nurtured literally hundreds of young violinists, including three of his children. This book is dedicated to his memory.

Picture credits:
page ii Simon Fraser University News Service
page xi (top) Canadian Music Centre
page xii (top) P.R.O. Canada; (bottom) François Varin and Frisco Photo (Montreal)
page xiv (top) *Bancroft Times*
page xvi (top) Fred Phipps, CBC Photo; (bottom) Robert Skelton

Murray Schafer in the early 1960s

The founders of the Ten Centuries Concerts, Toronto 1961.
Left to right: Harry Freedman, Norman Symonds, Harry Somers,
Gordon Delamont, Schafer

Schafer at the Electronic Music Studio, Simon Fraser University, circa 1968

Schafer with school children, Montreal 1971

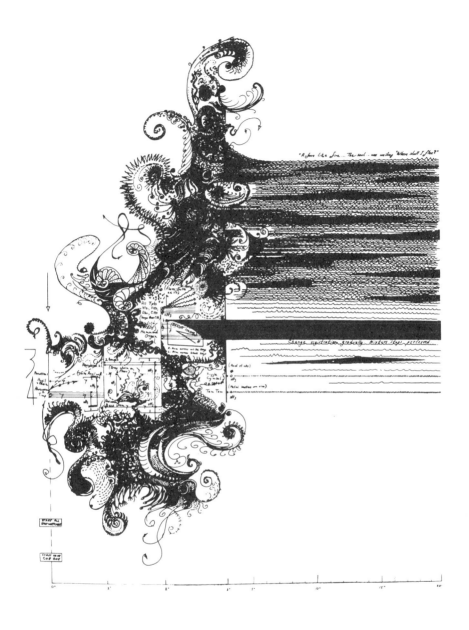

Divan i Shams i Tabriz, opening page of score (© Copyright 1977 Universal Edition (Canada) Ltd.)

Schafer and Yehudi Menuhin with the sound sculpture in Schafer's barn, during the shooting of the television series 'The Music of Man'

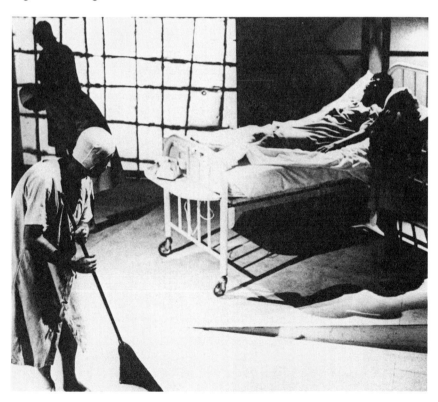

From the Stratford Festival production of *Patria II*, 1972

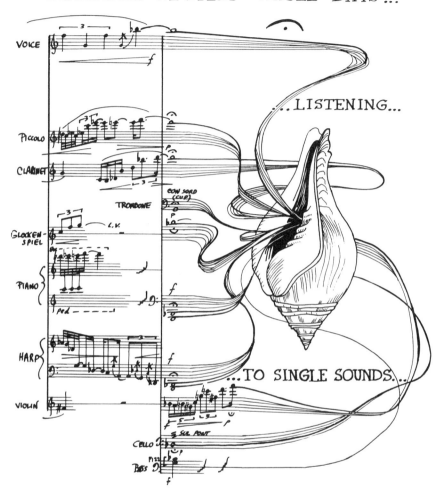

Smoke: A Novel, page 44. The music shown is from *Hymn to Night*.

From Les Grands Ballets Canadiens production of *Adieu, Robert Schumann*. *Left to right*: Annette av Paul, Vincent Warren, Maureen Forrester

From the University of Western Ontario production of *Apocalypsis*, showing b.p. Nichol as John and Paul Dutton as Michael, with the Four Living Creatures and the Chorus of Elders

R. MURRAY SCHAFER

1

Biography

Since 1975, Murray Schafer has made his permanent home in a one-hundred-year-old log farmhouse in Monteagle Valley, a few miles north of Bancroft, Ontario. Bancroft is a small town some three hours' drive north and east of Toronto, on the edge of the Muskoka-Haliburton cottage region, but not really part of it. The farmhouse, empty when Schafer bought it, has been made habitable with some difficulty; the farm itself is not picturesque. The region is rich in character, however – full of associations with Group of Seven canvases and, for him, with personal memories of boyhood summer holidays. Schafer's move to Monteagle Valley after a ten-year stay at Simon Fraser University in British Columbia was a removal from social entanglements, but not a retreat. He finds there the quiet country soundscape that is so precious to him and freedom to work without interruptions in the spacious studio built onto the farmhouse. The move marks a daring and yet calculated decision, typical of Schafer, to do whatever is necessary to allow the primary activity of his life, composing music.

Composing is Schafer's first vocation. Yet this statement might surprise some who know Schafer's name. He is widely known as a music educator. His books and his pieces for young students have made him a palpable if controversial force in Canada, as well as in Europe, the United States, Australia, and New Zealand. In literary circles, Schafer is a serious scholar, an authority on Ezra Pound, whose opera *The Testament of François Villon* Schafer produced for the BBC in 1962; he has also published a study of the German author and musician E.T.A. Hoffmann. Finally, others know Schafer as the author of *The Tuning of the World*, the founder of the World Soundscape Project, in fact the virtual inventor of 'soundscape' research – a hybrid study that crosses acoustics, geography, psychology, urbanology, and aesthetics into a new discipline dedicated to improving the acoustic environment in which we live. Some who know Schafer in his other roles would perhaps be surprised to learn that he is a composer at all; but all his activities have as their centre the composer's one concern: sound.

No success is possible in so many different areas without a deep personal drive to produce not just ideas but concrete results. Yet one impression of Schafer is curiously persistent: that he is more concerned with concepts than with works, more an original than a craftsman. He is still, in some circles, just a rebellious crackpot. Schafer's musical training has not been orthodox; his has never been a temperament to submit passively to anyone else's system, and it is truer of him than of most of us to say that he is self-taught. In addition, his unmethodical approach to music education is suspect. 'I am dismayed,' he says, 'by people who see me in action for about an hour at a workshop and then come to the conclusion that my sole ambition is to smash down the past. They get the impression that Schafer simply makes whoopee in the Music Room but that after a few exciting flings at this or that there is nothing more in his method.'[1] Also, because some of Schafer's best-known pieces have been written for students who have scarcely carried their instruments for a year, it is suspected that he would have them stop there. Because he accepts John Cage's principle that any sound can be heard as music, it is feared that he would throw away conventional music. A biographical essay by Peter Such dwells on Schafer's early rebelliousness at school, his poor academic performance, and his dismissal from the University of Toronto.[2] No one can deny the significance of any of these facts, but even a brief acquaintance with his work makes it clear that throughout his career, Schafer has applied himself stubbornly, with a rare intellectual integrity, to whatever discipline, musical or otherwise, was necessary to strengthen his art.

Born in Sarnia, Ontario, on 18 July 1933, Raymond Murray Schafer was raised and schooled in Toronto.[3] His mother is a competent amateur pianist, and his father taught himself enough at the keyboard to play through, say, the first movement of the *Moonlight Sonata*. An accountant for an oil company, Mr Schafer was unusually sympathetic to the arts, encouraging his son's artistic aspirations. He had done a number of pastel paintings as a young man, and young Schafer's first love was painting and drawing. Until the age of eighteen, he intended to follow a career as an artist, while his musical tastes were derived mainly from pop tunes heard on the radio. Schafer's one brother, Paul, has also pursued a career in the arts, as an administrator and cultural theorist. Paul Schafer has served as assistant director of the Ontario Arts Council, and he helped organize the Arts Administration program at York University in Toronto.

Murray Schafer's earliest exposure to serious music was confined to the conventional piano lessons and singing in a boys' choir – but both experiences were of considerable consequence. The choir was that of Grace Church on-the-Hill, Toronto, conducted by John Hodgins. Schafer sang there from about the age of ten until he was eighteen. Not only was his musical training under Hodgins valuable, but he developed a feeling for choral music that has been apparent throughout his career; Hodgins also gave young Schafer organ lessons for a very short time. Schafer's piano lessons began when he was six, under the guidance of a local teacher named Mrs Lindsay. At first he valued them mainly for teaching him how to play 'Bumble Boogie' incessantly at choir practices; but, although he later developed an ironical disdain for the piano ('an over-decorated hearse'), he became a proficient pianist, studying with the well-known Toronto musicians Douglas Bodle and Alberto Guerrero. Eventually he earned the diploma of LRSM (Licentiate of the Royal Schools of Music, London, England), the only music certificate that he possesses. At the age of fifteen, he began theory lessons with John Weinzweig. He did not seriously consider writing music until he was eighteen, though he confesses to one youthful indiscretion in the form of an operetta, which he never completed.

Schafer's ambitions in the field of graphic arts were qualified by one circumstance. When he was very young, he developed glaucoma in his right eye. After two unsuccessful operations at the age of eight, the eye was removed. The consequences of this must remain speculation, and are perhaps slight; but it seems plausible that his interest in the visual arts may have contained an element of compensation, and that his later decision to turn to music was influenced by his affected eyesight. Schafer has never really abandoned art, however, as a glance at the remarkable pictographic notations of *Lustro* and *Patria* will prove. Possibly the loss of his eye made Schafer more sensitive than other people to the functions of the various organs of perception – the kind of sensitivity that would attract him to such philosophers of perception as Paul Klee, Ezra Pound, and Marshall McLuhan, all of whom shaped his thinking in later years.

Some of Schafer's pleasantest childhood memories are connected with sports, especially football. As a youngster, he threw himself into this passion with the same all-consuming determination that characterizes his personality generally, and even in football his traits of originality and initiative are clear. Eventually, he became good enough to try out for the Balmy Beach team of the old Ontario Football League (though the team had at that point, he admits, fallen on hard times). What is more unusual, he trained himself as a football strategist: he bought every book he could find on the subject and then, still unsatisfied, entered into correspondence with a number of prominent sportsmen, including Frank Leahy, the celebrated coach at Notre Dame. Schafer's specialties were elaborate razzle-dazzle plays and sneaker plays of a kind no longer in fashion; but after finishing high school, when he tried his hand himself at coaching a young team in the High Park YMCA League, he achieved a remarkable record: in five years, his teams scored 545 points, with only one touchdown scored against them.

Less pleasant are his memories of school: his own accounts are fairly Dickensian. Schafer felt that his teachers misunderstood him, that they showed no sympathy at all with his artistic ambitions, that they simply embodied the rejection of artistic values by Canadian society as a whole. For their part, the teachers resented Schafer so much that they several times recommended that he leave school altogether. He was considered a complete academic failure. Among several depressing stories that Peter Such relates about Schafer's experiences in the Toronto school system, perhaps the most revealing is his encounter, at the age of fifteen or sixteen, with the official 'guidance counsellor':

MURRAY	I'd like to be a painter.
COUNSELLOR	A house-painter? Well ... that's very steady ...
MURRAY	No. I mean the other kind of painter.
COUNSELLOR	Oh. Well. You know there's lots of money in commercial art if you're prepared ...
MURRAY	No. I didn't mean a commercial artist.
COUNSELLOR	Oh. You mean painting portraits. Well. That's a ...
MURRAY	No. I want to be an abstract painter like Picasso.
COUNSELLOR	Now look here, young man. You're going to have a wife and family and you're going to have to look after them. How are you going to support them with the kind of money you're going to make from those dizzy paintings?[4]

If this episode really represents Schafer's experience with Canadian public education, there is little wonder that he later determined to do what he could to impress on the schools the legitimate claims of the arts.

If Schafer's discovery of art was precocious, his appreciation of literature and music emerged only later. Two incidents in particular have assumed in the composer's memory the status of conversion experiences. One was his reading, in grade eleven, of Dickens' *Great Expectations*. He was so moved by the experience of real literature that the following year in school, still avid, he committed the entire text of *Macbeth* to memory. Schafer's true discovery of music came at about the same time and with even greater suddenness – though not through the devices of the Toronto school system. On a May morning drive to the country with his family in their first car, the radio picked up Beethoven's *Emperor Concerto*. He heard for the first time. With something like Pauline intensity, Schafer's conversion to classical music was accomplished.

Schafer completed grade twelve, but he did not attempt the rigours of Ontario's grade thirteen.[5] Instead, from 1951 to 1953, he determined to pursue his musical training first at the Royal Conservatory of Music and then at the University of Toronto Faculty of Music. He was ineligible for academic programs at the university because of his high-school record, but after the first year he was able to enroll in the Artist Diploma Course, a non-academic course primarily intended for performance students, which at the time included an option for composition. Schafer was still uncertain about a future in music, and understandably so.

Although Schafer's stay at the university was curtailed prematurely, it was not without value. He studied piano with Alberto Guerrero, the Chilean master who also taught Glenn Gould and John Beckwith. Guerrero, a man in his late sixties when Schafer knew him, was an inspiring teacher who showed interest not only in his student's digital technique but in his mind as well. Schafer remembers him as a man who listened with sincere attention, and who directed him towards French culture and the music of 'Les Six.' When Guerrero died in 1959, Schafer wrote a brief *In Memoriam* for string orchestra.

A more unusual pursuit for that time was the study of harpsichord under Greta Kraus. Schafer, like many students, found her love for older music infectious, and he has ever since preferred the harpsichord to the piano. Her insight was especially valuable at a time when the revival of baroque music was just beginning to stir, though it was still something of an esoteric taste. Schafer's first major composition is a *Harpsichord Concerto* written with Greta Kraus in mind. At the

University of Toronto, Schafer also benefited from Arnold Walter's lectures in music history, despite the friction with Walter that later developed. But most important, Schafer found in John Weinzweig a sympathetic instructor in theory and composition.

Aside from his stature as a composer, Weinzweig is one of the most influential teachers in Canadian music; the long list of his students at Toronto includes names like Harry Somers, Harry Freedman, Norma Beecroft, Robert Aitken, and Gustav Ciamaga. Weinzweig was the first Canadian composer to feel the influence of Stravinsky and Schoenberg, or to take interest in the scores of the great modernists like Bartók and Varèse at a time when Canadian music (in Toronto at least) was still dominated by the Anglo-romantic tradition of Sir Ernest MacMillan and Healey Willan. In the early 1940s, when Weinzweig began to teach, he was, according to Brian Cherney, 'regarded by many established musicians as a fifth columnist, bent on destroying the traditional nineteenth-century musical language.'[6]

Ten years later the situation had not much changed. In Schafer's words, Weinzweig

was the first fluorescence of genius to become visible on the Canadian music scene ... Back in 1950 most of John's colleagues were busy composing music for those over fifty who had never been under fifty, and so he became the only teacher to whom those under fifty could go ... Toronto critics called him the Donald Duck of music, and preferred the oscitations of Brahms; but for us he was a Parnassus of one ... If I were asked to name his principal service to Canada it could be this: that he rode out the first storms of criticism alone, until he could educate enough other composers to offer him the companionship of the Canadian League of Composers.[7]

Certainly no one else in Toronto could have given Schafer a better introduction to modern styles. 'I do not know if he was a good teacher,' says Schafer; 'I only know that he was considerate and that things he had to offer were not purchasable anywhere else in Canada at that time.'[8]

Weinzweig had been responsible for all of Schafer's training in theory from about the age of fifteen. Entering on composition, Schafer studied analysis and orchestration, not composing his first pieces until he was eighteen or nineteen. Weinzweig's twelve-tone technique was at this point beyond him: his earliest works are timid excursions into polytonality. He had discovered by this time the Paris of the 1920s, and was drawn by 'Les Six,' as much by their milieu as by their music. He remembers feeling that life would suddenly become meaningful as soon as he could get to Paris. At the same time, he was aware that other young composers – Somers, Freedman, Beckwith – were far ahead of him in technique, and he felt diffident at first about his music. Under Weinzweig's direction, Schafer produced a number of works in a neo-classical style: the piano piece *Polytonality*; the song *A Music Lesson*; an unpublished *Trio for Clarinet, Cello, and Piano*; and finally the whole of the *Concerto for Harpsichord and Eight Wind Instruments*, a piece far more polished and sophisticated than its composer's experience could possibly lead one to expect.

Schafer's exposure to music before 1956 was determined as much by the nature of Toronto's musical taste as by the limitations of his own. Certainly he heard, he says, 'a great deal of English music, performed by Lord Largo (alias Sir Ernest MacMillan),'[9] and he recalls with pleasure participating with his church choir in the massive annual *Messiah*. The church choir also gave a performance of Benjamin Britten's *St Nicholas Cantata*, under Britten's direction. But very little contemporary music could be heard – if anything, an occasional piece by Stravinsky or Copland. Schafer recalls some listening to recordings at the Faculty of Music. He heard some twelve-tone works, piano pieces of Schoenberg, and Berg's *Lyric Suite*. Ives and Bartók were just emerging from obscurity; Schafer remembers hearing a couple of pieces by Bartók and dismissing them as uninteresting. Chancing upon a work by Varèse, young Schafer decided the man was absolutely mad.

But Schafer's curiosity was expanding. It drew him into contact at the university with Marshall McLuhan, several of whose classes he attended in the company of a friend, Cam Trowsdale, later to become concert-master of the CBC Vancouver Chamber Orchestra and a CBC broadcaster. McLuhan's manner with his students was even then oracular. The sessions could hardly be called 'discussions' in the ordinary sense of the term: students would ask questions, and McLuhan's responses would land at some distance from the original point of take-off. The talk touched on matters of aesthetics, James Joyce, Ezra Pound, and McLuhan's incipient communications theories, and the experience doubtless helped make new heroes of Joyce and especially Pound – whose fortunes were just then at their lowest ebb after his arrest for supporting Mussolini during the war. (Pound, imprisoned in St Elizabeth's Hospital for the Criminally Insane in Washington, was corresponding with McLuhan at the time.) McLuhan was by no means a celebrity in the early 1950s, except locally; but he had already branched out from his earlier New Critical thinking into communications, an area just then emerging as an independent study. *The Mechanical Bride* had appeared in 1951, marking the start of McLuhan's study of pop culture and his sense of the arts as an index to culture as a whole. McLuhan was then openly antagonistic to pop vulgarity (a satiric attitude that he later suppressed – though never, I think, entirely). Schafer was very early attuned to McLuhan's basic assumptions.

Not all Schafer's academic experiences, however, were equally joyous. He resented some of his courses, and he betrayed his resentment by insulting behaviour. Arnold Walter, director of the Music Faculty, demanded that Schafer apologize in writing to certain instructors; Schafer refused, and he was quietly ejected.

Schafer's behaviour was indeed insulting, and he acknowledges a degree of responsibility for his dismissal. He was perhaps a 'fringe character,' he says. But at the same time he felt mistreated by 'an educational system that was angled straight down the centre.'[10] And the system was inflexible; for example, Schafer's petition to be excused, as an 'already experienced chorister,' from Richard Johnston's mandatory choir class, was refused. Then, when he refused to sing, ostentatiously reading an art book at the back of the room, Johnston, who was standing on a chair to conduct, stomped on it in a rage – and went through the seat. Schafer sealed his fate by laughing when Johnston, lunging forward, literally fell on his face. This incident is only one of a number that preceded Schafer's dismissal.

Years later, in 1968, Schafer received a surprising request. Arnold Walter was retiring, and several of his former students who had achieved prominence were invited to give their tributes at a testimonial dinner. Would Murray Schafer be pleased to attend? The reply is worth quoting at length:

Dear Arnold Walter:
A curiosity, perhaps, that I of all people should write, for my premature release from the Faculty of Music after two of the most uncomfortable years in my life scarcely qualifies me as an alumnus. However, a few years ago, to my extreme mystification, I began receiving notices on stationery of the Music Alumni Association and was forced to the conclusion that indeed somehow I had 'graduated.'
I still have strong impressions of your history lectures. In fact, of all university

lectures I recall only yours on history and McLuhan's on poetry and music –
these with some whimsy because they were so poor. Yours were calculated,
ruminating, Spenglerian. If anything, they gave me a respect and care for the
accuracy of scholarship and, as you know, I have done some of that, as
respectfully and carefully as possible.

But my strongest memory is of that day in your office on College Street when
you kicked me in the pants and sent me flying out of the Faculty of Music. With
that action you became a chief influence in my life. It was the best thing that
could have happened. Your institution became a symbol of something against
which I could react positively and coherently. In one of his essays entitled 'Why
I Write,' George Orwell gives as his first reason: the desire to prove to parents and
teachers that they were mistaken. It is an utterly important function of the
teacher to act as an abrasive against which his students can react. Sometimes
this can be accomplished pleasantly, sometimes unpleasantly; but in the long
run, how it is accomplished is quite without importance. Looking back now,
however, it is obvious that my current deep involvement with music education
could only have come about as a reaction to my own experiences. It is time to
thank you for what you have done. We had some petty disputes which it was
useful for me to dramatize in order to harness my own life-energies. We have
matured. Let us be friends.

I am sorry not to be able to be at your testimonial dinner, much as I should like
to.

Finally, the hope that your retirement will bring you pleasures and freedoms
to compose, research, and provide wise counsel to the nervy young Turks.

With all best wishes. Yours sincerely,

R.M. Schafer[11]

Schafer's letter, apart from its telling self-analysis, perhaps suggests
some of the hurt that he felt at being barred from learning, and from
privileges that attended a finished degree. (A few years earlier, in 1964,
Walter had denied Schafer access to the university's excellent new
electronic music studio, and when Schafer re-applied as a student to
gain access, he was again refused – for lack of academic qualifications.
He was at the time artist in residence at Memorial University in
Newfoundland. Within a few years, however, Schafer was admitted to
the studio and used it frequently. Arnold Walter, too, later invited
Schafer to lecture at the Faculty of Music and supported him in certain
grant applications.)

Turned out of school, Schafer decided on Europe. For nine months in

1955 he worked on board a Great Lakes oil tanker, saving his money for Vienna. Before he left, he picked up as much of the language as he could from a German-speaking neighbour in Toronto.

Schafer's decision to go to Vienna was largely influenced by Greta Kraus, who had family there and generously arranged for Schafer to stay with them. The city, traditionally the musical heart of Europe, may have seemed attractive, and even, as the home of Schoenberg, a place where advanced musical styles could be imbibed freely; but sadly, when Schafer arrived at the Vienna Academy, he quickly realized that he could not be interested in the kind of music being taught there. Schoenberg and Berg and Webern were gone without a trace. The only music that could be heard was the mainstream of Viennese tradition, from Mozart through Bruckner and Strauss; even Mahler and Bach were little performed. Furthermore, 1956 was the bicentenary of Mozart's birth, and the attendant glut of that composer's music left Schafer with a distaste that he still senses. Schafer continued to broaden his interests, however. He decided to study medieval German, so he searched out at the university a 'curious lady whose chief ambition was to translate *Beowulf* into *Mittelhochdeutsch*, and who spoke a strange, Chaucerian English.'[12] The outcome of this study was the *Minnelieder* (1956), a group of thirteen songs to texts by medieval German poets. Schafer's attraction to the *Minnesänger* stemmed from his interest in Ezra Pound, a champion of medievalism. Schafer's interest in the mezzo-soprano voice resulted from his friendship with Phyllis Mailing, a young voice student whom he had known in Toronto and who would later become his first wife. Schafer now looks on the *Minnelieder* as the best of his early pieces – 'the first work I would regard as a useful contribution to music.'[13] For two years afterwards, he wrote no new music. The piece reflects the composer's experience in Vienna, and more than one listener has detected in it the ghost of Gustav Mahler – a presence equally noticeable in the *Kinderlieder* (1958). Schafer's contact with the advanced stages of the Hapsburgian *Schwärmerei* has yielded more unpredictable results in his later music, notably his ambivalent homage to Richard Strauss, *Son of Heldenleben* (1968). Schafer still feels a fondness for Vienna, returning occasionally to see his publishers at Universal Edition or to lecture at the Vienna Academy, but mainly to recover the atmosphere.

While in Vienna, Schafer greatly expanded his literary and artistic interests. He read deeply in German romantic authors – Hölderlin,

Novalis, Tieck, Büchner, Rilke – and he was particularly fascinated by the versatile author-composer-caricaturist E.T.A. Hoffmann. In fact, during this period he completed his study of Hoffmann's musical romanticism, including a draft of his book, but he was unable to find a publisher. The volume that appeared in 1975 as *E.T.A. Hoffmann and Music*, a revised version of the first text, has been praised by one scholar as 'an evocative book by a man of learning, imagination, feeling and wit.'[14]

At this same time, Schafer developed an intense interest in the work of the Bauhaus artists, Paul Klee in particular. He claims these artists among the strongest influences on his own development. Klee and Schafer have roots deep in German romanticism; both reveal a pervasive love of nature and a respect for the role of the subconscious in creation. Klee's satiric edge parallels Schafer's. And Klee's debt to the art of children and the mentally disordered suggests further parallels in Schafer's music – his compositions for children, or his preoccupation with extreme mental states.

The Bauhaus experiment stands behind many of the mature Schafer's ideas. The Bauhaus, created in the 1920s 'to unite the arts through the promulgation of egalitarian feelings that hovered somewhere between medievalist romanticism and expressionist socialism,'[15] suggests Schafer's impulse not only to combine the arts but to unite his art with larger social or political concerns. Like the Bauhaus, Schafer seeks to combine artist and technician, to humanize the machine. Both build on a reformed education. Schafer's interest in the nature of sound resembles the Bauhaus study of basic elements of drawing, like the studies of line and colour in Klee's notebooks. Schafer is deeply sympathetic with the technological bent of Bauhaus teaching: 'Although the Bauhaus had great teachers, it didn't produce really great students. Their achievement was the discovery of the whole field of industrial design.' Accordingly, Schafer's soundscape studies 'would not produce great composers but people who could design a ring for the telephone.'[16] At least one project, his 'Basic Course,' is modelled directly after the basic course in visual design that Johannes Itten developed for his first-year students, 'aimed at purging the student of all conventionally acquired knowledge in order to introduce him to workshop theory and practice.'[17] Finally, Schafer has admired the architectural spaces of Walter Gropius for breaking away from visual perspective: 'The liberated viewer as he moves about the building through time has become the governing aesthetic criterion.'[18] Schafer has pursued this idea, first in his stereophonic compositions and then in his theatrical works, influenced consciously by the theatrical spaces designed at the Bauhaus, particularly the *Totaltheater* conceived by Gropius for Erwin Piscator.[19]

Through the late 1950s, Schafer travelled widely about Europe, making one especially fruitful excursion into the communist countries of the Balkans. His curiosity was twofold: he wanted to hear the fabled folk-music of the region, and he wanted to observe the cultural conditions under communism. Describing himself as 'essentially a non-political man,' Schafer was still strongly attracted by communist theories, and he desired that the trip might force some decisions. Westerners were much less common in the area than they are now, but while Schafer suffered the usual snarls of red tape, he was impressed by the hospitality. In 1959, he visited the Composers' Union in Bucharest, studying the government's generous system of patronage. In Sofia he spoke with Bulgarian composers who defended their backward-looking styles: 'We are humanists, and are ready to sacrifice our pride, even our individuality, for the sake of writing music that will inspire the nation,' explained Ljubomir Pipkov. 'Before 1945 we were a nation of farmers. Most of us had never heard a symphony orchestra, let alone a composition by Schoenberg.'[20] From Bulgaria, Schafer travelled to Yugoslavia, then to Hungary, where he met Zoltán Kodály and László Lajtha. Lajtha was particularly kind, welcoming many visits from the young Canadian; Schafer later returned the kindness by arranging some performances of Lajtha's music in the West.

These experiences profoundly affected Schafer's political outlook, for whatever his dissatisfaction with capitalist commercialism, he did not find Marxism an acceptable alternative. He recalls this feeling at the time as 'somewhat indecisive,' but it has since solidified. The paradoxical position of an *avant-garde* Marxist like Luigi Nono gradually revealed itself as untenable. Communism coerces the artists, the visionaries, the 'fringe elements' into conformity with its own needs, and it outlaws all forms of protest. Schafer was struck by the way casual conversation was undermined by a system in which criticism of the Musicians' Union could be construed as treason. Schafer still respects many features of communism as ethically superior to their capitalist counterparts, but he refuses to equate economic equality with spiritual conformity. His own career would have been out of the question in such circumstances. So instead of adopting Marxism, Schafer in 1960 wrote two atonal songs with orchestra, *Protest and Incarceration*, on smuggled texts by political prisoners, and decided to carry on his quarrel with capitalism from the inside.

While in the Balkans, however, Schafer (like Bartók and Milman Parry before him) travelled with recording equipment – much less suspicious to officials than a camera – pursuing his curiosity about the folk-music both at first hand and through the various cultural institutes. One of his most unusual possessions is a tape from a region of western Bulgaria where the major or minor second is accepted as a consonant interval. The effect of the peasant women with their stridently focused Slavic voices singing in parallel seconds is unforgettable. Once asked about his most profound musical experiences, Schafer recalled 'listening to the peasant musicians of Rumania, Bulgaria and other truly musical societies such as one does not find here.'[21]

Schafer spent much of his time in Europe not in the cultural metropolises but in provincial areas where he could become more closely acquainted with the people. After leaving Vienna, he stayed six months in France, but, disappointed by Paris, he quickly removed to Angers. Having made friends with the hotel proprietor's son, he was allowed to live there without rent – in the unheated servants' quarters. For warmth, he went to bed early and read the works of André Breton, Jean Cocteau, and René Char. Later he spent a period in Trieste, staying in a villa overlooking the Adriatic with an aristocratic eighty-year-old lady, Signora Mosetti, who showed him the haunts of Winkelmann and Duino Castle, where Rilke wrote his elegies. For a while in Trieste, Schafer taught English at the local Berlitz school – the identical job once held by James Joyce.

In the midst of his European wanderings, Schafer returned for a few months to Canada. Typically, his brief homecoming was not unproductive. Working with two other young composers, Milton Barnes and Morris Eisenstadt, Schafer mounted a program of chamber music, including his own *Trio for Clarinet, Cello, and Piano* and *Three Contemporaries*, performed by Phyllis Mailing and Weldon Kilburn. John Beckwith, reviewing the concert in the *Canadian Music Journal*, was cool towards the *Trio*, but he acclaimed the songs: '*Three Contemporaries* was the success of the concert, and is as original a work as this commentator has heard from the pen of any Canadian lately.'[22] After describing the work in detail, Beckwith, having discussed eight composers in all, prophetically identified as 'the most accomplished writing in the group' that of Bruce Mather and Murray Schafer.

Coinciding with this success, Schafer somehow won the confidence of The Canada Council and returned to Europe with a scholarship to study composition. (An earlier application, for a Pound-inspired project to study relationships between Arabic and troubadour poetry, had been turned down.) Schafer's destination this time was London. There he spent two years, and he was more successful in hearing the music that he needed to hear. In Europe, he recalls, 'Vienna was a washout and in Paris one heard only French music. But in London at that time all kinds of music were available as they were in no other European capital.'[23] There was a great deal of contemporary music, both the classics (Schoenberg and his followers were being pushed vigorously by the BBC) and music of younger composers. This exposure to more contemporary music immediately began to show itself in Schafer's own style.

For a tutor in London, Schafer had originally decided on Matyas Seiber, the Hungarian composer and a noted teacher; but Seiber died tragically in an accident in 1960, so Schafer turned to Peter Racine Fricker, a former Seiber pupil who had gathered a substantial reputation as a composer. Fricker's personal approach was agreeably informal, never evoking any of Schafer's former rebelliousness. 'He was independent, certainly, which I approved of, but no more than that,' Fricker recalls. 'I don't know if I taught him anything, since he was already a most competent and intelligent musician, but it was interesting to work with him. I found him to be a lively and stimulating personality.'[24]

What emerges most clearly from Schafer's published interview with Fricker is the English composer's passionate belief in form. Fricker's music, says Schafer, shows 'great craftsmanship and a fastidious concern for design, though its appeal is urgent and consuming.' Fricker says of his own procedure, 'the work begins to take shape before I write a note of it ... This is what I teach my pupils too: that before they can write the second bar, they must know all the implications of the first bar. The entire work is responsible to the original fragment whatever that may be.'[25] Fricker set Schafer to analysing scores of Webern and Dallapiccola, and also Guillaume de Machaut, a task he found much to his liking. None of Schafer's music much resembles Fricker's, but the influence was crucial. The sudden adoption of serialism in *Protest and Incarceration* (already written before lessons with Fricker commenced) marks a clear break from the earlier works. In *Brébeuf,* Schafer for the first time sustains a single formal concept across a long span of time. Under Fricker's guidance, Schafer produced some of his most abstract and architectonic compositions – the strict canonic writing of the *Five Studies on Texts by Prudentius* (1961–2) and the two *Untitled Compositions for Orchestra* (1963), or the serial and isorhythmic procedures of the *Canzoni for Prisoners* (1961–2). This last piece employs a device favoured by Fricker, a row of more than twelve notes (Schafer's has seventy-six). Fricker also interested Schafer in Prudentius, having himself already set that author in his *Elegy of St Eulalia*.

The interview with Fricker forms part of another large project of this period. In London, assuming the role of free-lance journalist, Schafer gathered a series of taped interviews with British composers, which he sold to the CBC. These became the basis of his first book, *British Composers in Interview*, published by Faber in 1963, covering sixteen composers from John Ireland to Peter Maxwell Davies. Schafer chose the composers carefully, he says, so that 'each one, if not necessarily a great composer, is nevertheless characteristic of a particular school. In other words, Malcolm Arnold is there because he writes a certain kind of music which, regardless of what I think about it, is a part of today's musical scene.'[26] The book was reviewed favourably and prominently – it drew a seven-page editorial from J.A. Westrup in *Music and Letters* – and, while most of the interest seemed to concentrate on the dwindling audience for the *avant-garde* in England, Schafer's performance as an interviewer was highly praised.[27] Arthur Jacobs, in *Opera*, described the interviewer as 'very much a musical journalist: he evidently took some trouble in studying his chosen composers in advance, talked to them on a level of intellectual equality, and was therefore able to ask questions that are individually pertinent. And sometimes *impertinent* too, thank goodness.'[28]

Out of these interviews, Schafer formed a number of friendships, the closest with Michael Tippett. Schafer visited Tippett frequently during this time, finding him a companionable mind, ready to converse over dinner or on long, reflective walks in the country about a broad range of common interests beyond music – German literature, Greek tragedy, Freud and Jung. Many parallels with Schafer's thinking appear in Tippett's book *Moving into Aquarius*.

Ever since the radio interviews, Schafer's activities as a radio journalist almost amount to a separate career. But one project, which has had important consequences, went beyond simple journalism. In June 1962, the BBC broadcast Schafer's production of the opera *Testament of François Villon* (1924) by Ezra Pound, with the role of Villon performed by the young John Shirley-Quirk. Pound's Villon settings make up a unique document of the 1920s, one that should be better known to musicians. Pound was a strictly amateur composer, yet he had to create a style of his own because he was dissatisfied with settings of verse by professionals. His solution through much of the opera is a simple monophonic line, vaguely medieval-sounding, yet strikingly modern in its occasional dissonance, pointillistic treatment of the orchestra, and scrupulously notated verbal rhythms. Wanting to chart the nuances of Villon's poetry exactly and lacking the notation, Pound got help from the American composer George Antheil, who painstakingly wrote down the rhythms with the skill of a musical ethnographer. The result is a unique and (against all odds) perfectly viable composition.[29]

Schafer's involvement in this project is typical of his initiative. From London he had written Pound, who had been released from St Elizabeth's in 1958 after thirteen years of imprisonment. Pound, shy of visitors, sent back a discouraging reply, but in the summer of 1960 Schafer went to call on him anyway at his home in Brunnenberg Castle in the Italian Tyrol:

I knocked. No one seemed to be in. Then high above me from one of the towers Pound poked out his head and said simply, 'So you've come.' I went up. He was in his undershirt and quickly apologized for not having any of 'the old vino' to offer me. He then promptly took to the horizontal on his bed and while I sat at his desk we had the most relaxed of our several conversations. We spoke of Arab music, which interested him because of its rhythms and its unharmonized melodies.[30]

Schafer visited with Pound for several days, talking about music and other subjects and listening to Pound recite poetry. Pound, says Schafer, was 'a generous conversationalist; he listened. He asked questions. There was no monologue but an exchange of ideas – at least one flattered oneself to think so.'[31] Before Schafer left he received Pound's permission to use the manuscript of the *Villon*. Then, says Schafer, 'with remarkable ingenuousness he handed me an open brown envelope. "Something to read on the train. When you get back to London give this to Tom."' Pound meant T.S. Eliot. It contained the typescript of a set of *Cantos*, the last portion of Pound's lifework that he would ever complete.[32]

When Schafer returned to London, having failed to interest the CBC in his project, he persuaded D.G. Bridson, a long-time Pound admirer at the BBC, to produce the opera, and he put Pound's music into performable condition. He also wrote an article on 'Ezra Pound and Music' for the *Canadian Music Journal*, for a long time the only available information on the subject; it has been reprinted in English, French, and German.[33] He also gathered a collection of Poundiana that became the basis of his massive edition of Pound's musical writings, a major achievement of literary scholarship. This task was no simple armchair scholarship, either, for Pound was in the habit of publishing in fugitive little magazines, and an important body of the musical reviews appeared in the town newspaper of Rapallo, Italy, where Pound lived in the 1930s; no Italian library kept copies, and Schafer, after considerable detective work, ultimately turned them up in dusty cardboard cartons at the tourist office in Chiavari. Furthermore, Schafer has contacted many of the now-forgotten musicians that Pound knew. Finally, with a generosity equal to Pound's own, he turned over the entire collection in 1970 to an unknown graduate student from Toronto (*ego scriptor*), who requested the material for a doctoral dissertation.

While in London in 1960, Schafer was married to mezzo-soprano Phyllis Mailing. They had known each other from the early 1950s as students at the Royal Conservatory in Toronto, where she had studied voice with George Lambert, Aksel Schiøtz, and Weldon Kilburn. As a major interpreter of Schafer's music, her influence on Schafer is great, but mostly of a general nature, resulting from the pervasive presence of her singing voice in the household. She kept him in close contact with the performer's viewpoint, not only giving him a working model of the singer's range, tessitura and dramatic potential, and capacity for innovative techniques, but keeping him mindful of simple, practical things like the desirability of cuing notes in the accompaniment. Since their divorce in 1971, she has continued to pursue a successful concert career.

In 1961, having spent the better part of six years in Europe, Schafer returned with his wife to Toronto. His return to Canada has proved final, though it has not been quite like a permanent settlement, since he has spent periods in Ontario, Newfoundland, and British Columbia. His return to Canada is celebrated in a cantata for baritone and orchestra *Brébeuf* (1961), one of his few pieces on a self-consciously national theme, a sort of Canadian *Erwartung* that ranks with the best of his works. *Brébeuf* did not mean, however, that Schafer had become a nationalist composer. Soon after his return, he published in *Tamarack Review* 'The Limits of Nationalism in Canadian Music,' an article explaining reasons, musical and cultural, why the obvious avenues to a national music are closed in Canada. The article was not Schafer's definitive statement, but seems more self-defence against Canadian pressures on his homecoming.

Content to remain in Canada, Schafer was not content to leave

Canadian culture as he found it. He quickly made contact with the local musical scene, taking a job with the Canadian Music Centre in Toronto, cataloguing, duplicating, and occasionally, when a request was not specific, filling it with scores by the most *avant-garde* composers. Toronto offered more varieties of music, perhaps, than it had a decade earlier, but Schafer was not alone in thinking there should be more. In the spring of 1962, five composers – Harry Somers, Norman Symonds, Gordon Delamont, Harry Freedman, and Schafer – were conversing casually about music left unperformed because it was 'uneconomical,' or because it would not fit comfortably on conventional concert programs. This conversation was the origin of the Ten Centuries Concerts, a remarkably successful series that constructed its programs from unusual repertoires and from neglected historical periods. Schafer became president of the organization. Local ensembles of all kinds were invited to participate, which they did enthusiastically. Tickets for the entire series sold out immediately. For two years, Schafer devoted a large share of his time to organizing concerts, hiring musicians, worrying about finances, and solving the inevitable practical problems. The series continued for five years, though after two Schafer relinquished his position to Norma Beecroft when he moved to Newfoundland. It is fair to say that the Ten Centuries Concerts were a major contribution to the city of Toronto's cultural coming of age. So much so that by 1963 Schafer could even remark, 'There's a terrible tendency in Canada to exaggerate what is going on in Europe today ... There are plenty of concerts in Vienna, sure, but so what? Right now there's more right here than you have time to go to.'[34]

Schafer carried in his mind two models for the Ten Centuries Concerts: the Invitation Concerts of the BBC Third Programme, covering a similar (though somewhat narrower) repertoire, and an unusual series that Ezra Pound had sponsored in Rapallo in the 1930s, emphasizing new music and early music resurrected from manuscripts in nearby libraries. (Pound's concerts were in fact an early stage in the revival of Vivaldi.) 'There are two frontiers of music,' wrote Schafer, 'the music of our own time and the music of antiquity, and Ten Centuries Concerts is dedicated to them both.'[35] Accordingly, the first season included a thirteenth-century *chant fable*, renaissance songs, baroque sonatas, percussion pieces by Chavez and Varèse, new Canadian works, and various styles of jazz. Schafer's predilections were reflected in the programming of Machaut's Mass and Schumann's *Kreisleriana* with readings from E.T.A. Hoffmann. But the most remarkable aspect of programming was the care to create meaningful juxtapositions: 'Many were the meetings,' says Harry Freedman, 'we sat thrashing out the relative merits or faults of combining a medieval work with a modern one or a secular work with a religious one.'[36] Thus the medieval *Aucassin and Nicolette*, combining dialogue and song, was paired with the *Sprechgesang* of Schoenberg's *Pierrot Lunaire*; Bach's *Musical Offering* with jazz improvisations on King Frederick's theme; renaissance Christmas music with Stravinsky's *L'Histoire du soldat*. Schafer himself had two works premiered in the series, *The Geography of Eros* in 1964 and *Five Studies on Texts by Prudentius* in 1965, both sung by Mary Morrison.

The second of these occasions was one of the few in which a Schafer premiere has been upstaged. Following the Prudentius songs were pieces by Gerald Gladstone and Jack Behrens, both involving numbers of flutes accompanied by an enormous metal sculpture by Gladstone that was attacked and beaten on the stage with mallets. The 'percussionists' were Schafer, John Beckwith, and Bruce Mather. When the audience began to giggle, so did the flutists. From all evidence, the affair was not the highest artistic achievement of the Ten Centuries Concerts, although the musicians involved remember it vividly; but it was accepted with good humour within the context of experimentation that the concerts offered. A few years later, when Schafer moved to Simon Fraser University, he remembered Jack Behrens and invited him to join the faculty there.

In the fall of 1963, Schafer and his wife moved to St John's, Newfoundland, where he became artist-in-residence at Memorial University. He was not required to teach, but he quickly organized a number of activities around the musical talent that he found there – free lunch-hour concerts and a brass consort formed of Salvation Army musicians. Schafer rehearsed them in a repertoire of Gabrieli and Pezel, and they eventually performed on the CBC. Involving as many local musicians as possible, Schafer found unusual music for them to play, including some pieces from the fourteenth-century Ars Nova. There was never trouble finding audiences, a fact that confirmed Schafer in his faith that persons having no musical prejudices are willing to tolerate the best that can be given them. The position in St John's gave Schafer more time to compose than he had in Toronto, but it also placed him in contact for the first time with students in the classroom.

Schafer's ideas about music education had long been forming, but his first public statement was made on 9 October 1962, at a banquet for secondary-school music teachers in Toronto. His 'scattered thoughts,' as he called them, included pleas for greater emphasis on listening skills and less on academic theory that angered conservative members in the audience. 'Since we live in a society where the performance of music is left to the few,' he said, 'it is obvious that most students should be trained as listeners.' More provocative still was his adamant rejection of teaching that sticks safely to the classics. Children, without adult preconceptions, can be delighted by music of the *avant-garde*, or any kind of music from the past: 'It is the duty of teachers to open this unlimited number of doors for children. And in the process contemporary music should be included ... The biggest problem in the way of building up student interest in this sort of fare is the prejudices of the teachers.'[37]

This speech came just after Schafer, along with a number of other composers, participated in programs that eventually became known as the John Adaskin Project of the Canadian Music Centre, an ongoing project to bring composers into school music rooms and inspire them to write pieces for students. Then, after his first term in Newfoundland, Schafer was invited to try out his ideas by C. Laughton Bird, the adventurous director of music education for the borough of North York in metropolitan Toronto. In 1964, Schafer taught a two-week summer course for students aged from thirteen to seventeen called simply 'Musicianship,' and he was given a free hand to experiment; the course, which was repeated the next summer, formed the basis of the first of Schafer's five educational pamphlets, *The Composer in the Classroom* (1965). These pamphlets have now been translated whole or in part into German, French, Hungarian, Hebrew, and (by Toru Takemitsu) Japanese. Schafer's actual contact with students was slight when he began, but he discovered a natural rapport with the young, and since 1965 he has had ample time to exercise it. His innovative classroom techniques have made him controversial, but they have established a reputation that is truly international, though, as he remarks somewhat wistfully, he sees 'no evidence of their having any real impact whatsoever in Canada.'[38]

Schafer's compositions for student musicians attempt to replace rote learning with encouragement to improvise creatively. He has written nothing that could be called an *étude*. Music in the schools, he explains, is 'far too frequently made a means of exhibitionism'; too often it means 'little more than memorizing *Monkey in the Tree* for some year-end social function.'[39] In his first observations of music classes, Schafer noticed that players were so intent on reading their own notes that they never listened to anyone else. 'What we need here is a notational system, the rudiments of which could be taught in fifteen minutes, so that after that the class could immediately embark on the making of live music.'[40] So Schafer began to compose pieces that students could begin to play immediately, and that called for a degree of imaginative involvement. *Invertible Material for Orchestra* (1963) is designed as a 'practice piece' involving random combinations of one-pitch rhythmic patterns. *Statement in Blue* (1964) is a graphic score demanding freely improvised solos. Most ambitious of all is *Threnody* (1967), for youth orchestra, youth choir, five narrators, and electronic sounds – a moving dramatization of the atomic bombing of Nagasaki from the viewpoint of children the same age as those performing the piece. In works like these, and in all his deep concern for public education, Schafer has demonstrated his commitment to the place of serious music in society.

During his second year in Newfoundland, Schafer accepted a commission from Pierre Mercure and CBC Television in Montreal that would mark a turning point in his career. The work was to be an opera that would be telecast across the country. *Loving*, part of which (*The Geography of Eros*) had already been performed, was produced on CBC television in May 1966. It is Schafer's first 'opera,' and in it culminates the stylistic experimentation that had occupied his entire career up to this point. In his early works Schafer had virtually surveyed the available modern styles, moving successively from polytonality (*Harpsichord Concerto*) to atonality (*Protest and Incarceration*) to studies in sonority (*Canzoni for Prisoners*).[41] The Prudentius songs move towards stereophony and electronic tape. *Invertible Material for Orchestra* incorporates chance, and *Statement in Blue* graphic notation. *Loving* shows Schafer for the first time in command of the full range of the techniques of the *avant-garde*; here he is especially interested in a range of vocal effects moving from singing to speech, with a variety of whispers and whistles in between; in addition, the stagecraft involved the multiple media of music, language, dance, and (in its CBC performance) the television camera. Of all his works to this point, *Loving* most clearly marks the full development of Schafer's individual style.

For a number of reasons the telecast of *Loving* was not wholly successful. Pierre Mercure, the brilliant composer and a skilled producer for televison, steered the performance sympathetically through the formidable musical and dramatic demands of the score. Then, tragically, he died in an automobile accident less than a week before the taping. Consequently, two important sections of the work were never screened, although the music had been recorded. The truncated condition of the piece, however, could hardly be blamed for the poor audience response. Serious musicians applauded *Loving*, and in French Canada some favourable comments were heard. But pop TV critics sneered. Roy Shields in the *Toronto Daily Star* must have echoed bewilderment and resentment from across the country. The idea of this 'musical whatsit,' he wrote, 'is to disarm the audience by conning them into the belief that here is a courageous, penetrating and avant-garde musical experience that is probably going to be beyond their lowly comprehension.'[42] It was. The supposition that such a work as *Loving* could have a popular audience was of course mistaken, if it ever existed; but the situation points to some curious paradoxes in Schafer's position. The theme of *Loving* is hardly recondite, but that only made it more vulnerable ('girls in tights flitting about, moaning and groaning'). Schafer's score is not overwhelmingly abstract, at least in the context of the 1960s. But how to explain this in a country containing 'vast stretches where the very names of Bach and Beethoven are odd novelties'?[43] As Schafer has gradually become more interested in his social function as a composer, the contradictions have become knottier. Artists, as Ezra Pound has remarked, may be the 'antennae of the race,' but most Canadians tuned *their* antennae to another channel.

One consequence of this experience was an academic report, *The Public of the Music Theatre: Louis Riel: A Case Study* (1972). Schafer's document analyses the audience of Harry Somers' opera, which like Schafer's is bilingual and was broadcast by the CBC (radio 1967, television 1969). The statistics are as depressing as the response to *Loving*; the work, which had a well-deserved triumph in its stage production, held only 13% of the total audience, and what is more, received an 'enjoyment rating' of only 29, the lowest for any show that season. One Winnipeg critic announced that he chose to save his eyeballs by not watching at all. Opera, Schafer writes, is 'far removed from the hearts of a people working close to the land in an attempt to open up a new country ... The majority of Canadians still consider opera inappropriate and are apprehensive of its value and charm. It seems thrust on them from "above" or "abroad."' Yet even so, *Louis Riel* reached and pleased greater numbers by television than it did in the opera house; so Schafer's study, like others, concludes that television 'could play an important role in discovering new audiences for opera; in fact, probably the most important role in the contemporary situation'; but he notes as well 'the increasing difficulty of accomplishing eccentric undertakings of all kinds in the face of the increasingly totalitarian thrust of "pop" culture.'[44]

In the decade from 1965 to 1975, Schafer pursued his various interests from the central base of Simon Fraser University in Burnaby, British Columbia. There not only did he produce his remaining four music education pamphlets, continue his work on Pound, rewrite his Hoffmann book, and develop the wholly new World Soundscape Project, but he also faced for the first time the daily routine of a teaching schedule. Incredibly, despite all these involvements, the decade has also been his most productive thus far as a composer. Simon Fraser seems to have been the right place for a man of Schafer's temperament. A brand-new university in a brand-new campus perched dramatically on a mountain top just outside Vancouver, it was willing to test some of the new thinking about university education that had developed in recent years and signalled its willingness by hiring a number of teachers on the basis of merit other than an academic degree. All did not go smoothly, of course. The campus was disrupted in its first years by student unrest and administrative confusion; more unexpectedly, Schafer soon discovered that the solid concrete structure of the building proved ideal for the transmission of the construction noise that continued for five years and more after classes began. But, despite complaints, Simon Fraser was on the whole generous, and Schafer's years there released an astonishing productivity while broadening his intellectual range.

Schafer was a member of the new university's Centre for the Study of Communications and the Arts, an experimental interdisciplinary department designed by Archie MacKinnon, a protégé of McLuhan, to break down traditional barriers between the arts and sciences. In its best moments, it was a new Bauhaus. The original faculty included, besides Schafer, a television producer, a social psychologist, a mechanical engineer, a theatre director, and a biologist. At first, Schafer was given enormous freedom in his teaching, for the university's academic organization was still fluid; and because advancement was wide open, he progressed from lecturer to full professor in the space of five years. Furthermore, the institution, blessed with a large budget, was soon able to provide Schafer and his colleague Jack Behrens with one of the best-equipped electronic sound studios on the continent. Schafer benefited from his daily contact with colleagues in various disciplines, and he himself would lecture as often on Buckminster Fuller or Constantin Doxiadis as on aesthetic topics.

For the first few years, Schafer taught a music course run in conjunction with the education faculty along principles set down in his *Ear Cleaning* pamphlet. He also had charge of a 'sensitivity course,' which met on Saturday mornings at ten o'clock and continued until everyone was exhausted – sometimes five in the afternoon or even nine at night. 'When we wanted to study the eye,' he writes, 'we gathered together a physiologist to tell us about the physiology of vision, a psychologist to tell us about the psychology of vision, and a painter and an architect to share with us their insights into the aesthetics of vision.'[45] In later years, Schafer taught Communications 100, an introduction to interrelations between the arts, technology, and society. A typical assignment: 'During the course of this semester, go to one of the following two corners in Vancouver, and remain there as an observer for a minimum of one hour. At the top of your assignment, give the date and time you were there. You may record your impressions, observations, reflections, in any form you wish: written, taped (oral), visual, photographic, cinematographic, etc, etc, etc. Use your imagination.'[46] The course, answering the charges of C.P. Snow's celebrated 'Two Cultures' lecture of 1959, moved Schafer's own artistic thinking more and more towards the exploration of sound as sound and the place of sound in the social structure.

Schafer's academic specialty in the Communications Centre was gradually defining itself: the acoustics of the environment. He taught what he believes to be the first course in Canada on noise pollution; and out of this thinking about environmental noise came the inspiration for the World Soundscape Project, founded at Simon Fraser in September 1972. With a large grant from the Canadian Donner Foundation, plus money from Unesco and private sources (including Schafer himself), the Soundscape Project has set out to gather information about all aspects of the acoustic environment. The World Soundscape Project is far more than a mere campaign against noise pollution. Noise is a nuisance, to be sure, but however stubborn its sources, it is surely the most biodegradable pollutant in the atmosphere. The problem is not to eradicate noise but to encourage an aesthetically desirable acoustic environment. Like the Bauhaus, Schafer aims to bring aesthetics to industry and give birth to a new area of industrial design.

The World Soundscape Project is central to Schafer's thinking, gathering together all the diverse influences of his past. John Cage's proposal to treat environmental sound as music is, of course, an essential component. So is the acute aural sensitivity of Ezra Pound. The various approaches to environmental studies taken by the Bauhaus, McLuhan, Buckminster Fuller, Doxiadis, and others have all contributed. And Schafer's educational ideas have been from the beginning concerned more with the nature of sound itself than with music. The synthesis of all these forces, however, has the true novelty of original creation. Apart from composition, the soundscape concept is surely Schafer's most enduring invention.

As he became more deeply involved in academic work, however, Schafer became more and more jealous of time for his own projects. In 1968, a Canada Council grant allowed him to take a leave of absence from the university. Told that the grant also included travel money, Schafer took advantage of it to visit a place that had long fascinated him: Iran. Ever since his youthful notion to study Arabic influences on troubadour poetry, Schafer had been attracted by Islamic culture. In Vienna, discovering an Egyptian student living across the hall, Schafer studied the language with him, picking up a modest Arabic vocabulary and rudiments of the language. His visit to Iran, however, was one of the great let-downs of his life, largely because of the degree of Westernization that he found there (the muezzins used amplifiers); but the experience had many high points. He discovered the work of the thirteenth-century Sufi mystic Jalal al-Din Rumi, and he visited Konya, in Turkey, where Rumi founded the Sufi sect. He visited the acoustically perfect Shah Abbas mosque at Isphahan. His experiences, recorded in an interesting 'Middle-East Sound Diary,' strongly colour the important book on the world soundscape, *The Tuning of the World* (1977). They are also reflected in several of the pieces composed after his return, notably *Lustro* (1969 – 72), which uses texts of Rumi and Tagore, and the large choral work *In Search of Zoroaster* (1971), a quasi-ritualistic study of Persian religion.

During the ten years at Simon Fraser, Schafer emerged from obscurity to prominence as a composer. *Requiems for the Party-Girl* (1966), perhaps his best-known work apart from the pieces for youth, has been recorded three times and performed by Bruno Maderna and by Pierre Boulez. The full-length version of *Requiems, Patria II*, received a spectacular stage production at the Stratford Festival in 1972. *Gita*, performed at Tanglewood in 1967, was praised by the American critic Irving Lowens as 'the high point of the Fromm Festival.'[47] The same year, Schafer prepared electronic works for two of the pavilions at Expo '67 in Montreal. *From the Tibetan Book of the Dead* was warmly received at the Aldeburgh Festival in 1967. In 1969, Schafer's work with a grade-seven class was made the subject of a half-hour film by the National Film Board, *Bing, Bang, Boom*, which won first prize in its division at the New York Film Festival. It captures the magnetism of

Schafer as Pied Piper of the classroom in a way that his written pamphlets cannot. The *String Quartet No. 1* appeared in 1970, as well as *Sappho* (a failure) at the Coolidge Festival in Washington, DC. In 1971, Schafer signed a contract with Universal Edition. Within the space of a few weeks in 1973, Schafer had four major premieres: *In Search of Zoroaster* at Dartmouth College (and the following week in Toronto); *East* in Ottawa at the National Arts Centre; *Arcana* at the Montreal International Competition; and the full seventy-minute *Lustro* in Toronto with the Toronto Symphony.

In the midst of this crowded period, in 1971, Schafer separated from his wife, Phyllis Mailing. He had met Jean Reed, who had recently moved to Vancouver from England with her two teenage sons and had taken a job as secretary in the Communications Department at Simon Fraser. They were married, after their two divorces had been settled, in September 1975.

Schafer's departure from Simon Fraser in 1975 was sudden but not capricious. Earlier, in 1971, he informed the university administration that he considered his salary exorbitant and arranged to teach only one semester per year for half pay. But meanwhile the university was changing, becoming more formally structured, more conventional; and as it did, Schafer grew less and less happy. First the Faculty of Education, recoiling at the prospect of Schafer students in the local school systems, decided (as Schafer puts it) that 'they preferred autoharps and painting snowmen to invention'[48] and replaced his 'ear cleaning' course with a traditional music education program. The sensitivity course collapsed when the students got lazy and refused to help clean up the debris. Then the Communications Centre itself came under pressures, internal and external. The original members, always faced with the task of having to define for others their *raison d'être*, either left or fought to organize their own departments. In 1970 the centre split into an Arts Centre, offering only non-credit courses, and an orthodox Communications Department. Because the Arts Centre offered only sessional contracts, Schafer stayed with the Communications Department and was obliged to find an academic specialty – hence his course in noise pollution. But finally, annoyed with the university's lack of commitment to its arts programs, the incessant scramble for budget money, and the general academic congealment, Schafer resigned.

In the summer of 1975, Schafer moved with Jean to Ontario, where they worked together on the farmhouse in Monteagle Valley. Ironically, if he had hoped to have more time for composition, the actual move kept him from completing any new pieces in 1975. Renovations on the house were more difficult than at first anticipated, with the result that (as he says) he 'did nothing but pretend to be a carpenter from June till November.'[49] Eventually, however, the house took shape, including a large, quiet, well-equipped studio. He works there on his music and his several literary projects, while Jean helps with the tasks of editing, indexing, and preparing manuscripts for the press. The move to the country reveals in Schafer not merely a streak of romanticism, always visible enough anyway, but a rare kind of courage. Asked how a composer can support himself in Canada, Schafer replies, 'He can't.' Royalties from his music are insignificant, though he earns some income from his books. Grants from the Canada Council and the Guggenheim Foundation (in 1974) have provided a further, but adventitious, source of money. And Schafer has accepted visiting professorships from a few universities. Still, his farmhouse, within fairly easy reach of Toronto, Ottawa, and Montreal, is cheaper to live in than an apartment in the city and, more important, offers an environment where Schafer can make his own life.

Whether Schafer's music will be changed by his move remains to be seen; but he has already hinted strongly at new lines of interest. Very likely, lacking the facilities of Simon Fraser's Sonic Research Studio, he will make less use of electronic sound. His attitude has always been guarded: 'Most composers have come to believe that electronic music has not lived up to its expectations as a pure art form. Whatever future it may have will probably be in conjunction with "live" music or with the other arts, such as the dance or films.'[50] More important, perhaps, will be Schafer's involvement with his immediate environment: his move, he says, 'represents some kind of decision in terms of finding that parochial culture, even if it means going down and conducting the village choir again, and seeing what you can build up in the way of expressing something which the people are capable of doing.'[51] Consequently, Schafer has found time to organize a community choir of about twenty or thirty voices in Monteagle Valley, teaching them a small repertoire that extends to composers like Weelkes and Schütz. Since many of the members do not read music, those that do teach those that do not; cassette recordings are also useful for this purpose. Besides the local choir, Schafer's dilapidated barn behind the farmhouse has proven a rich source of raw materials for various experiments in sound sculpture. Seen in the right way, the parochial world is inexhaustible.

Schafer's move is most decidedly a revolt against the culture of urban technology. 'I'm really beginning to feel,' he says,

> that maybe we should begin to find a totally new kind of musical art form, one which corresponds more closely to that rural wilderness environment that is so much a part of our heritage. It would be very interesting, somehow, to make a simpler art form with the materials that were available rather than having to use materials that are either imported or that cost a lot of money. It is what, I suppose, Levi-Strauss would call 'bricolage,' taking the materials of the environment and putting them to new uses ...
>
> Last summer, with a couple of young friends, we started to build some 'sound sculptures' in our barn with old ploughshares from a whole sort of junk yard of waste metal that I have. We got very excited because we were reconditioning all this old material and building new 'musical structures' out of it ...
>
> I think I'm more interested in doing that than in perpetuating many other kinds of music. In the last lecture to my communications students, after they'd had four years of communications and they were going to graduate and go out into the world as communicators of one kind or another, I said, 'Remember that practically everything you've learned depends on one thing.' And their eyes would light up for the first and last time. 'It depends on this: going to a plug – pull it and you're out of a job.'
>
> We begin to think in terms of energy conservation and so forth and we wonder: Should we really be perpetuating the recording industry in its consumption of petroleum? Should we really be so dependent on electronics? It means that we're going to have to go on producing more and more electrical energy in order to power all those gadgets. Or shouldn't we get back to the great beauty of human power – just the human lip blowing a simple flute ...[52]

2
Writings

Romanticism: *E.T.A. Hoffmann and Music*

Schafer belongs to that small group of composers whose intellectual attitudes are nearly as important as the sounds they combine in their music. Certain obvious comparisons spring to mind: Berlioz, Schumann, Wagner, Ives, Cage. Like all these composers, Schafer has produced a body of prose explaining his artistic acts. Like most of them, he places himself squarely in the musical tradition that we call romantic. Schafer's own brand of romanticism, however, must be defined with some care.

His romanticism has often been noted – for better or worse. Despite his youthful starting point in Stravinskian neo-classicism, Schafer's mental map of history sometimes seems to jump directly from Bach to Schumann, and he confesses a distaste for Mozart. His agents advertise, truthfully, that his music is modern in idiom but romantically expressive in its appeal.[1] He has been called a 'charming anachronism,' 'a Romantic in a world of anti-Romantics,'[2] and indeed the anti-romantics have had their say. John Rea, in a whimsical essay,[3] attacks Schafer's musical and intellectual stance by drawing parallels with Wagner; the fact that he lumps Ezra Pound, Marshall McLuhan, and John Cage together as 'Wagnerites' suggests that he leaves certain distinctions unspoken, yet many of Rea's parallels are just, and he really errs in confining himself to Wagner when he could throw in Hoffmann, Schopenhauer, Nietzsche, Rilke, Winckelmann, Pater, Ruskin, and a long list of others for good measure. Schafer's achievement has been to reinterpret the attitudes of nineteenth-century romanticism in contemporary musical language.

Schafer acknowledges his romantic affinities as few of his contemporaries have done. *E.T.A. Hoffmann and Music* is an extended treatment of the subject. Although not published until 1975, the book was largely completed in Vienna in the late 1950s: really his first book, it represents an effort to define 'romanticism' in his own mind. The book may disappoint readers primarily interested in Hoffmann's texts; Schafer translates only nine of Hoffmann's musical pieces, and the bulk of the volume is Schafer's distillation of early romantic attitudes. Still, Schafer's is the only book-length study in English of Hoffmann's musical romanticism.

From the first, Schafer's ambivalence is apparent: he is 'tempted to agree' that the romantic century 'really did represent some pinnacle of musical expression never again to be attained'[4]; but he blames the neglect of musical styles before and after the romantic on the longevity of nineteenth-century institutions like the orchestra and the opera house, and on the public's desire for escapism. Our attitudes have been changed by the experiences of this century: 'The spectacle of Beethoven playing c-sharp minor *arpeggios* by moonlight on the Danube is difficult to bring into view now that moonlight has been replaced by neon and all the rivers are polluted' (page 4). Without becoming embroiled in the semantics of the word, the reader of Schafer's study can discern both his 'romantic' affinities and his reservations.

Hoffmann's major character, the mad composer Johannes Kreisler, defined the new role of the composer in society, 'and at the same time exposed the tragic consequences of a compulsive and overindulgent philosophy of music' (112). Far from being a meek servant of the aristocracy, the romantic composer is superior to his society, the explorer and teacher of ever-new modes of perception. Hoffmann, unlike many German aestheticians (whose great weakness was to regard art 'in the pure state of antisepsis, stripped bare of all sociological considerations'), 'was never guilty of ignoring the social implications of art' (141). The artist, like Shelley's poet, becomes unacknowledged legislator of the world, not imitating life but teaching life to imitate his art. Hence the romantic's need for inventing a new form in each work, for shaping his own texts, and for explaining his work in writing. Schafer, asked to describe his favourite music, once replied, 'Music that speaks directly; music that is created perilously; music created by composers who risk everything; dangerous music.'[5]

This danger, as Kreisler shows, is not just aesthetic: it touches the composer's very sanity; and yet music must serve the composer's personal phantasmagoria, never merely the whims of his patron. 'The ultimate liberation and secularization of music,' says Schafer, 'is a nineteenth-century achievement – probably the greatest single artistic achievement of that century' (9). This separation of music from aristocratic and ecclesiastical patronage, symbolized in Mozart's letter to the archbishop of Salzburg, is balanced by a sacramental attitude towards art itself. According to M.H. Abrams, the romantics tried to preserve religious values, 'but to reformulate them within the prevailing two-term system of subject and object, ego and non-ego, the human mind or consciousness and its transactions with nature.'[6] 'The close identification of music with religion can be sensed everywhere in German romanticism,' says Schafer; but the religion is not of the church. Much of Schafer's music, too, expresses a personal religious vision, as when he calls *Threnody* 'a religious piece for our time,' or *Lustro* his *Parsifal.*[7] Or else the romantic's rejection of patronage is balanced by nationalist feelings for the people; nationalism is one romantic issue that Schafer has been slow to resolve, and only recently has he clarified his role as a Canadian composer.

From an unsympathetic viewpoint, the romantic's private world may seem mere escapism, or even madness. But when older social institutions become unacceptable, the individual is forced on his own resources, forced to become a romantic. His problem, as Jacques Barzun says, is 'to create a new world on the ruins of the old ... The task of reconstruction manifestly does demand energy, morality, and genius,' so that romanticism on the whole is 'infinitely more constructive than escapist.'[8] The romantic creates (in McLuhan's term) an anti-environment that passes implicit judgment on society. Some of the ingredients of Hoffmann's created world – night, mystery, dreams, madness, music (41) – recur in Schafer's private fantasies, especially *Loving* and *Patria*. His work is preoccupied with the problems of ego versus non-ego – with individual liberty (*Canzoni for Prisoners*) and psychological symbolism (*Loving*) on the one hand, and on the other with absorption of the ego into something Other, say, Nature, or some mystical Oneness. Schafer's soundscape theory goes directly back to Hoffmann, for whom 'nature was like an enormous orchestral score, respiring mysteriously' (7), and filtered through Cage, who declared that environmental sound is music. Many of his works (*Gita*, *Lustro*) deal explicitly with mystical forfeiture of the self. In all, he shows the romanticist's 'desire to mold musical form as closely as possible on psychological and dramatic truth.'[9]

This effort to build a new heaven and new earth accounts for the apocalyptic tone of many romantics, including Schafer. Apocalypse, first mentioned in *Protest and Incarceration*, reappears in the Prudentius songs, which outline the entire biblical myth, and finally in the enormous choral work *Apocalypsis*. *In Search of Zoroaster* deals with a parallel Persian myth. And *Threnody*, dealing with nuclear warfare, tempers the hopeful romantic apocalypse with a vision of total destruction.

From his modern standpoint, Schafer seems wary of the self-destructive element in romanticism. 'The romanticist seems either unwilling or unable to face everyday reality squarely. At worst the dichotomy of these two existences created unbearable pressure and led to madness and suicide' (6). Schafer's works, like Hoffmann's, are populated with such figures, victims of the irrational – hallucination (*Brébeuf*), madness (*Patria II*), suicide (*Patria I* and *Patria II*), attempted suicide and madness (*Adieu, Robert Schumann*), megalomania (*Son of Heldenleben*). Here, romanticism is not so much Schafer's mode of expression as his subject-matter. As composer, he stands fascinated, but at some ironic distance, both feet firmly in this century.

To the romantic, music is 'the means by which the incalculable demonic forces of the universe burst in on the calculated life of man, setting up tremendous and destructive upheavals in his personality' (143). Nowadays, delirium is suspect. 'The more temperament and abandon the interpreter of romantic art brings to his subject the more embarrassed the audience becomes ... Who has ever wept at music? Today we are dispassionate; weeping is sentimental. Yet in 1805 people bragged about it' (4). Romantic music takes itself seriously – Hoffmann regretted the playfulness of Haydn – but today we are less inclined to apostrophize 'du holde Kunst.' Schafer, swayed perhaps by Pound, is always ready to trade delirium for discrimination.

The romantic attributes art to the irrational forces of the mind; but the road to Xanadu is littered with fragments. Schafer, like most moderns, sees mainly hard work and craftsmanship. Unlike hapless romantics of two centuries who have tried to heighten their perceptions artificially, Schafer wholly separates artistic experience from psychedelic experience: art does not resign intellect. And while Hoffmann may have sought inspiration in alcohol, Schafer slyly observes that from the evidence of the diaries he never wrote much on the days when he got drunk; rather, Hoffmann often used the word *Besonnenheit* ('presence of mind') in his writings (22–3).

The romantic musician lays claim to greater powers of perception and more intense powers of feeling than the ordinary person. Though sometimes expressing this feeling through understatement, more often he aspires to intensity through increased instrumental forces, volume, and sonority. The device that most interests Schafer, however, is synaesthesia, the appeal to many senses through many arts at once. The composer who sought this form of intensity most strenuously, of course, was Wagner, but origins of the idea lie in earlier writers like Hoffmann, whose essay 'The Poet and the Composer' 'laid the foundation for all romantic opera, and particularly for Wagner's later works' (112): 'For Hoffmann, the nervous system of music was stretched over the visible, tactile, and olfactory world, reconstituting the elements in dazzling but irrational patterns' (153). Yet while it is ever the musician's fate to hear 'unification of the arts' and think 'Wagner,' this reflex has obscured several crucial distinctions. Schafer writes of Wagner warmly but not uncritically: 'Wagner's idea of the *Gesamtkunstwerk* was noble but premature,' he says; in *Parsifal* there is 'more crush than exaltation.'[10]

The basic tenet in Schafer's thinking is neither intensification of feeling nor even a multiplication of sense impressions in synaesthesia: it is the education of the senses. In this way, Schafer is typically the modern aesthete – always remembering that that much-abused term derives from the Greek word meaning 'to perceive.' To train the perceptions is the function of the artist. In Ruskin's words, 'The greatest thing a human soul ever does in this world is to see something, and to tell what it saw in a plain way. Hundreds of people can talk for one who can think, but thousands can think for one who can see.'[11] Eliminate the visual bias and the remark stands: the musician is not the man who feels sounds most intensely but the one who perceives and conveys them most clearly. This aesthete need be no escapist: he brings his heightened perceptions before the world as cogently as he can.

The twentieth century: *Ezra Pound and Music*

Schafer's romantic outlook has been filtered through the anti-romantic, anti-Wagnerian reaction of this century. The relevant sources here are both musical and literary. Schafer's earliest works were modelled after neo-classical fashions set by Stravinsky and 'Les Six' and articulated by Jean Cocteau, whose *Cock and Harlequin* Schafer read with enthusiasm. The influence of Ezra Pound (who also admired Cocteau) accentuated many of these same tendencies. If Schafer's uncertainty of direction at the beginning of his career is only natural, and if he soon turned to serialism like many other neo-classical composers of the 1950s, he still preserves many of the predilections of his earliest models.

Neo-classical attitudes appear throughout Schafer's work. He shares the neo-classicists' liking for small-scale forces and objective, often transparent sonority. He likes the harpsichord and actively dislikes the piano. He regards the orchestra as an outmoded relic, and though he has written for it (mainly on commission) he dislikes the medium. Even large-scale works like *Loving* and *Patria* demand modest instrumental forces. His orchestration is often (though not always) spare, and he once (for example) criticized Vaughan Williams for 'thickening the middle-orchestra texture,' producing 'a sort of musclebound mumble.'[12] Through the 1960s, Schafer favoured linear textures, declaring that 'every line of a polyphonic composition must live on its own; there should never be any "fill" in music.'[13] Recently he has tended towards more massed or veiled sonorities; but his instrumentation persistently favours winds and percussion, and he allows the strings little room for cantabile.

On most of these points, Schafer found support in his study of Ezra Pound. Pound's musical aesthetic, formed in London and strongly influenced by Arnold Dolmetsch's revival of early music, anticipated the Parisian neo-classicism of the 1920s even before he arrived there to compose his opera and sponsor his protégé George Antheil. In music as in literature, Pound demanded art free from 'emotional slither.' He was a vigorous anti-Wagnerite. 'There are two aesthetic ideals,' he wrote,

the Wagnerian ... i.e., you confuse the spectator by smacking as many of his senses as possible at every possible moment; this prevents him from noting anything with unusual lucidity, but you may fluster or excite him to the point of making him receptive ... The other aesthetic ... aims at focusing the mind on a given definition of form, or rhythm, so intensely that it becomes not only aware of that given form, but more sensitive to all other forms.[14]

Characteristically, Pound, like Schafer, is didactic rather than hedonistic. Pound 'asks for complex acts of discernment, not for immolation.'[15] Music alerts, refines, and expands the powers of hearing. Pound and Hoffmann would join in condemning everything that subordinated art to mere entertainment. Both were artists who dared to spearhead historical movements, teaching their followers new modes of perception. The artist's function is pedagogical; consequently, the artist is liable to expect some mental exertion from his audience, and truly, as Schafer notes with approval, 'Pound has never been one to let his work slip off into his audience's laps without demanding some effort on their part.'[16]

One of Schafer's central aesthetic problems has been to harmonize a romantic notion of synaesthesia with Poundian modernism. Pound himself rejected synaesthesia: he scoffed at 'kindergarten stories about colours being like tones in music'[17] and prided himself on refusing to speak about one art in terms of another; nonetheless, Pound did compare his *Cantos* to a fugue, and his mosaic of ideograms does present a multiplicity of sensations, each to be measured and discriminated by the reader. Schafer, too, discriminating between different functions of synaesthesia, rejects mere intensification of experience, the 'grotesque synaesthetic debaucheries of Des Esseintes' (hero of Huysmans' *A Rebours*). This is Wagner's error:

Wagner assumed that the various art forms mirrored one another and that to superimpose as many of them as possible would produce the maximum emotional effect. Operatic effects, even the most subtle, are always muscle-bound and obvious because the arrows of all the arts are being shot in the same direction.[18]

A better model is the Roman Catholic mass:

All the senses are summoned up: vision – the architecture of the church, the colour of the *vitraux*; hearing – the music of the choir and the instruments, the ringing of bells; taste – the transubstantiation of the bread and wine; smell – the incense; touch – devotion on the knee ... What strikes us here is that at no time are the senses bombarded aimlessly; everything is neat and integrated. In the Catholic mass there is no sensory overload.[19]

Schafer's desire to purify the senses has led him to examine the most basic materials of each artistic medium. The same impulse led Pound to his well-known classification of poetry into 'melopoeia,' 'phanopoeia,' and 'logopoeia,' that is, poetry that appeals primarily to the eye, the ear, or the verbal sense. To Pound, the most interesting poetry develops some single sensory aspect of language to some ultimate refinement: thus he recommends Provençal troubadours for melopoeia, Chinese for phano-poeia, and certain individual ironists like Jules Laforgue for logopoeia.[20] Pound's criticism, like some of Schafer's, is often couched in an arresting if reductive language that aims at basic concepts: 'I prefer,' says Schafer, 'to start with the most elementary gestures of each art form,' borrowing an example from the Bauhaus artists: 'The extended study Kandinsky, Klee and the others at the Bauhaus gave to the basic elements of the graphic arts (Kandinsky, for example, spends almost 40 pages in discussing the significance of the dot in his book *Point and Line to Plane*), needs to be duplicated in the other arts – in music, for example, by a prolonged study of the single tone.'[21] This aim to purify, even re-define, the basic sensory vocabularies of the arts informs Schafer's theories of soundscape and music education, as well as much of his music.

As a poet, Pound's primary musical interest is rhythm, and Schafer has made high claims for Pound in this area, particularly for the brief, overlooked *Treatise on Harmony* (1925). 'A superior work of theory can alter our entire conception of music,' he writes. 'If this is true then Pound's book deserves mention along with Schoenberg and Schenker, for no book on the subject so cogently forces us to see harmony as a study in movement.'[22] Pound's treatise, however opaque, remarkably anticipates Stockhausen's theory of unity in electronic music; both attempt to relate pitch and timbre, the vertical factors of sound, to the horizontal factor of rhythm, mainly through frequency of vibrations. Pound holds an important place in the early history of noise music, after Russolo and Pratella. He opposed the futurists but took them seriously; with the intuition of a poet obsessed by rhythm, he saw that noise in music threatened the horizontal functions and forced a redefinition of them. His treatise and Antheil's early experimental work are the first attempt to solve the problem of rhythm in a music conceived purely as *objet sonore*.

Schafer has suggested that such a conception of rhythm is a key to the correspondences among the arts: 'The various senses are bound together by the biological and neural rhythms of the human anatomy. The real meeting place of all the arts is therefore *rhythm*, particularly in those basic rhythms which condition the resolving powers of the senses, and of the body (heart, breath, motor rhythms, sleep, etc.).'[23] Schafer's theoretical ideal of synaesthesia, then, seems to be a kind of rhythmic counterpoint of one sense against another, each sense impression kept clear and distinct, but all ultimately unified through the fundamental bodily rhythms. Part of Schafer's educational theory aims at such an ideal, but whether it has ever been achieved, or can be, is another question.

Pound's influence on Schafer extends naturally to his choice and handling of texts. Here, Pound's poetry and criticism prove more useful than the poet's music; for although Pound's too-little-known opera, *The Testament of François Villon*, is valuable in its own right, it little resembles Schafer's stage works. Pound laboured to capture the verbal rhythms of Villon precisely, to transfer them into musical notation inviolate. To do so, Pound developed an amazingly finical notation (with George Antheil's help) that anticipates in its complexities the rhythms of total serialism. Schafer, however, observes that if the text remains superior, musical interest must be severely attenuated, as in troubadour lyric or Pound's *Villon*; generally, 'it is the music which penetrates the literature and not the other way around.'[24] So Schafer in his own music, though accepting Pound's observation that music history is a gradual evolution towards more precise notation, turns instead to indeterminacy and graphic notations. Pound's authoritarian view of the composer robs the performer of his rightful place, often resulting in unnatural delivery of the music. The problems forced by Pound's experiment gave Schafer a negative example. The only positive influence, perhaps, is Pound's defiance of conventional opera and his effort to redefine the genre. Both are motivated by abhorrence of the self-indulgences of opera and a wish to remake the entire tradition.

Pound's redefinition of poetry has proven a more valuable model. Schafer's sensitivity to his texts can be attributed to the poet's influence perhaps only in a general way, though he credits Pound's *Testament* with teaching him much about the relationship of notes to words. But the rhythms of Pound's verse are penetrating. 'Every composer,' writes Schafer, 'knows the value of a line in which the arrangement of tensions and relaxations is so precise, so honest to the ideas it expresses that it suggests its own music effortlessly ... The contemporary composer's interest in asymmetrical texts in order to attain freedom for his vocal line may be largely traced back to the *vers libre* adventure in poetry.'[25] Pound's *vers libre* relies on what he calls 'absolute rhythm,' a shift of attention from regular metre to the actual sound of the verse line, which is unique for every line whether metrical or not. The 'absolute rhythm' of the line, not the metre, is responsible for the line's expressiveness, and it is nearly always asymmetrical. Hence Pound's defiantly asymmetrical settings of Villon's regular octosyllabics. Schafer's settings too employ complex, asymmetrical rhythms, but these rhythms always bear some discernible expressive relationship to the sense of the text. Schafer deplores the disjunction of text and music apparent in much contemporary music. 'The arrogance of most contemporary composers in smothering the verse they set,' he notes, 'is counterpointed by the documentary and other unsingable qualities of much contemporary verse.'²⁶ His pamphlet *When Words Sing* is a highly original exploration of verbal expression, and his handling of texts, especially since *Loving*, has plied the sundry modes of articulating words from singing to speech.

Schafer's texts, too, show Poundian influence. Some grow directly out of Pound's enthusiasms: the lyrics of the *Minnelieder*, the Tagore songs, the two settings of Sappho. Others, more curious, simply reflect Pound's omnivorous curiosity: the Latin of the Prudentius songs, the Sanskrit of *Gita*, the Persian of *Lustro*, the Egyptian hieroglyphics of *Arcana*, the Tibetan of *From the Tibetan Book of the Dead*. Obviously the polyglot texture of *Patria* owes much to Pound's *Cantos*. Yet, strangely, Schafer has never set any of Pound's own verse, though he does portray him in *Three Contemporaries*. If, as Irving Lowens has written, Schafer 'uses language with the precision and grace of a poet,'²⁷ much of the credit must go to his study of Ezra Pound.

The *avant-garde*: Schafer and John Cage

Schafer blends the disparate influences of Pound and German romanticism in the context of mid-century *avant-garde* thinking. The man who most fully represents this thought is John Cage. This is not to equate Schafer with Cage: Schafer's music certainly sounds very different, but, like nearly every composer since the 1960s, he has worked in the awareness of Cage's revolutionary aesthetic. The influence appears directly in the Soundscape Project and in the music education theories; it appears in the music indirectly, transformed there by Schafer's romantic insistence on the expressive, metaphorical nature of sound.

Cage's contribution can be summarized under three leading ideas: chance; synaesthesia, or mixed-media forms; and a merging of art and life, leading to Schafer's soundscape. Chance music is probably the phenomenon most firmly associated with Cage. Here Schafer has been cautious. Aleatoric techniques have given him useful tools in the classroom, but, even there, Schafer encourages students to manipulate and combine sounds intentionally rather than randomly. Sounds do not just exist, they mean. He judges some sounds preferable to others, unlike Cage, who (theoretically at least) welcomes all alike. He is too much a formalist (a legacy from Pound and the Bauhaus) to abandon control over the sounds of his pieces. While his pieces, like Cage's, depend greatly on originality of concept, he never takes Cage's elaborate precautions to ensure randomness. 'The pleasant serendipity that chance brings to over-organization,' he declares, 'ends in boring chaos when protracted indefinitely.' 'The human being,' he says, 'is ill-adapted to withstand the colossal boredom of chance'; we are 'fundamentally anti-entropic,' that is, random-to-orderly arrangers.[28] Schafer's music is product, not process.

The one chance device most useful to Schafer is graphic notation. Schafer finds here an outlet for his talented pen, a teaching tool (teachable to musically illiterate schoolchildren), and, most important, notations that free him from the twelve pitches and periodic rhythms of conventional music. Schafer examines all these issues in his article 'The Graphics of Musical Thought.' Graphic notation means freedom from the increasingly finical notations of the serialists, and therefore a medium for music conceived purely as sound object. For many textures, graphics are really more accurate than conventional notation.[29] They give the performer leeway and imaginative stimulus, but (and this is where Cage would demur) Schafer reserves full control as composer. Cage attempts to efface the composer entirely, his notations often devised by random procedures and serving no expressive intention; but Schafer's graphics always have a clearly expressive, clearly meta-phorical projection of some musical purpose. His music may sometimes be indeterminate with respect to performance, but never with respect to composition.

Although Cage, like Schafer, is sometimes superficially regarded as 'Wagnerian,' his interest in mixed media is no attempt to muddle one sense with another; different media simply co-exist in the same situation simultaneously. Like Schafer, Cage combines sound with the other senses only after he has first apprehended sound as sound. But where sound to Schafer can be either tonic or toxic, capable of expressiveness or debasement, sound to Cage is just sound. No one is better than another. Cage emphatically rejects the expressive function of music: 'No purposes. Sounds.' 'Someone said, "Art should come from within; then it is profound." But it seems to me art goes within.'[30] Consequently, as some of his music proves, Cage fears no over-indulgence of the senses; nevertheless, he is concerned, like Schafer, with acuity of perception, and much of *Silence* is taken up with pinpointing aural experience. Cage would agree with Schafer, I think, that 'we separate the senses in order to develop specific acuities and disciplined apprehension. Music is a collection of elegant acoustic events ... But a total and sustained separation of the senses results in a fragmentation of experience.'[31]

The contemporary redefinition of music to include all sounds and noises and frequencies is really a further abstraction of hearing from the other senses. The twelve chromatic pitches imply a quasi-visual framework for frequency bound up with convenience of notation, just as the periodic rhythms of conventional music are bound up with mensural notation. Noise music, electronic music, Cage's music – they often dispense with these frameworks for frequency and rhythm, leaving the ear entirely on its own, with no support from vision or the other senses. So, instinctively, composers have turned to mixed media for corrective balance, and such music is usually heard in connection with dance, film, theatre, or just with flamboyant performers.

Cage's marriage of chance with musical theatre led in the 1960s to the Happening. 'We have eyes as well as ears,' says Cage, 'and it is our business while alive to use them.' 'Theatre is all the various things going on at the same time. I have noticed that music is liveliest for me when listening for instance doesn't distract me from seeing.'[32] At times Schafer sounds like Cage on this subject: 'We are seeing the end of art music as we have known it'; 'I think I shall see the day when there are no composers';[33] 'The younger generation is more interested in mixed media affairs which have to do with environments and have very little to do with concert halls, live musicians or the complex acts of aural discernment required by the traditional art of music.'[34] But Schafer has absorbed a great variety of multimedia influences – Eisenstein, Jaques-Dalcroze, Meyerhold, Piscator; and, for reasons already given, he has refused to abandon himself to chance. He dislikes the term 'total theatre' because 'it has become associated with the messy excretions of mixed media. Mixed media is not always synonymous with mindless slopping, but it happens frequently enough to keep us in suspense ... The incoherence of most mixed media activities today results in a glutting of the senses to the point where discrete acts of discernment are no longer possible.' The Happening is by definition non-repeatable – 'hence it is at variance with the fact of art.'[35] While Patria may owe something to the random events of the Happening, Schafer keeps his theatrical illusions under firm control and notates the score with exactitude.

Cage would respond that art is not different from life. Art is 'an over-simplification of the situation we are actually in.' 'Music should add to the disorder that characterizes life, not the order that characterizes art.'[36] To a point, Schafer would agree. While he has not given up the composition as artifact, he has welcomed the notion of environment perceived as art; to Schafer, art may penetrate life, but not the reverse.

When Schafer looks forward to 'a situation in which "art" and "life" would be synonymous,'[37] his emphasis falls on ordering the environment. He anticipates a time when, in Cage's words, 'we will be able, without scores, without performers and so forth, simply to sit still, to listen to the sounds which surround us, and hear them as music.'[38] The best way to grasp the soundscape concept is to regard the world 'as a large musical composition.'[39] The apparently extreme nature of this view has led David Cope, in his survey of recent musical trends, to place comments on the World Soundscape Project at the end of a chapter called 'Antimusic.'[40]

But no one has to be an anti-musician in order to care for the acoustic environment. This care is common to all of Schafer's antecedents. Hoffmann heard nature as music and worshipped the sound of the Aeolian harp; in 'Die Automate' he contemplated a machine that would extract the most nearly perfect possible music contained in natural objects. Pound and Antheil, both aware of Russolo's noise music, developed a notion of 'workshop orchestration,' a rhythmic reorganization of the factory to make conditions more tolerable.[41] And Erik Satie, Cocteau's musical ideal, created an artificial acoustic environment in his *musique d'ameublement*, which in turn inspired Cage's 'centrally located pulverized Muzak-plus ... performed by listeners who do nothing more than go through the room.'[42] Schafer is natural heir to such ideas; but, as he warns, 'there are those who think the Omega point can be produced at once by playing patty-cake with paints in the vicinity of electric guitars.'[43] Schafer's utopianism, like that of his Bauhaus masters, is ballasted with a demand for technical knowledge. If composers are going to claim a part in harmonizing the environment, they need a new craftsmanship. Schafer's World Soundscape Project, 'the first treatment of the acoustic environment as a macrocultural composition,'[44] is a step towards that end.

The Tuning of the World

In *The Tuning of the World*, Schafer defines acoustic ecology as 'the study of sounds in relation to life and society.' He wants tools to analyse environmental sound, to compare different soundscapes, and to suggest measures for improving them. If we are in fact, as McLuhan tells us, turning from a visual to an aural culture, then such study should become increasingly important. The central impulse of Schafer's study is aesthetic, although it touches areas of the sciences and social sciences, from medicine to law. His interest is not primarily medical, although he notes the real hazards of noise in terms of deafness and stress. Practical concerns like these, however, are inseparable from the aesthetic because both depend on the same scale of measurement, the human ear.

Aesthetic control of the acoustic environment may seem merely idealistic. Sometimes Schafer contrasts the horrors of modern society too glibly with some suppositious golden age. The language of science jostles with mysticism – 'the creation of the world was but one pulse in a great universal symphony' (226). Aesthetic preferences compete with scientific objectivity. Above all, we instinctively mistrust the engineered society that Schafer envisions. One wonders, for example, what percentage of the population really would prefer Satie to Muzak (though a while ago I did hear the *Gymnopédies* in a supermarket). Schafer himself has contemplated a dystopian composer, 'a complete villain, perpetrator of God knows what evil noises, as he sits brooding in the rare altitude of his Parnassus of one.'[45] The answer to this charge, however, is simple. The villain already exists. He has designed the snowmobile, the electric guitar, and the supersonic transport. Our soundscape is already controlled by engineers. Someone is needed to press the claims of aesthetics, harmonizing with technology to create a humane acoustic environment, just as the visual artists of the Bauhaus did earlier in this century.

The want of even elementary tools for this purpose led to the coinages in Schafer's vocabulary. Vision is supported by the bias of language, but hearing requires new words: 'soundscape' for 'landscape,' 'earwitness' for 'eyewitness.' Fortunately, these are not themselves cacophonous, and they may be (I hope) catchy enough to enter the language. If they do, the Soundscape Project will succeed, for the word will then call the thing into being on a large scale; until now, sound has seldom been treated as a 'thing' of social concern.

Schafer, like Rudolph Arnheim and E.H. Gombrich in the visual arts, has tried to put the findings of perceptual psychology into a form useful to the creative artist. As Sigfried Giedion has written, in the works of an original creator 'new parts of the world are made accessible to feeling':

The opening up of ... new realms of feeling has always been the artist's chief mission. A great deal of our world would lack all emotional significance if it were not for his work. As recently as the eighteenth century, mountain scenery was felt to exhibit nothing except a formless and alarming confusion ... Right now there are great areas of our experience which are still waiting to be claimed by feeling.[46]

Schafer proposes the soundscape as one such area.

If John Cage first called for the musical perception of ambient noise, Schafer pursues the task more systematically. Soundscape research measures ambient noise levels; it identifies 'keynote' sounds, the continuous backgrounds, like urban traffic noise or electric hum, that the ear filters out. Schafer adapts terms from audio technology to soundscape studies: he speaks of the 'signal to noise ratio' of an environment; in some environments, which he calls 'lo-fi' as opposed to 'hi-fi,' no signal can stand out clearly from the ground. Such a situation demands a new kind of unfocused listening, a scanning process that, instead of concentrating on signal, scans the whole field for events of momentary interest. This listening process is clearly relevant to music like the stochastic pieces of Xenakis, or to any music in which texture replaces figure (Schafer's *Arcana* or the second string quartet). This century, in fact, has seen a reversal of the traditional figure-to-ground relationship. Since Russolo, it has become gradually easier to hear noise as music, while at the same time the proliferation of radios and Muzak has relegated conventional music to background – has reduced 'a sacred art to a slobber' (98).

Whether his emphasis is artistic or social, however, the sound-scape researcher faces the same problems of analysis. Beyond basic terminology, Schafer offers systems for the classification and notation of sounds. Notation is a serious obstacle. No existing system – acoustic, phonetic, or musical – is adequate. Phonetics records only verbal sound; musical notation can manage the oriole but stands helpless before the Harley-Davidson; and acoustic graphs are unreadable except by experts. The difficulty is great enough with the laboratory specimen, but sound events in the environment are not conveniently separable.

Beyond their physical attributes, however, sounds have symbolic and aesthetic qualities. Sound symbolism arises naturally from the sound source, if recognizable; some are so deeply ingrained as to be considered archetypal, like the waves of the sea or roaring wind. Such natural sounds have an ineffaceable emotional value. Bird song will always suggest a delicacy of sentiment that speaks through its various manifestations in music from Janequin to Messiaën. Other sound symbolism is intrinsic to the sound itself, quite apart from its source. Loudness always suggests power. The lilt of a folk-song deriving from the muscular rhythms of physical labour communicates its symbolism quite apart from the text. Bell sounds, nearly universal among mankind, have an archetypal significance, evoking 'some deep and mysterious response in the psyche which finds its visual correspondence in the integrity of the circle or mandala' (176). In the modern city, where church bells are smothered by traffic noise, we are losing touch with many archetypal resonances. While primitive peoples can reproduce natural sounds with uncanny accuracy, we may recognize, say, 'bird,' but we rarely know which bird; as Schafer remarks, 'We perceive only what we can name ... When the name of a thing dies, it is dismissed from society, and its very existence may be imperiled' (34).

Given the relativity of sound semantics, aesthetic laws of environmental sound are exceedingly hard to determine. Yet their existence is undeniable. 'The Moozak industry does not hesitate to make decisions about what kinds of music the public is most likely to tolerate, nor did the aviation industry consult the public before it entered on the development of supersonic-boom-producing aircraft' (146). When does sound become noise? Cultural and geographical features are involved. Citizens of developing nations do not express the same dislike for machine noises as North Americans; tropical societies are less sensitive to outdoor noise than northern societies (perhaps the reason why the inventor of soundscape research is Canadian). If Schafer's definition of 'noise' as 'unwanted sound' seems circular, it does at least demand an awareness of context.

'Clairaudience, not ear-muffs.' Schafer's motto proclaims his ideal of good acoustic design. Noise control in the past has been fairly limited to noise-abatement measures, necessary but by themselves ineffectual. They must be accompanied by a greater awareness of acoustic design on the part of not only legislators but engineers, architects, and any professionals who control the urban environment.

Acoustic design should aim at certain aesthetic balances: between artificial and natural sounds; between human and technological sounds; between high and low, loud and soft, continuous and discrete sounds; between sound and silence. Physiological measurements may be taken as modules, like Le Corbusier's modules for architectural space. Noting that the unaided human voice cannot be raised above the pain threshold, Schafer concludes that 'God was a first-rate acoustical engineer' (207). But modern man has lost touch with basic biological rhythms; the designer ought to become aware of rhythmic modules based on breath, heartbeat, footstep, nervous system.

Unfortunately, acoustic design must contend with the fact that loudness equals power, and modern society is power-hungry. Just as in the city skyline the cathedral has bowed to the bank tower, so in the soundscape the church bell has given way to the machine. Schafer develops from this observation a theory of 'sacred noise': 'To have the Sacred Noise,' he says, 'is not merely to make the biggest noise; rather it is a matter of having the authority to make it without censure. Wherever Noise is granted immunity from human intervention, there will be found a seat of power' (76). Accordingly, the loudest noise in primitive society is most likely heard at its religious celebrations; the loudest machine in medieval society was the cathedral organ. But with the industrial revolution, the factory stole the sacred noise from the church; and then the Beatles stole it again from the factories of Liverpool. Now it is possible to see that industry is not God, that its blessings are not unmixed. Meanwhile, competition for noise power continues.

Paradoxically, one of the most serious offenders in this power play is the music industry. Our environment is wired for sound, and often it is impossible to move beyond earshot of music. E.T.A. Hoffmann complained likewise of the ubiquitous musical amateurs of Germany (see 'Der Musikfeind'), but then music was tied to music makers limited to mere human volume and endurance. With electronics, music can exceed the pain threshold; it can fill any conceivable space; it can continue without pause for breath or sleep. The dangers of this situation are so clear that in 1969 the International Music Council of Unesco passed a resolution condemning wired-in music: 'We denounce unanimously the intolerable infringement of individual freedom and of the right of everyone to silence, because of the abusive use, in private and public places, of recorded or broadcast music.' Schafer remarks, 'for the first time in history an international organization involved primarily with the *production* of sounds suddenly turned its attention to their *reduction*' (97–8).

We now suffer from what Schafer calls 'schizophonia,' the splitting of sound from its source, resulting in a distorted perception of auditory space. Singing is no longer 'tied to a hole in the head'; it can issue from anywhere in the environment, at any volume, for any length of time. Of course benefits of this technology are undeniable, quite apart from the genuine pleasures of recorded music; we have increased our awareness of auditory space in ways comparable to our heightened perception of visual space through telescope and microscope. As long ago as 1937,

John Cage welcomed the ability to write a 'quartet for explosive motor, wind, heartbeat and landslide.'[47] But the implications of schizophonia are still little understood. Radio is a wall against the outer world, and an instrument of power over it, like the motorcycle or the unmufflered car. Radio and Muzak become a form of audioanalgesia, reducing music from an art to a mass pacifier (rather like Aldous Huxley's 'sexophones' in *Brave New World*). But even more, the pop music industry, with a budget like the Pentagon's, exerts its sound imperialism on a global scale, uprooting the soundscapes of local cultures and substituting a featureless, internationalized smear. Faced with such a reality, composers and music educators must become as much concerned with the prevention of music as with its creation.

The most serious threat of all, however, is the airplane: 'As every home and office is gradually being situated along the world runway, the aviation industry, perhaps more effectively than any other, is destroying the words "peace and quiet" in every world language. For noise in the sky is distinguished radically from all other forms of noise in that it is not localized or contained' (85–6). On the ground, zoning laws prevent builders from raising hamburger stands on residential streets; but the sonic equivalent of MacDonald's golden arches roars overhead without censure.

Legal aspects of the problem are complex. Law is based largely on visual units having clear boundaries, but auditory space has no boundaries: it overlaps indefinitely. While legal controls are essential, the real solution is better acoustic design. Schafer hopes that greater public awareness of the problem will eventually create pressure for solutions, and much of his music education theory, his call for 'ear cleaning' in the public schools, is given to this end. Meanwhile, planners remain ignorant. Insensitivity shows up in as simple a matter as the telephone: 'Who invented the telephone bell? Certainly not a musician' (241). Why must technological noises always be ugly?

Schafer's ideals are utopian perhaps. Governments are torpid confronted even with medical facts. Aesthetic standards are harder to sell, as the ugliness of our visually dominated society warns. And Schafer's book never really solves the question of aesthetic relativism. To society as a whole these industrial sounds mean material comfort, progress, power. As Schafer observes, Western man abhors silence:

Man likes to make sounds to remind himself that he is not alone. From this point of view total silence is the rejection of the human personality. Man fears the absence of sound as he fears the absence of life ... Since modern man fears death as none before him, he avoids silence to nourish his fantasy of perpetual life. In Western society, silence is a negative, a vacuum (256).

Some evidence (like the *Silence* of Cage's title) suggests that this condition is changing as the ego-dominated technology of our culture is called into question. But, on the whole, aural sensibility seems likely to retain its present low priority in the scale of cultural values, except when noise is shown to be a medical issue, or when infringements upon the quality of life are sonic-boomed into the public consciousness.

The Tuning of the World is not primarily a book about music, but Schafer occasionally speculates about relationships between music and the acoustic environment. Was the Alberti bass really suggested by horses' hoofbeats? Was the Beethoven sforzando a response to urbanization? Was sonata form created by the same exploratory impulses that produced colonial imperialism? Many composers of the 1920s consciously mimicked machines, but were jazz men aware that their flams and paradiddles were influenced by the railroad? *Something* has happened 'between Pope and Pound,' between Mozart and Stravinsky, Schafer declares, and very likely it includes 'the accumulation of syncopations and offbeats in the soundscape' (227). Technology's influence on music has not been studied. Perhaps it is significant that choral societies developed in the north of England just when mechanization severed singing from manual labour. It is probably not accidental that athematic music appeared just when the phonograph made infinite repetition possible. The music of Penderecki 'leaves the impression that it was conceived somewhere between the airstrip and the Autobahn' (113). So it is not surprising that the opening of *Music for the Morning of the World* reminded Eric McLean of an air-conditioner hum.[48] (One of the keynote sounds of our society is the hum of electric current, which centres in North America on about B♮, a drone that can become a kind of tonality.) Music can become a tool for soundscape propaganda, like the roaring snowmobile of *North/White*.

Otto Luening, the American pioneer in electronic music, has noted that 'the novelty of electronic sound production as an end in itself is no longer relevant. The task is now to develop the capacity to perceive these new sounds ... Avoidance of this responsibility can only lead to noise pollution and bring an unfortunate confusion to the new art form.'[49] Composers need to be sensitive to the new potentials of technology in order to understand how new technology is altering our perceptions. Asked in interview whether his music and his soundscape researches connect, Schafer replied:

They do insofar as a lot of things that I've learned about the soundscape are probably reapplied in musical expression. For example, we discovered when we measured the water of the Pacific Ocean lapping against the West Coast of Vancouver Island that the breakers come in approximately every eight to ten seconds ... It happens to correspond approximately with our breathing when we're in a relaxed state, and one can develop that musically in terms of an articulation – in phrasing, for instance – that has a parallel to wave motion. I really feel that in this sort of way art can intimate, I won't say a higher reality, but it can intimate alternative modes of existence, alternative modes of living. And that may be one of our tasks as artists: to suggest other states of consciousness ... in terms of say, the tempo of music, the kinds of frequency areas one deals with, the kinds of textures and the way in which sounds are put together.[50]

These ideas apply directly to *East* and the *String Quartet No. 2* ('*Waves*'). They do not necessarily make these works great music, but they do give them a novel theoretical underpinning. And they hint of possible future developments in Schafer's career.

Creative Music Education

Schafer's commitment to music in society shows most clearly in his contributions to music education. Here, in simplified form, all his ideas come together. His writings, which have gained him celebrity – or notoriety, depending on one's viewpoint – are part of a larger movement of experimentation in education during the 1960s. Professional educators in other countries, like George Self, Brian Dennis, and John Paynter in England, have made innovations much in the same spirit as Schafer's. Since the first excitement, however, financial crises in education combined with a philosophic retreat to conventionality have lessened interest in Schafer's methods. 'I do not know whether my work is taken seriously or not,' he confesses.[51] But even if he sees his work rejected, Schafer is still famous in the profession as an innovative trouble-maker.

The rejection is not surprising. As one writer puts it, 'the general defensiveness of music educators toward their colleagues in other aspects of music and education' is self-acknowledged.[52] Among teachers, they must fight for their music programs against the pressures of more 'practical' subjects; among musicians, they must fight for equal status as professionals. Also, like many other musicians who consider themselves 'advanced' when listening to Bartók, they are often embarrassed by their ignorance of genuinely contemporary music. Schafer, then, appears to them in the threatening guise of a contemporary composer who, an outsider, vents the private grievances of his own education in invectives against their already defensive profession. True, he has done little to ingratiate himself. But his criticisms, if sometimes radical, are not unfamiliar; and his correctives offer a fund of suggestive possibilities even to the teacher not yet ready to swallow Schafer whole.

A few misunderstandings do need to be cleared away. First, *Creative Music Education* does not outline a 'method.' It is mainly a casebook of transcripts intended as models for imitation – but not duplication. The book contains surprisingly few statements of principle, at least until the end. It is unsystematic, repetitive, and as hard to abstract as it is to summarize in prose. Schafer has more than once refused publishers' requests that he turn his booklets into a 'method.' The very attempt would destroy the heuristic process. This process is certainly not the only way to teach, but it is a good way and too little used. The teacher's function is to pose the problems, direct the dialogue with as much Socratic wit as he can muster, and gradually disappear, while the students pursue their discoveries. Education should be 'programmed for discovery rather than instruction,' Schafer writes, quoting McLuhan (228). 'Teach on the verge of peril' (221). Success, then, depends enormously on the teacher's charisma. In Schafer's hands, it works; but it gives insecurity nothing to hide behind.

Secondly, Schafer proposes his activities as a supplement to traditional music teaching, not as a replacement – though he is strangely reluctant to soothe anxieties of traditionalists on this point. His choral classes scarcely include ordinary singing: 'If anything we leave off at about the point this begins. (The qualified teacher can go on easily enough from there)' (161). His techniques differ from 'the mainstream of education,' but neither stream 'should be considered a replacement for the other' (223); accordingly, he proposes a curriculum integrating the two (273–4). But here again he chafes the educator's sensitivities, for while he is not concerned with traditional training, he insists that such training be conducted by 'the professional musician who has earned a living ... in a keenly competitive profession.' 'One of the black spots in school policy (at least in North America) is the systematic exclusion of such people from teaching' (243).

Schafer's book, however, limits criticism of conventional programs to occasional sniping and concentrates instead on deficiencies that he, along with a few others, sees. The root problem is ignorance of contemporary music. Music education is simply out of touch with modernism. Here, the visual arts have the advantage. 'There is in music ... no equivalent to the Basic Course which Johannes Itten developed for the first-year students at the Bauhaus' (228). The teaching of the arts should relate 'directly to the contemporary practices of that art,' agrees Elliott Schwartz; 'there are few respectable art programs that haven't made use of collage techniques, photographic images, abstraction, and pseudo-cubist representation.'[53]

This charge is hardly original with Schafer. According to Bennett Reimer, 'the notion that children – of *any* age – should be "protected" from certain styles, these usually being the more puzzling contemporary styles, is one which a more mature profession would find intolerable.'[54] Even the educator who insists on having *all* kinds of music is often seeking only to legitimize his personal capitulation to pop. Rarely is he ambitious to tell the students about Boulez. Schafer advocates a wide variety of styles – new, old, non-Western (237–41) – though he tentatively excludes pop music, not because it is necessarily bad, 'but because it is a social rather than a musical phenomenon' (223). But Schafer's primary concern is not with what music gets taught. Instead, he wants the classroom to nurture curiosity: 'Don't be content to stand still in your musical tastes,' he pleads (5). 'I do not mean that we should merely shovel music by contemporary masters into the classroom. Rather, I am concerned that young people should make their own music' (237).

Essentially, Schafer's answer is to take John Cage into the classroom. The problem is to convince educators that he belongs there.

As we have seen, Schafer, though cautious with Cage's ideas in his music, has embraced them heartily in his soundscape theories. Likewise, Cage seems more useful as a fund of pedagogical devices than as a maker of musical artifacts. His three principles – chance, environmental sound, and mixed-media forms – emerge in the three areas of music education that Schafer claims for attention:

1 Try to discover whatever creative potential children may have for making music of their own;

2 to introduce students of all ages to the sounds of the environment; to treat the

world soundscape as a musical composition of which man is the principal composer, and to make critical judgments which would lead to its improvement;

3 to discover a nexus or gathering-place where all the arts may meet and develop together harmoniously (227).

Schafer discovers in Cage's redefinition of music as 'sounds, sounds around us whether we're in or out of concert halls,' (96) and in his childlike insistence on fundamental questions, a stimulus to the young mind just beginning to think about music. Cage's concern with sound as sound points to Schafer's 'ear cleaning.' His indeterminacy, improvisation, and graphic notations can be made more accessible to untrained performers than traditional music. And his inventiveness inspires inventiveness in others. Just as Cage energized a whole generation of composers (many of them very unlike himself), so he can be used to fuel creativity in the classroom. Consequently, everything in Schafer's teaching, he says, is 'calculated either to sharpen the ears, or to release latent creative energy, or both' (90).

Interested chiefly in the general music program, Schafer sees music education as being preoccupied with performance. 'Our system of music education is one in which creative music is progressively vilified and choked out of existence' (41). 'Most students never listen at all to one another ... where there are twenty clarinets or sixteen flutes all tootling away at the unison line of their Beethoven-Browns and Handel-Jacksons' (33). Again, the same criticism comes from within the profession; public displays and competitions, involving deadening over-rehearsal, all promoted by the 'slick techniques of salesmanship ... employed by portions of the performance "establishment,"' have become 'a source of embarrassment' to serious educators.[55] Furthermore, Schafer laments 'the genius syndrome' of gearing performance programs to the star performer; 'music education, geared down to the average human intelligence, may have its own rewards' (224).

Schafer's emphasis on universal creativity dominates his booklets. It includes a philosophical approach, examining basic conceptual problems: 'We must keep returning to the beginning. What are the basic ingredients of music? What are the pristine elements out of which it can be structured' (224)? The first dialogue of *The Composer in the Classroom* uses the question 'What is music?' to stretch the tolerances of the students. *Ear Cleaning* expands this definition by contrast with noise and silence and explores the components of musical sound one by one – tone, timbre, amplitude, melody, texture, rhythm. *When Words Sing* repeats much of this process with vocal sound.

But Schafer's approach even to philosophic questions is active. He avoids passive listening, either to music or to lectures: 'All our investigations into sound should be verified empirically by making sounds themselves and by examining the results ... An actual contact with musical sound ... is more vital than the most gluttonous listening program imaginable' (49). Here, Cage's chance methods liberate student improvisations from the constraints of harmony and melody. *The Composer in the Classroom* leads a group of students from their first questions about sound to the creation of an original, group-improvised composition. (The film *Bing, Bang, Boom* records this same process). Schafer relies heavily on imitative and descriptive sounds to encourage acceptance of sounds as music; but he also emphasizes the general affective associations of sounds, and, noticing that some things cannot be imitated directly, moves through a study of sound textures. Likewise, *When Words Sing* begins with vocal imitation ('nature concert') and verbal onomatopoeia, and moves through a classification of choral textures and the problems of making musical sounds reflect a verbal text. Always, Schafer (unlike Cage) stresses the expressive nature of sound and urges students to discriminate between sounds critically. Both booklets culminate in a complete composition – the first in a group-improvised 'Mask of the Evil Demon' (on a text that Schafer had used in *Kinderlieder*), the other in his own *Epitaph for Moonlight*.

Schafer's methods emphasize direct training of the perceptions, so that pure informational content is somewhat beside the purpose. If some traditional music programs stress performance, others 'with a heavy emphasis on theory, technique and memory work' become 'predominantly knowledge-gaining' (228). The hand operates the pencil, while the ear falls asleep. Truly, Schafer is not anti-information; in the context of his heuristic procedure, however, information turns into information retrieval. In a discussion of the music of the spheres, for example, one student happens to ask about radio signals from outer space. Schafer's response: 'There's an observatory in town. Why not phone up an astronomer and ask him about it?' The student does, and returns in fifteen minutes with a wholly unplanned expansion of the original theme (135). So too, when a class wants to know about smell, Schafer invites a cosmetician and a pestologist to visit. This is admittedly a spotty way to transmit bodies of fact, but it has advantages of vividness, as well as demonstrating that if the student has a question, then there is likely to be – somewhere – an answer.

The soundscape theory, of course, grows naturally out of Schafer's concern with sound as sound. His booklet *The New Soundscape* should be supplemented with *The Tuning of the World*, and the ideas need not be repeated here. But the teacher, even if unwilling to believe that the whole nature 'of the theory and practice of music ... is now going to have to be completely reconsidered' (97), will find the soundscape concept perhaps the most accessible part of Schafer's work, appealing as it does to the scientific orientation of the student and his social conscience, as well as expanding his understanding of what constitutes music. Also, in a school system committed to competition and practical achievement, there is an added argument for Schafer's insistence on the 'inalienable right to stillness' (103).

Schafer's third area of concern, media study, is the least adequately developed. It emerges mainly in *The Rhinoceros in the Classroom*, the last of the booklets, which is also taken up with reprints of scattered general statements on music education. But these ideas too grow naturally out of his interest in training the senses, 'cleaning the lenses of perception,' through creative exploration of their capabilities – all senses, not just hearing. Like the soundscape concept, Schafer's interest here is less with music itself than with its place in the world. 'The collapse of specialisms and the growth of interest in interdisciplinary undertakings should not go unnoticed by those engaged in any kind of music education' (244). This kind of enterprise, he feels, is most important in the early grades, where

we should abolish the study of all the arts. In their place we should have one comprehensive subject, perhaps called 'media studies,' or better 'studies in sensitivity and expression,' which would include all yet none of the traditional arts.

Yet, at a certain point we could still separate out the individual arts as separate studies, though always bearing in mind that we are doing so in the interests of developing specific sensorial acuities ... Ultimately, we might return to a reconfiguration of all the art forms into the total work of art again – a situation in which 'art' and 'life' would be synonymous (232).

This radical reorganization of arts education suffers from the same dangers that he notes in other experiments with synaesthesia: 'An over-indulgence in them brings about a confusion of the senses, and unprofitable piling-up of resources rather than an acuity of sensorial experience' (244). To this I would add that concentration on purely sensuous, non-intellectual perception is always liable to abuse, and that reliance on extra-musical associations sometimes brings Schafer dangerously close to the old-fashioned method of drawing pictures to illustrate Beethoven.

Nonetheless, Schafer's mixed-media concepts have had practical application in his Sensitivity Course at Simon Fraser, and with some success. *The Rhinoceros in the Classroom* provides a few tantalizing glimpses of this course, like Schafer's multimedia canon:

Four students took up positions at four drawing boards, and another four stood in front of them. Those in front were instructed to make sounds with their voices, and those at the drawing boards were asked to translate their hearings immediately into visual patterns. As the first four vocalized, sometimes in surprising or entertaining ways, the second four dashed paint around their papers ... Then we added four dancers who were asked to ignore the sounds they heard and concentrate on moving their bodies into the shapes they saw appearing on the page. Finally, four more students were given percussion instruments ... (268).

To some, such activities must seem foolish. But within the context of contemporary theories of art they need not be – especially if one considers the sensory deprivation imposed by most schooling. Schafer's ideas here would be more persuasive, I expect, if we possessed a fuller account of his Sensitivity Course, its successes and its failures.

Schafer's main interest is the general music program as opposed to performance; but in his compositions for young ensembles, instrumental and choral, he has also helped to correct 'the obvious and painful anemia of the school performance literature.'[56] He observes that many *avant-garde* compositions (he mentions those of Udo Kasemets) are also suitable, even more suitable, for amateurs than professionals: 'The problems are not digital problems ... They're mental problems, heuristic problems, such as what sound do you actually hear, when you hear that sound, you add this sound' (60). Schafer's educational pieces are integral to his own development as a composer, so I have discussed them in later chapters, but as a group they embody most of his educational ideals.

Though Schafer's pieces make some concessions to simplicity (he avoids serialism), they remain aggressively contemporary. To students unfamiliar with such music, they introduce a new experience and stretch tolerances. The improvisational demands encourage the performers' creativity, as well as the critical judgments of everyone in the group. The music simply cannot be played without attentive listening. *Minimusic*, especially, is a listening exercise based on 'Music and Conversation'(33–40). Some pieces involve social views (*Threnody*) or environmental concerns (*Miniwanka, Train*). All employ one common device, graphic notation.

Again, Schafer's views are controversial: 'I have tried to make the enthusiastic discovery of music precede the ability to play an instrument or read notes, knowing that the right time to introduce these skills is when the child asks for them' (225). He approves of the blind music master in Iran, teaching six students to play the santour by rote: 'Not a word is spoken. Not a note is written down' (247). The debate about when to teach musical notation still rages, and the success of the Suzuki violin method argues merit in Schafer's position, though critics complain that the rote repetition there is mind-numbing, and that older students experience more serious frustrations in learning notation than the very young. But if conventional notation is not going to disappear, graphics have nonetheless proven their worth. Schafer's graphic compositions retain their pedagogical and musical merits, whatever his views on the notation controversy. They may be taken as the practical vindication of all Schafer's educational theories – or they may simply remain proven contributions to the tiny repertoire of *avant-garde* music for young performers.

The Canadian composer: *Music in the Cold*

Question: 'Is there, or ought there to be, a distinctive Canadian music?' Answer: 'There isn't and there oughtn't.'[57] Schafer has been slow to make peace with his own nation. His blunt rejection of nationalism in 1969 was not his last word on the subject, nor his first: but it does suggest his internationalist bias and freedom from sentimental politics. Still, the question of Canadianism has concerned him persistently, often with ambivalence. Such ambivalence, of course, is part of the Canadian experience. But Schafer's remained awkwardly unresolved until his soundscape theories gave him a basis for understanding his relationship to his environment without committing him to an outmoded chauvinism.

In 1961, home from Europe, Schafer published an article detailing why the obvious avenues to a national music are not open in Canada. 'Canada may not have produced her Beethoven yet,' he remarks, 'but she will certainly never produce her Smetana.'[58] The music of Indians and Eskimos is too primitive to be useful. The Eskimos are 'an astonishingly unmusical race,' he says, comparing their singing to 'Sir Winston Churchill clearing his throat' (72). Even more damaging are the cultural attitudes inherited from the early settlers: 'The first emigrants to Canada were philistines. They were men of energy and vision, but they are culturally bankrupt. The vast majority came not to propagate European culture but to escape it, and this hostility to the fine arts has, though we hope it is now overcome, nevertheless, left us suspicious of the value of the culture we do possess' ... (73–4). To Canadians, 'culture' belongs in Europe: 'If God had intended Canada to have culture, Mozart would have been born there.'[59] Conversely, from the vantage of Europe, Canada is all but invisible culturally. We appear a kind of suburb of Chicago. What would have come of Stravinsky, Schafer asks, if the Rite of Spring had been premiered in Vancouver? 'Canada is not taken seriously as a place where music is generated.'[60]

In North America, Canada faces not only indifference but active aggression. Unfortunately, the United States does have a distinctive culture: 'It is baseball, Tin Pan Alley, and shut-in church broadcasts on Sundays.'[61] American pop culture cannot be stopped at the border, and our only defence against its totalitarian thrust is the government. 'Unlike the u.s.a., Canada is not primarily a free-enterprise nation; on the contrary, its best achievements have resulted from public enterprise – usually brought about in an effort to withstand American pressures.'[62] Despite his tendency to think internationally, Schafer's soundscape research revealed to him the threat of the multi-national monied powers. 'We were all in favour of internationalism,' he says, 'until we realized that what it really meant was that we were going to be drinking Coca-Cola in Persia, that one airport was going to be exactly like another, and that every piece of commercial crap was going to be spread around the world in greater and greater volume.'[63]

If the Canadian composer is prevented from expressing a simple nationalism, both by the problematic nature of the nation itself and by the international colour of current affairs, nothing prevents him from responding to his physical environment without reference to political boundaries. This response is inevitable anyway. 'If you are looking for Canadian identity in music,' he argues, 'you have to ask yourself what we have in our total acoustic environment that makes us different from other people in the world.'[64] The right question is not whether Canadian composers are better than others, but what makes them different. The answer lies in the soundscape.

'Typical Canada is a Canada of wilderness,' he continues. 'The average Canadian carries around with him in his head a vision of spaciousness.' This may be responsible for the most intensely Canadian feelings associated with, say, the 'deep and haunting' whistles of the national railway, so different from the 'bright and piping' sound in Europe: 'Is it the long haul from East to West across thousands of miles of lonely and spectacular landscape that makes the E-flat minor Canadian whistle seem so appropriate?'[65] Metaphors from the soundscape perhaps provide a key to Canadian music. The music of Serge Garant has 'a hard, glittering quality that seems to me analogous ... to the glittering of snow and ice.' The music of Harry Somers shows 'a rough sort of hard line in the melodic writing that you don't seem to find in other parts of the world, except maybe among Scandanavian composers.'[66]

Schafer's *Music in the Cold* is a text, neither poem nor prose, but possibly unique in Canadian literature: a power fantasy in which Canada takes over the world. Beginning as a poor, bare, frozen land, Canada learns to sell off its resources, becomes populated, founds arts councils, gets too rich – in short, turns into the United States. Schafer's satire broadens as Canadian culture, no longer provincial, becomes the international norm:

We became the most powerful nation in the world.
We lived in glass houses hundreds of feet in the air.
We no longer went South.
We *were* South.
We paddled barefoot in the broadloom and planted rubber trees in our kitchens.
We flushed our toilets twenty times a day and showered twice.
(All the sewers had to be widened.)

Then the ice age arrives. Everything freezes. Canada returns to its pristine, unpopulated state.

In this brief work, Schafer projects from Monteagle Valley, Ontario, his apocalyptic vision of a Canada purified, brought back to its original austerities. 'The art of the North,' he says, 'is the art of restraint.' 'The art of the North is composed of tiny events magnified.' Musical form 'will become clear as an icicle.' As for the artist, his mind is 'as cool as an ice box.' Against a portrait of corruption, Schafer draws the Canadian values that speak through his music – a virtuous toughness, a moralistic asceticism, a conviction that less is more, a fear of too much growth, too much wealth, too many people, a horror of excess.

Given this much leave, I might play my own game of metaphors. If one theme stands at the heart of Schafer's music, it is, I think, the feeling of disorientation in space, of being lost in vastnesses of space and time. This is not the confident expansiveness felt in American composers like Copland or Roy Harris. Schafer's most typical figures are Brébeuf, hallucinating in the wilderness (in Canadian vernacular, 'bushed'), or the mute Characteristics Man in the urban labyrinth of *Patria I*. The chase through 'Phantasmagoria' in *Loving* is another instance. But this sense extends metaphorically. Schafer twists acoustic space, notably in the mystical antiphonies of *Lustro*. The stage design for *Patria II* sets the audience above the action, looking giddily down; *La Testa d'Adriane* depends partly on optical illusion. Often the time sense, too, is skewed. 'Incarceration' describes the experience of endlessness in prison, while other works express near stasis (*From the Tibetan Book of the Dead*) or hypnotic repetiton (second string quartet). *Canzoni for Prisoners* consists of bewildering overlays of simultaneous tempi. Most of Schafer's mature music is without meter at all. His favourite semitone cluster is a sound without a centre. Tape-delay techniques suggest cavernous echoes. And the slow semitone glissando – perhaps his most distinctive soundmark – seems like a tone that doesn't quite know where it belongs.

Perhaps most remarkable about all this is that, in spite of his disorientation, his ironies, Schafer has preserved a youthful, romantic optimism. At the end of *Music in the Cold* he describes his own 'new heaven and new earth':

The dream of unlimited wealth must be put aside.
The dream of international celebrity must be forgotten.
I will build a new culture, fresh as a young animal, fresh as new grass,
a culture huge in dreams but simple in materials.
Every culture implies faith in its available materials.
Underlying every action is a faith in some technology ...
The old technology of waste is gone.
What then remains?
The old virtues: harmony; the universal soul; hard work.
I will live supersensitized, the antennae of a new race.
I will create a new mythology.
It will take time.
It will take time.
There will be time.

3

Early works 1952–9

Schafer's development as a composer from the earliest works to *Loving* suggests no pattern that can be called logical or 'organic.' Rather, it shows a process of trying out available modern styles in succession, gradually assimilating various stylistic languages. During the first several years, Schafer modelled his music on the neo-classical composers of the 1920s – Stravinsky, Milhaud, Poulenc. This style, which seemed adventurous at the time, found support in the teaching of John Weinzweig, whose non-serial works, like the Copland-inspired ballet *Red Ear of Corn* (1949), stem from the same background. The very existence of these early neo-classical works must surprise anyone familiar with Schafer's mature music, particularly since several have been published belatedly in the 1970s. But the surprise is surely agreeable when one discovers anything as charming and well-crafted as, say, the *Kinderlieder*. These are apprentice works, to be sure; they were long in the writing, and derivative. Yet many are already viable enough as music to be considered on their merits, not merely as parts of a process leading to better things.

  Three works survive from Schafer's earliest days as a composition student: *Polytonality* (1952), which remains his sole contribution to the literature of the piano, and two songs, *A Music Lesson* (1953) and 'Benjamin Britten' (1954), the latter now forming a part of *Three Contemporaries*. Schafer recalls that when the Britten sketch was given at one of the Saturday afternoon presentations of student compositions, he proclaimed that it represented his belief (appropriated from Stravinsky) that music should express no feeling, but that it might have didactic or informative value. ('So that's the way you feel?' asked someone. 'Yes,' answered the composer. There were hoots of laughter.) Yet for all the jejune theorizing, these pieces now seem amusing, urbane trifles – certainly not the intended impression, for Schafer himself was impressed with his own daring modernism at the time. *Polytonality* is called 'a didactic piece' in the composer's holograph (not in the printed version); the text of *A Music Lesson* initiates the audience into the mysteries of modern music: 'Polytonality is the simultaneous combination of two or more tonalities. Do not condemn it, try to understand it. Listen to the false relations. Listen to the tone-colour in these chords: [the piano illustrates]. It's not exactly dissonant; in fact, it's rather pleasing.' Considering that Pierre Boulez was writing *Le Marteau sans maître* at this same time, Schafer's plea may simply reflect his own naïveté; but really it reveals just as clearly the backwardness of musical Toronto when Schafer began his studies. It is worth noting, too, that Schafer has never lost his faith in music as a didactic medium.

Despite the composer's *avant-garde* airs, the technique of these pieces is limited to simple superimposed triads, most often a major second apart. Even when the singer proposes that we should 'try to visualize these melodies horizontally in terms of counterpoint instead of vertically in terms of harmony,' Schafer's counterpoint is rudimentary – and was to remain so for many years. The striking feature of *Polytonality* is not the harmony but the basso ostinato, which persists through the entire piece. *A Music Lesson* tentatively superimposes one metre in the voice on another in the piano. But nothing in these pieces even hints that the composer had sufficient resources to sustain a large composition. Yet the next two years brought a four-movement *Trio for Clarinet, Cello, and Piano* and the pleasant *Concerto for Harpsichord and Eight Wind Instruments*.

The trio, which seems to have resembled Milhaud's lightweight *Suite* for clarinet, violin, and piano, is no longer available for inspection. The Harpsichord concerto, however, is the *chef-d'oeuvre* of Schafer's study with Weinzweig. It was conceived for Greta Kraus, with whom Schafer was studying, and, though she has never performed it, it has been given by both Kelsey Jones and George Malcolm. The piece, says one writer, 'has all the rhythmic bite of Stravinsky with the infectious wit and humour of Poulenc or Roussel.'[1] It does make a cheerful sound, most attractive on first hearing, and it must be examined not so much for anticipation of maturity as for vestiges of inexperience. Vestiges there are, of course. Individual themes, recalling the *boulevard* manner of 'Les Six,' are short-winded, while the whole work seems too long, especially the middle movement. There are awkward transitions between tempi, and some pointless scale passages. And while most of the woodwind writing is idiomatic, showing the composer's instinct for combining sonorities, the two bassoons are used too much in the lowest register and not at all in the highest. The texture of the whole seems too busy, betraying the student who has yet to learn how to make less accomplish more. All of these faults granted, however, the harpsichord concerto still makes a strong impression, quite belying its status as a student composition.

Schafer's principal model here is Manuel de Falla's *Concerto for Harpsichord and Five Instruments*, though he also borrowed ideas from the harpsichord concerto by Poulenc. Between Falla's work and Schafer's there are several parallels. Both are in three movements: the first in sonata form, toccata-like; the second processional in feeling, with broad harpsichord arpeggios (these also show up in Schafer's first-movement development); the third a concise, dance-like finale in alternating 3/4 and 6/8 (and in Schafer, 4/4). Both works feature ornamentation reminiscent of baroque harpsichord idiom. Similarities extend to the small instrumental ensemble and its astringent, staccato rhythmic character combined with bright, folkloric fragments. Unlike Falla, however, Schafer dispenses with strings altogether and calls instead for an unusual group of eight instruments (two flutes, oboe, clarinet, bass clarinet, two bassoons, and horn), often combining bass clarinet with the bassoons to strengthen the harpsichord bass.

Throughout the concerto, Schafer repeats and juxtaposes ideas rather than developing them. He is still uncertain how to extend a single idea and multiplies their number instead. The ideas themselves are more rhythmic than melodic, and the two outer movements sustain interest largely through their rhythmic spark; but the first movement, depending on different tempi for contrast, loses the momentum of the unitary tempo most characteristic of this style. This movement follows the outlines of sonata form, deploying loosely related ideas. The first idea begins in irregular metre, then settles into 4/4, though the metrical irregularity recurs (example 3.1a, b). A pattern of running sixteenths continues from this idea in the more gently moving second idea (example 3.1c). A third idea (or second key area) at a still slower tempo pits the harpsichord with Stravinskian bassoon staccato against an oboe line that combines the angularity of the first idea with the rhythmic pattern of the second. Other patterns appear in the movement; but despite this abundance the development is based on two additional ideas – slow arpeggiated parallel triads in the hapsichord placed against some high, rapid bitonal figures that make effective use of the lute stop.

3.1 *Concerto for Harpsichord and Eight Wind Instruments*: themes from first movement: a/ bars 1–3; b/ bars 22–3; c/ bars 129–30

The recapitulation is handled mechanically: molto ritardando to a pause followed by a simple roulade in the winds leading back to example 3.1b.

The solemn and rather static second movement bears the inscription 'Zur Erinnerung an Paul Klee.' The composer had no specific work by Klee in mind, but the movement is mosaic in structure, perhaps suggesting those canvases in which Klee juxtaposes blocks of subtly modulated colour. Like the second song of *Three Contemporaries*, this movement suggests both Klee's rather austere lyricism, represented by bare, sustained lines in the winds, and his angry streak of sarcasm, figured mainly in the highly ornamented harpsichord writing (the first solo entrance is marked 'Brutal'). This movement is most remarkable for its colourful use of the wind ensemble and for a dramatic middle section involving repeated thirty-second note triads, fortissimo, widely spaced by rests.[2]

The third movement returns to the insouciant patter of the first, based chiefly on a theme in 4/4 cleverly superimposed on an accompaniment in 3/4. This finale is the most satisfying movement of the three, more concise than the second, and more successful than the first in sustaining its rhythmic drive through to the end.

The harpsichord concerto and the *Sonatina for Flute and Harpsichord* (1958) are Schafer's only works in a classical mould. Schafer can hardly be said to have neglected instrumental music, but his predilection for vocal writing appears early, and his most impressive early works are three sets of songs, all composed for Phyllis Mailing: *Three Contemporaries* (1954–6), *Minnelieder* (1956), and *Kinderlieder* (1958). All (except 'Benjamin Britten') were written without supervision after Schafer's enforced departure from the University of Toronto Faculty of Music in 1954.

Three Contemporaries, the earliest, is in many ways the most revealing. It marks the first sign of the composer's aptitude for inventive, ear catching novelty. Each song is a satiric sketch of some contemporary artist connected with Schafer himself: Benjamin Britten, Paul Klee, and Ezra Pound. The prose texts by the composer proceed from the academic to the romantic to the rebellious, while the satiric tone follows suit as the subjects draw closer to the composer's sympathies.

The Britten sketch, which was written at the same time as *Polytonality* and *A Music Lesson*, was originally entitled 'Benjamin Butter': 'Benjamin Britten is a most distinguished composer. Born in nineteen thirteen in Lowestoft, he received a scholarship in composition at the Royal College of Music. Among his many works are the operas *Peter Grimes* and *Albert Herring*. Benjamin Britten is a most distinguished composer.' This dry text is accompanied by a witty parody of Britten's dryest manner, accentuated by musical allusions to the two operas mentioned. The Klee sketch, set in German (with alternative English), is a more serious statement compiled from Klee's diaries, proclaiming the artist's fondness for simplicity while complaining that his 'literary nature' suffers 'devastating changes from tender lyric to bitter satire.' The Pound sketch depends on irony incomprehensible without knowledge of Pound's imprisonment in an American federal hospital for the criminally insane. The text, a mocking echo of the Britten number, speaks of Pound's 'generous scholarship from the United States government' making him 'part of the great American institution.' As John Beckworth described it, 'the last phrase of the vocal part takes the rising motive "Ezra Pound" suddenly up over an octave and the vowel in "Pound" breaks into a derisive howl. This moment is highly original and theatrically most effective.'³ Altogether, *Three Contemporaries* is a firmly conceived unit, the earliest indication of Schafer's dramatic flair.

Minnelieder, a group of thirteen songs for mezzo-soprano and woodwind quintet, is a surprisingly successful marriage of Schafer's neo-classical influences with that of Gustave Mahler. This union was the outcome of Schafer's decision to take his non-Germanic style to Vienna in 1956, where he studied the *Mittelhochdeutsch* that gave him his texts. The Mahler influence seems plainest in the *Ländler* rhythms of 'Uf der Lindenwipel' and 'Mahnung,' the triadic German folk-song idiom of several of the numbers (most noticeably 'Verwirrung'), and also some of the high, soft, sustained lines (in 'Frouwen Wonne,' for example) reminiscent of Mahler's vocal writing.

The other composer whose presence is felt here is Britten; for while Schafer jibes at Britten in *Three Contemporaries*, their affinities are striking: the literary perception, for example, that matched Wilfred Owen's poems to the liturgy in the *War Requiem* is equalled by some of Schafer's best dramatic inventions. Both composers blend a cosmopolitan literary culture, a theatrical bent, and a base in Anglican church music. In *Minnelieder* specifically, not only did Britten contribute the revolving minor triad figure to 'Verlangen' (from *Winter Words*) and the conception of the large last song 'Des Dichters Grabschrift' (which resembles the last number of the *Serenade for Tenor, Horn, and Strings*), but also he perhaps encouraged Schafer's development towards greater transparency of texture and firmer control of tonal feeling. Schafer's management of the wind ensemble in *Minnelieder* is far more functional and uncluttered than in the harpsichord concerto.

Schafer's miscellany of medieval love poems is arranged in no discernible plan, narrative or otherwise; but 'Des Dichters Grabschrift,' the longest, is placed last in order to preserve the fine dramatic effect of Heinrich von Morungen's poem, which breaks off plaintively as the singer breaks the string of his lute. Thus *Minnelieder*, like most of Schafer's works, ends *en l'air*.

These poems are brief, even epigrammatic: some are a mere four lines; 'Herzenschlüzel' lasts only sixteen bars. In most cases Schafer sets the whole poem, though in a few he selects stanzas. All are through-composed. Some are sectional; 'Mahnung,' contrasting expressions of hope and disappointment, seems almost two separate songs; others, however, describe conventional ternary forms. The temptation with such miniatures is to be over-elaborate, and to a degree Schafer succumbs. Since most of the songs are built on at least two contrasting ideas – a new idea for every line or two of text, usually in different tempi – the music loses momentum in closing figures and transitional vamps, while the whole group seems to total more than thirteen songs. The wind quintet, too, creates the need for developing five identities rather than just one in the accompaniment, further discouraging conciseness – though naturally Schafer exploits the compensating colouristic possibilities. He also shows the needed skill for inventing brief, incisive figures, like the wistful mordent of 'Herzenschlüzel' or the delightfully tipsy waltz that ends 'Verwirrung.'

The songs are unified by a high degree of stylistic consistency. The texture throughout is homophonic, with little imitation of any kind. Tonality never falls in doubt, though some songs fluctuate between modes or cadence in an unpredictable key. There is much ostinato; harmonic rhythm is quite static, with quartal and added note harmonies and a few bitonal or bimodal passages. Throughout *Minnelieder*, Schafer shows a predilection for the flatted sixth and second degrees of the scale, and a tendency to avoid the leading note in both voice and accompaniment; this Phrygian colouration produces a downward pull that reflects the disheartened mood of most of the verses, even when the tempo is fast, as in 'Mahnung.'

Despite the pandiatonic style, *Minnelieder* is Schafer's first tentative – extraordinarily tentative – venture into twelve-note serialism. The series turns up in the first five bars of the introduction, but thereafter it returns simply in connection with related chromatic motifs. These do scarcely more than hint at a unifying theme, and they provide relief from the otherwise diatonic-triadic style. But Schafer's procedure here already shows his tendency to think of the series in thematic terms (example 3.2).

Perhaps the most winning feature of *Minnelieder*, however, is the vocal writing. The composer, employing a comfortable mezzo range (rising to g″) shows a fine command of the vocal registers and a new interest in sustained melodic line. The triadic idiom of German *Lied* provides the basis, spiced with chromaticism or bitonal clash with the accompaniment. Schafer is noticeably fond, too, of phrases that sweep dramatically in one direction an octave or more, and particularly of phrases that rise to a high cadence, pianissimo ('Sommer,' 'Uf der Lindenwipel,' 'Frouwen Wonne'). Schafer himself still regards *Minnelieder* as the most successful of his early compositions. 'I feel no less fondness for it,' he says, 'than I do for some of my other best pieces.'[4]

Kinderlieder, while less ambitious, seems to me the most accom-

3.2 *Minnelieder*: series and themes derived from it: a/ 'Sommer,' bars 16–22; b/ 'Wip unde Vederspil,' bars 1–3; c/ 'Der Falke,' bars 1–4

plished of these early works. These nine songs with piano accompaniment were composed in Toronto in 1958, after Schafer's return from Vienna. Though they too were written for Phyllis Mailing, they specify soprano voice, not mezzo, and the tessitura is higher than in the *Minnelieder* (the voice touches a pianissimo A♯″ and never descends below c′. Seven of the poems are by Bertolt Brecht, three of them taken from the collection called *Kinderlieder* published in 1956, the last year of Brecht's life; the non-Brecht poems are traditional but compatible with Brecht's in tone. All are childlike and imply a child speaker, but they broach innocently Brecht's favourite themes: 'Mailied' is a child's view of his parents marching in a May Day political parade; 'Patriotisches Lied' avows that there is no conflict between love of country and international good will; 'Die Vögel im Winter' rewards the labours of three charmingly proletarian birds – and so on. The naïve political aspect of these songs is a strangely diffident anticipation of protest-minded works of the 1960s like *Threnody*.

Schafer's unpretentious settings capture the tone of these verses perfectly. The melodies (which never breathe a hint of Kurt Weill) resemble those of *Minnelieder*, but they show their folk-song affinities even more clearly, four of the nine songs using a modified strophic form.

The harmonic language too is like the *Minnelieder*, but more diatonic, without the modal darkening. The accompaniment is suitably ingenuous, and it never wastes time. The empty-headed inconsequence of 'Hollywood' is parodied superbly in running sixteenth-notes that never seem to arrive anywhere. The naïve sentiment of 'Patriotisches Lied' is suggested in broken triads that sound like a beginner's étude. 'Die Vögel im Winter' allows the singer to characterize the voices of the three hungry birds and the child who feeds them. But perhaps the most striking number is 'Die Maske des Bösen,' which begins with the voice whispering tonelessly over the piano accompaniment and then (in Phyllis Mailing's performance) rises in a kind of *Sprechgesang* scream on 'Maske des bösen Dämons' before returning to the normal singing voice. Remarkably, the effect does not seem out of character with the general musical style; it does anticipate, however, more radical extensions of the singing voice that were to follow in a few years.[5]

The *Sonatina for Flute and Harpsichord* belongs to the same year as the *Kinderlieder* and exploits the same vein of elegant simplicity. While the piece brings nothing new to the composer's technique, it shows that by this time, if he had wanted to, Schafer could have continued indefinitely adding well-made compositions to the recital repertoire. Along with *Kinderlieder*, it signals the young composer's consolidation of his craft within the confines of his early style. But Schafer, apart from his pedagogical interests, has shown little sympathy with the *Gebrauchsmusik* ideal; what is more, these works must have suggested to him the limitations of his style. Already, *Three Contemporaries* and 'Die Maske des Bösen' hint at dramatic aspirations. But the deeper elements of passion and anger in the composer's personality needed more than a genteel neo-classicism for their expression.

In Memoriam: Alberto Guerrero (1959) marks an initial effort to reach deeper levels of feeling. Guerrero's death drew from Schafer his first work using strings at all, and the most attractive of his three works for string orchestra. The piece aspires rather short-windedly to Mahler's full-throated adagios, but the expressive glissandi and other effects also foreshadow Schafer's later writing for strings – dissonant clusters, glissandi, and special pizzicato effects filtered through the middle-European *avant-garde* but ultimately derived from Bartók.

But to inspect *In Memoriam: Alberto Guerrero* for evidences of transition is beside the point. What is certain is that, in the music that follows, Schafer opens into a wholly different world. The first bars of *Protest and Incarceration* (December 1960) leave no doubt. With practically no advance warning, Schafer in three closely related vocal works plunged into atonality. *Protest and Incarceration* is followed by *Brébeuf* (May 1961), a cantata for baritone and orchestra, and *The Judgement of Jael* (August 1961), a cantata for soprano, mezzo-soprano, and orchestra. Meanwhile, Schafer had moved to London and begun his study with Peter Racine Fricker.

4

Stylistic experiment 1960–5

In a 1976 interview, Schafer remarked on the changes in his music after 1960:

Yes, it began to change, but very gradually. I'm a slow learner, and so I reflect on things and think about them for a long time before there's a noticeable change. I think the changes are on the whole organic. I've used the word before – I like it; it seems to me the way I am ... If I think back to that period of 1960 and the kind of 'imitation Berio' I was writing then, and I think of what I'm doing now, there have been enormous, staggering changes.[1]

Certainly the composer's development through these next five years was a remarkable process of modernizing; but considering the conservative nature of the early pieces, the process seems more like Alice crossing the chessboard than any organic exfoliation. This is a period of acquiring techniques rapidly – but not uncritically. Schafer accepted the techniques of the *avant-grade* only as they revealed their expressive purposes. After *Loving* (1965), differences in technique from one work to the next are less perceptible and pursue a path less heavily travelled, more distinctly Schafer's own.

The young composer had always, even in *Polytonality*, desired to be up to date, but now his study with Fricker offered him a disciplined model, plus exposure to quantities of recent music. His travels in eastern Europe exposed him to folk-music traditions that have inspired many earlier composers and also to the negative example of music written in the service of a state. Besides, his visit with Ezra Pound surely strengthened any resolutions he may have had to keep in touch with the most recent developments of his art.

Schafer's works during this period are experimental – learning pieces in an even truer sense, perhaps, than his first works; for now one work after another opens up new techniques. Some, naturally, are failures. Schafer has admitted as much already, for in August 1968 he surveyed his catalogue of compositions and withdrew several, all composed in the 1960s. At the same time, however, this experimental period produced some works that will always stand among the composer's best: *Brébeuf, Canzoni for Prisoners, Five Studies on Texts by Prudentius.*

Schafer's first effort was to assimilate serialism. Different works apply the procedures in different ways, freely or strictly; but while Schafer has continued to use them, his practice has been from the beginning undoctrinaire. He has never been attracted to ideals of 'total control,' and he has expressed doubts even about the perceptibility of Schoenberg's methods:

Whether the unity behind these devices can be heard or not is very debatable. Schoenberg's critics said it couldn't and called his work 'Papiermusik.' Drawn into public defence of his method, Schoenberg once used the analogy of a hat, which, no matter how it is seen, always remains a hat. But the metaphor is specious on grounds of perception, for a hat remains a hat because it possesses a 'Gestalt' (i.e., hatness), and if it is possible to separate this quality of 'hatness' from the shape called a hat it can then be mistaken for a boulder, a flying saucer, a stove pipe – in fact, any number of things, depending on the angle from which it is viewed.[2]

In this essay, 'The Graphics of Musical Thought,' Schafer defends Schoenberg's theory only in so far as it produces audible *Gestalts* – and these, he adds, may also be produced with graphic notations.

This view suggests that Schafer considers the series mainly as a convenient mechanism for generating melodic or motivic material. Thus Schoenberg's ban against repeated pitches within the series has little meaning, as does the number twelve. Any melody may be turned into a series and so treated, and this is Schafer's practice. But his stated view suggests that he has little faith in any subliminal perception of the series on the microcosmic level of recurrent interval patterns – an assumption that underlies most twelve-note theory – even though many of Schafer's pieces (*Arcana*, for example) require such an assumption for their rationale.

Furthermore, Schafer's serialism is not a flight from tonality; he regards all of his music as tonal in some degree:

I don't think I ever threw away tonality entirely, because even if the music was serial, it was not serial in the conventional way, but in the sense of writing things with long extended series of rhythms, and using certain intervals, such as a minor second or a perfect fourth, in all their possible permutations. This kind of procedure gives a certain tonal quality to a piece. There was a tonal feeling in a lot of my music all the way through: there still is.[3]

Schafer's tonality, however, has always – even since the ostinato of *Polytonality* – been more closely allied to the drone of non-Western music than to the modulating key centre of European tradition.

Protest and Incarceration, a pair of songs for mezzo-soprano and orchestra, marks a new beginning in many ways. Not only is it Schafer's first full-fledged serial work (not counting *Minnelieder*),[4] but it is his first with full orchestra, and the first in a sequence of openly political declarations that followed in the 1960s, culminating in *Threnody*. The tentative social criticism of *Three Contemporaries* or *Kinderlieder* here gives way to passionate, direct denunciation. Indeed, the serial technique itself is an implied protest against state control of music in the communist countries that Schafer visited in 1959, although the texts are non-doctrinal, referring to the repression of dissent under any political system.

The texts, by jailed East European poets, were translated into English and given to the composer by a young Romanian woman whom he met in 1959. They had been smuggled out of prison and were being circulated underground in hand written copies. The words give the composer clear dramatic suggestions. After the opening section, 'Protest, or Birthday Wishes for a Dictator' builds two agitated sections on the idea 'Grow, my timid voice, grow as a daemon, grow as a great bird'; these frame a curse evoking the horned beast of Apocalypse. The curse and the final section ('Now you must grow, my voice, little by little') build through wider and wider intervals, climaxing on full-voice B♭″ and A″. 'Incarceration,' the inevitable consequence, offers musical contrast, a mood that is 'not so much desperation as bewilderment,' the prisoner disoriented in undifferentiated time ('empty days without form'). Here Schafer concentrates on narrow intervals in the lower middle range, employing for the first time the eerie slow semitone glissando (example 4.1b) that marks several works of this period – notably *Canzoni for Prisoners* and the *Untitled Composition for Orchestra No. 1*.

The glissando, especially the slow semitone glissando, is one of Schafer's most distinctive fingerprints. It is related to his fondness for

4.1 *Protest and Incarceration*: series and vocal entrances: a/ *Protest*;
b/ *Incarceration*

semitone clusters and for semitone groups in his tone rows, as well as to
his use of drones. Schafer has noted a rationale for this effect in the work
of the American experimentalist Harry Partch, one of the first composers to chafe against the tyranny of the discrete scale, who argued that
'discrete steps were never in man's cries, never in the cries of other
mammals, and practically never in the songs of birds ... We have in
addition wailing tug-boats, gliding foghorns, weeping train whistles and
soul-rending raid sirens ... But nowhere in the world is the convention of
discrete steps so academically rigorous as in the West.'[5] Schafer, noting
Partch's discussion of the human voice, remarks: 'European languages
do not seem to be given to long glides, but the American language is – the
"drawl" so many people make fun of.' Furthermore, as Schafer remarks

in *The Tuning of the World*, 'the flat line in sound produces only one embellishment: the glissando ... Then flat lines become curved lines. But they are still without sudden surprises.'[6] Schafer qualifies Partch's criticism of discrete intervals, however, observing that 'just as pure vowel sound admits consonants to delineate itself and form words, so the tonal spectrum admits "discrete steps" to identify its parts. This may not be artistic but it is logical, aiding man in recognizing and accepting things.'[7] Consequently, Schafer does not throw out the chromatic scale. But he does become increasingly fond of glissandi, electronic effects covering the tonal spectrum, and natural sounds.

In *Protest and Incarceration*, Schafer uses the series more for thematic purposes than for contrapuntal unity. The two songs use variants of the same row, which is neither schematic nor symmetrical in its distribution of intervals (ex. 4.1). It features groups of three adjacent semitones and three adjacent whole tones, other intervals being perfect fourths or tritones; excluding thirds entirely, it ensures acid chordal arrangements, while the adjacent tones allow for either stepwise motion in the voice or dramatic leaps of a seventh or ninth. 'Incarceration' transposes the original row down a fourth and rearranges the first four tones, anticipating the all-interval row of *Requiems for the Party-Girl* (see example 8.1). Unlike his later practice, Schafer uses this row in all four forms and in several transpositions; otherwise, however, he usually leaves it intact in the voice line and leading instrumental lines rather than distributed among the parts. He does not subdivide into hexachords or tetrachords, but does allow occasional changes of sequence and a few anomalous tones in the supporting parts. Both songs open with direct statements of row followed by parallel restatements in inversion. Such manipulations are hardly innovative; but the piece shows Schafer's native ability to make serial techniques serve clear expressive purposes.

Having once essayed conventional serial methods, Schafer immediately turned to a relaxed serialism in *Brébeuf* and produced one of his finest works. Though written in London, *Brébeuf* marks Schafer's repatriation to Canada after five years' sojourn in Europe. 'I had been looking for a subject with Canadian feeling,' he wrote in a program note, 'and it was Harry Somers who suggested the Brébeuf theme to me, one day when we were walking in the Jardin des Tuileries in Paris.'[8] Intrigued, Schafer characteristically turned not to a literary version, like E.J. Pratt's poem or Francis Parkman's narrative, but directly to the primary source, St Jean de Brébeuf's own account in volume 8 of the

seventy-three volume *Jesuit Relations*. Schafer's English text, adapted
from this source, deals mainly with Brébeuf's first Canadian winter in
1625 and his first penetration to the land of the Hurons in the following
year. Schafer also incorporated into the work many of the saint's visions
and premonitions of his own martyrdom, as collected from other
sources. The result is a descriptive narrative of a spring canoe trip,
interrupted by a series of hallucinatory outbursts. The other sources
derive from accounts by others commenting on the character of the
martyr and the circumstances of his martyrdom. Schafer's text, then, is
a collage of statements paraphrased from primary sources, rather like
Pound's redactions from historical documents in *The Cantos*.

Schafer's Brébeuf is the first in a series of suffering, idealistic solitaries,
prefiguring the protagonists of the *Patria* sequence. He represents the
saint as heroic, sincere in his devotion, but slightly mad, foreseeing,
almost willing, his own martyrdom (though historically he managed to
survive until 1649, twenty-three years after the journey depicted in the
piece). Brébeuf's antagonists are not just the Indians, savage and mis-
trustful as they are, but also the Canadian vastness itself, cold and
isolating. The brief first section represents Brébeuf's call: 'Last night in
a dream I saw a great cross in the winter sky large enough to hold many
people. I fell to my knees and prayed to God: "What Lord would thou
have me do?"' Winter is suggested by glitering tremolo scales in the
violins' highest register over sizzle cymbals, while the interlude leading
to section II represents the 'sudden dramatic break-up of the ice on the St
Lawrence River' during the Canadian spring, which requires not 'a
delicate flutter of sound' but a 'quite brutal strength.'9 'The Journey,' the
central and longest section, representing Brébeuf's trip by canoe into the
land of the Hurons, is a narrative built up of cool, realistic observation
('These savages smell terribly; dried out, withered ...') punctuated by
three 'hallucinatory outbursts,' each followed by a brief, fortissimo
orchestral interlude. These hallucinations ('And at once I beheld the
Spirit upon me and upon my hands appeared spots of blood ... !') set
against the outwardly receptive land ('The rivers are filled to overflow-
ing with fish; we lack nothing') throw into relief the power of Brébeuf's
obsession amid the vast, undifferentiated wilderness. The last section,
'The Arrival,' is again brief and quiet, the piece closing with Brébeuf's
ironic benediction: 'It is so quiet here, I kneel down to thank God for a
safe journey. May the progress of the faith increase from day to day and
the blessings of heaven flow down on this good land.' This irony is
underscored by muted strings in a brief epilogue, espressivo.

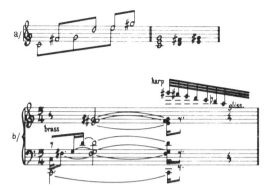

4.2 *Brébeuf*: a/ six-note cell showing harmonic implications; b/ opening bar

The form of *Brébeuf*, however, is more sectional than this account indicates, since the text is subdivided into seventeen paragraphs, and musical textures rarely continue for more than thirty bars or so, sometimes lasting only four or five. Tempo changes are frequent and unsystematic, with much accelerando and ritardando, striving towards the metreless idiom of later works. Thus the piece is conceived as a series of isolated dramatic vignettes closely bound to the text and linked together continuously, without reliance on structural repetition to give form. In this, *Brébeuf* shares a family likeness with many of Schafer's other works, from the through-composed numbers of *Minnelieder* to the detached dramatic moments of *Arcana* or *Requiems for the Party-Girl*. Nonetheless, *Brébeuf* still gives the effect of a fluid, unbroken continuity, sustaining a momentum more successfully than any of the composer's previous works. This effect results from the careful management of transitions – orchestral interludes are kept few and brief, while Brébeuf's narrative dominates the entire score – and from the derivation of the musical material from a single cell of six notes.

These six ascending notes form the pyramiding chord of the opening bar (example 4.2). Schafer treats this hexachord freely in different ways. It provides a direct source of melodic and harmonic material, used in all transpositions, often one superimposed on another. The original form predominates, though the inversion occasionally appears. The fifths of the hexachord give a sense of root position stability on c, complicated by the tritones c–f♯ and d–g♯. Or, conceived differently, the hexachord becomes a c major triad supported by major thirds on d and e.

4.3 *Brébeuf*: a/ six-note cell transposed a major second upwards; b/ scale derived from cell; c/ bars 8–9, violin ɪɪ

4.4 *Brébeuf*: voice lines, bars 2–7

But these original six notes also yield a scale with is own distinctive sonorities (example 4.3). This seven-note scale (example 4.3b) contains five of the original six tones, or all six if the original hexachord is transposed up a major second (example 4.3a). Strongly characterized by its four adjacent whole tones and two adjacent semitones, this scale in turn yields further material for the piece. For example, the first section is dominated by scale passages high in the violins (example 4.3c), while the voice line draws most of its tones from the same material, hovering especially around the semitone group. This group, pivoting on ᴀ, gives that note a dominant quality suggesting for the moment a tonal centre on ᴅ, the root of this version of the hexachord (example 4.4).

All the material of *Brébeuf*, then, is derived from the hexachord or the scale – or in other words, from the six notes of the opening bar (ex 4.5a). Thus Schafer, following Fricker's precepts, is for the first time working out the implications of his original material. But a brief passage will also show the freedom of Schafer's treatment. Here the first violin line directly states the hexachord on ɢ♯, flanked at beginning and end by ꜰ♯. The supporting harmonies are more indirectly drawn from the basic material, without regard to transpositions; but nearly every sonority is related as a possible rearrangment of tones in a possible hexachord, as indicated in example 4.5b. The complex superimposed chords are clarified by being distributed to brass and string choirs in the orchestra. The result, using in this instance five basic triads strongly

4.5 *Brébeuf*: a/ six-note cell and chords derived from it; b/ bars 69–74 showing chordal arrangement

emphasizing whole tones, perhaps helps explain why *Brébeuf* so often recalls Berg, who was also fond of whole-tone aggregates.

Schafer treats the voice gratefully in *Brébeuf*. The line is largely a passionate, quasi-melodic declamation, carefully bound to the rhythm of the text, rather like the lyrical moments of *Wozzeck*. The music calls for a dramatic high baritone voice rising to a top A♭′; one passage hovers cruelly around F′, and F♯″ and G′ for several bars. There are a few moments of parlando recitative and one short passage of *Sprechgesang*, but otherwise the singer is not called upon for special effects – except at the climax of section II, the third hallucination. Here, on the words 'I would embrace Death,' the baritone sings the last word on a high C″, falsetto, subito pianissimo. The effect is electrifying. *Brébeuf*, if it were better known, would be a welcome enlargement of the scant repertoire of pieces for baritone with orchestra.

The Judgement of Jael, a companion piece to *Brébeuf*, has been withdrawn, but it is interesting as a transitional sketch for *Loving*. Schafer's text turns the grisly story of Jael, the Hebrew woman who struck a nail through the temples of Sisera (Judges 4–5), from a song of triumph into a anti-war protest. In the first two sections, Deborah (soprano) calls the Israelites to war, and Jael (mezzo-soprano) claims the praises of her people; in the last, the two join to denounce bloodshed. The music is most remarkable for its demanding vocal techniques and its treatment of the orchestra.

In his first three works with orchestra, Schafer strengthens his grip on the medium. *Protest and Incarceration* called for a modest orchestra, with winds in pairs, piano, and harp; percussion is manageable by two players and not prominent. *Brébeuf* calls for a larger orchestra, with woodwinds in threes (including auxiliary instruments), four horns, three trumpets, three trombones, tuba, piano, harp, celesta, and at least four percussionists. Percussion is prominent, especially suspended cymbals and an assortment of drums, but it never commands the centre of interest. Both works are closer to Schoenberg and Berg than to the post-Webern composers, though both contain pointillistic passages. *The Judgement of Jael*, however, goes further, with its enlarged percussion, and furthermore, like *Loving*, it uses orchestration structurally. Deborah's song, beginning unaccompanied, is supported by four percussionists. Jael's song, for contrast, is accompanied first by strings alone, joined later by harp, celesta, and a few solo winds (including, for the seduction passage, what Stravinsky somewhere describes as the 'adolescent personality' of the saxophone). But the composer reserves full orchestra for the third section, where it enters fortissimo on a twelve-note chord.

The Judgement of Jael is even more notable, however, for Schafer's experimentation with vocal techniques; the piece is plainly a sketch for the vocal style of *Loving*. Schafer writes widely leaping grace notes, glissandi, *Sprechgesang*, calls for 'chest tone,' 'hard tone,' and 'vicious whisper,' and directs some passages to be spoken or cried out. The most extreme demands occur in section III, where the two voices are written in fiercely dissonant close intervals and intricate, mutually interfering rhythms. They pass words back and forth to each other and also use the medieval device of hocketing that Schafer observed in two works that interested him greatly at this time, Machaut's Mass and Ezra Pound's *Cavalcanti*. This rejected cantata acclimatized him to the *avant-garde* vocal techniques of his later compositions.

While he was writing these three large-scale vocal works, Schafer also produced two pieces for string orchestra, *Dithyramb* (1961) and *Partita* (1962). Neither is really successful. *Dithyramb*, the larger of the two, contains a profusion of notes and demands, it would appear, every special string effect the composer could think of; more important, it marks Schafer's awakening interest in counterpoint. In contrast, the *Partita* is concise, restrained in its use of special effects, and positively austere in its serial technique, using only the original and inversion of the row with no transpositions. Schafer is preoccupied here with making his series audible. The attempt at clarity succeeds, but on the whole the *Partita*, as an exercise in Webernesque brevity, does not – not because of its simplified serial technique, but because its rhythmic texture lapses back inappropriately to the neo-classical manner of the early works, especially in the last and longest movement.

Schafer's experimentation with stricter methods really ran counter to his temperament; but it did yield a few successful if somewhat uncharacteristic works, the only ones that might sensibly be called 'post-Webern.' *Canzoni for Prisoners* (1962), Schafer's first purely orchestral work, is technically an ingenious extension of serial procedures and rhythmic manipulations combined with the medieval device of *cantus firmus*. The result is a piece sombre in mood, rather long (eighteen minutes), with passionate high moments; best of all, it has a staying power that endures as its large-scale structures grow familiar.

Although the piece has no program, the occasion for its composition was political, the founding of Amnesty International in London in 1961. The organization particularly impressed Schafer because it expressed no ideology but dedicated itself to the rights of political prisoners everywhere. According to his note in the score, 'The prisoners I had in mind in the title were prisoners of conscience – that is, non-violent objectors in any land who are imprisoned merely because they disagree with the particular regime under which they are forced to live. As all political systems are united in eliminating radical thinking, no country has a monopoly on prisoners of conscience. They are closer than you think.'

The material of the piece is a series of seventy-six notes (example 4.6). Considering Schafer's concern with the recognizability of the series and the simplified techniques of the *Partita*, his decision to try such an unwieldy series might seem self-defeating, like some of Max Reger's serpentine fugue subjects. The result, however, is not mere music for the eye. For one thing, Schafer again curtails the usual manipulations, using only the original, plus a few transpositions in section II only; thus the series acts as an extended *cantus firmus*. Furthermore, he restricts

4.6 *Canzoni for Prisoners*: seventy-six note *cantus firmus*. Notes in parentheses appear as alternatives or are frequently omitted. Bracketed notes are recurrent groups or strings of semitones.

his intervals to minor seconds, fourths, and tritones, all but excluding thirds and whole tones (the minor third 46–7 is the sole exception). Then, the series contains repeated groups that help recognition (groups 1–3, 12–15, and 20–3). Several semitone groups also stand out in the texture (for example, bracketed groups 29–33, 51–4, and 68–76). The beginning of the series is clearly marked by Schafer's slow semitone glissando (glissando tones 4 and 10 are often omitted if the series is given to an instrument incapable of glissando). Finally, the series is allied to recurrent rhythmic patterns; the most striking of these is the group of the last six notes with equal rhythmic values, often as a sextolet, a recurrent effect that marks the end of the series like the lash of a whip. Other recurrent rhythmic groupings gradually become audible as the piece grows familiar. Schafer's series in *Canzoni for Prisoners* is thus motivic, even melodic, behaving as a row mainly in its octave displacements and its distribution among various instruments. This equivocal blend of serial procedures with conventional motivic development is typical of all Schafer's serialism. He carries the series to even greater lengths in *Lustro*.

Rhythmic design is just as important in *Canzoni for Prisoners* as the unusual tone row. Devices that recall both Messiaën's asymmetrical rhythms and Elliott Carter's 'metrical modulation' derive principally

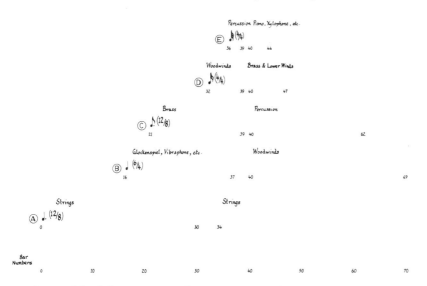

4.7 *Canzoni for Prisoners*: canonic arrangement of section I

from the *Ars nova* techniques of isorhythm and prolation. The piece contains five continuous sections, all in tempos proportionally related to the opening bars, and in each section the different rhythmic manipulations of the series generate a different texture.

Section I is a prolation canon in which each group of instruments enters at a successively faster rate, beginning with ♩. as the basic unit and accelerating to ♪, then subsiding again (example 4.7). This generates an eloquent climax at the middle of the section, bars 40–3, where four separate tempos begin simultaneously. Just before this point, unpitched percussion instruments add to the rising momentum, sounding the rhythms of the series at the fastest rate. Meanwhile, the strings, having completed the series at the slowest rate, rising from low to high, begin again at bar 34, winding down from high to low; thus they form a framing arch for the whole section, while they support the climactic bar with broad, sustained notes in the upper violins. The whole effect sounds complex in description, but it remains transparent to the ear throughout.

Section II is a wispy scherzando, very fast (♩ = 138), moving in sixteenth-notes in the woodwinds, piano, harp, and trumpet, all in their upper registers. The texture consists of isolated groups of notes – one or two, never more than six – widely separated by rests, so that the overall feeling is not sprightly but neurasthenic and exposed. The section begins as the lower strings are finishing the last cycle of section I; flute, clarinet, and oboe, spaced twelve beats apart (other instruments assisting later), begin the original series plus three upward transpositions of a semitone, but the highest series, having shorter rests, finishes first, and the first series last; this creates a more frenetic feeling mid-cycle. Just before the middle, the piano enters with new material in even staccato eighth-notes (a variant of the original row transposed up a minor third). This regular rhythm binds the texture together momentarily, leading to the pivot of the section, where pizzicato strings take up the piano row in retrograde while the woodwinds again begin simultaneously with four unevenly spaced transpositions of the original row. The end of the section is punctuated by a slowly accelerating parabolic glissando in the whole string section, from bottom to top, spanning sixteen bars.

Section III, scored for strings alone, is based on motifs from the two previous sections but much freer in treatment. The nervous sixteenth-note patterns of section II continue in one series (in thirty-seconds, since the tempo is halved), while a more sustained series recalls section I, breaking out from time to time in swooping glissandi. Again the greatest tension appears mid-movement, fortissimo, while the last twenty-two bars are played piano.

Abruptly the tam-tam, fortissimo, breaks the quiet and ushers in section IV, a remarkable rhythmic *tour de force*. Here, chords derived from the series are repeated nine times each (usually), staccato, with an internal rest whose position varies. Each group has a different tempo, and as one is overlaid on another all sense of stability collapses in a dizzy field of competing pulses. Instrumental alliances are made and broken as quickly as the rhythms shift. (The instrumentation of this section produces a brilliant metallic sound that suggests, like the manipulation of note values, the influence of Messiaën.) The result is a nightmare for the conductor, but it makes a bewildering, even sinister assault on the ear.

Section V draws together many of the previous devices and sonorities in two sustained crescendos accelerating to two shattering climaxes for full orchestra. Here, the seventy-six-note cycle is completed only once in each crescendo, with groups of notes freely repeated. Different groups of instruments, however, articulate the series in different note values. The fastest values, which recall the scherzando motifs of sections II and III, are fragmented and spaced wide apart; the slowest provide a base of sustained chords in the strings that propel the movement to a climax by becoming subtractively shorter, dropping from 26 beats to 24 to 20, and so on. In the second crescendo, the shortening of note values and telescoping of entries grow even more noticeable. The piece closes with a quiet epilogue, subito piano, featuring ghostly glissandi in the solo strings.

In 1963, Schafer produced a pair of sharply etched miniatures, *Untitled Composition for Orchestra No. 1* and *No. 2*, both closely related to *Canzoni for Prisoners*. *No. 1* lasts only four minutes and calls for a small orchestra using extremely sparse textures; *No. 2* is even shorter but requires a large orchestra for a texture of contrasting sound masses. *No. 1*, an eerie piece that has attracted many performances, is a clearly audible prolation canon like the first section of *Canzoni*, beginning again with the longest note values in the bass and developing through a series of complex superimposed tempi in constant acceleration. The theme also features quarter-tone sharping and flatting of sustained notes and rises to a queer bobbing figure over a minor tenth. *No. 2*, on the other hand, has so far never been performed, possibly because of the large orchestra demanded by so short a piece. But it is an interesting attempt to deal with orchestral sound masses contrapuntally – Shafer's only venture in this direction. The orchestra essentially pits strings against winds. The strings in long note values state the material, here not linear but a sequence of timbres and note clusters which the wind groups twice imitate in succession, using shorter note values. Neither of these compositions adds anything radically new to Schafer's development, but both are concentrated, clearly intelligible sketches.

Schafer's strictest piece written with Fricker is his *Five Studies on Texts by Prudentius*, for soprano and four flutes (also using alto flute and piccolo). These songs are not serial but rather they combine quasi-serial or isorhythmic manipulations of pitch with canonic writing of great melodic and rhythmic intricacy. In addition, they mark Schafer's first use of spatial arrangement in his music, requiring the four flutes to play from the four corners of the room (which must be of chamber proportions) with the singer on stage. When these songs were premiered, this effect was achieved with pre-recorded tape (Robert Aitken playing all four parts), so the piece marks the composer's first venture with electronic equipment as well.

The Prudentius songs pose fearsome but not insurmountable difficulties in performance. Not only are all five parts rhythmically exacting, but the spatial arrangement makes synchronization more problematical (except in the first song, where the parts move at independent tempi).

And the voice line extends from bottom A to top C♯″, making free use of the uppermost register at all dynamic levels. Nonetheless, Mary Morrison sang at the premiere, according to the *Toronto Daily Star*, 'with ease, grace, and no pretences whatsoever,'[10] and other singers have since negotiated the demands successfully.

The effect of the Prudentius songs is of great concentration and purity – a great deal of music condensed into a short time. Because the four flutes offer no contrast of timbre, the lines of counterpoint are extremely difficult for the ear to disentangle, so the stereophonic arrangement is essential; but the four flutes together (which might threaten to sound like a steam calliope run amok) in fact produce an ethereal, disembodied sound perfectly suited to the religious texts. Much of the meaning of the piece stems from Schafer's symbolical treatment of the texts. These were suggested by Peter Racine Fricker's settings of Prudentius, and the ensemble was modelled on the *Goethelieder* of Dallapiccola, a set of canonic songs for soprano and three clarinets. Prudentius is best known for his *Psychomachia*, a turgid fourth-century allegory that influenced much of the literature of the Middle Ages; but Schafer draws instead from the *Tituli historiarum* (Scenes from history), a collection of tiny quatrains apparently intended to accompany Old and New Testament scenes painted on church walls.[11] Rather atypically, Schafer uses the English translations of the Loeb edition rather than the Latin, so that the musical symbolism might emerge more clearly. Out of forty-nine poems, Schafer chose five which form, according to his note in the score, 'a miniature Bible in themselves, from the story of Adam and Eve to the revelation of St John, with the birth of Christ in the centre.' The songs thus outline the entire cosmic myth of Christianity.

1 In 'Adam and Eve,' the melodic lines are (Schafer remarks) 'serpentine,' and as each part enters at a marginally faster tempo, the free, unsynchronized lines perhaps symbolize the revolt against divine authority; furthermore, the spatial movement in this song is 'centrifugal,' the canonic entries moving around the room through the four flutes in sequence suggesting forces broken loose from a centre. Musically, the song is a five-part canon, two of the parts inverted, each entering on one of the first five notes of the canonic subject. The melodic line uses only three intervals: minor second, minor third, perfect fourth. Finally, the rhythms are arranged in a perpetual accelerando and ritardando, progressing from forte to piano and then reversed (example 4.8). The result is a curiously wave-like rhythm, fluid and yet controlled by the strict imitation.

4.8 *Five Studies on Texts by Prudentius*: 'Adam and Eve,' rhythmic arrangement

4.9 *Five Studies on Texts by Prudentius*: 'The City of Bethlehem,' canonic arrangement

2 In 'Moses Has Received the Law,' the lines are angular, and the spatial movement crosses the room diagonally, suggesting the severity of God's Old Testament commandments. This song is a melodic and rhythmic canon superimposed, with each of the two flute voices passed between two players. The melodic canon is at the unison; the rhythmic canon is at the distance of one bar, but displaced by one note on the pitch series in order to generate different melodic contours in each part. Intervals are minor seconds and major and minor thirds (each song preserves two intervals from its predecessor and alters one).

3 'The City of Bethlehem' is a solemn two-part palindrome on a subject that begins on a circle of perfect fourths, symbolic of perfection. The flute part is passed among all four instruments in reverse order from the first song – the Incarnation reversing the Fall. The melodic intervals are minor second, major third, and perfect fourth. The flute line is in note values 1½ times those of the vocal line. The second half of the song is a rhythmic and melodic retrograde of the first half, the whole pivoting around a bar of silence, the very centre of the piece, like (in T.S. Eliot's phrase) 'the still point of the turning world.' Just before and after this centre point, the voice touches its extremes of range, the low A before and the top C#″ after. The whole canon is a complex symmetrical structure (example 4.9).

4 'The Passion of St John,' which treats Salome's dance, might seem a less logical subject than the poem on St Paul that Schafer originally contemplated for this position. However, musically it offers an excuse for contrast with its dance rhythms and its thinner texture (only two flutes), and theologically it can be taken to suggest the continuation of

sin even after the Incarnation. The dance is not barbaric but ironically genteel, in tripping staccato. The canon is in three parts, one inverted. The melodic intervals are major and minor seconds and minor thirds. The last bars of the song, freely composed, lead without a break into the following song.

5 Curiously, 'The Revelation of St. John' marks the second appearance of St John's Revelation in Schafer's music before *Apocalypsis* (the other is in 'Protest'). Again the flutes enter in reverse order – the Second Coming, the second reversal of the Fall. The canon is based on a six-note series (intervals are major seconds and thirds and perfect and augmented fourths) repeated twelve times, each time a semitone higher. It is in two sections; the first is for the flutes alone, entering in varying degrees of diminution (not exact) and building to a climax; in the second section, the voice repeats the fourth flute line with modifications, and the flutes begin to repeat their material, but in fragmented form. The fluid rhythms here balance the fluid rhythms of the first song, as the piece builds to a frenetic climax in which the piccolo makes its only appearance, stridently. But the world meets its end pianissimo, the unaccompanied voice pronouncing Amen on the Db with which the piece began.

After such severities of technique, Schafer began to look in new directions. The pre-recorded tape for the premiere of the Prudentius songs pointed towards more adventurous experimentation with electronic sound. This medium seemed more attractive on account of the new Electronic Music Studio at the University of Toronto, although this was for a time closed to him. Also, probably in revolt against too many canons, Schafer began to consider the possibilities of chance. A number of short pieces in remarkably varying styles intervene between the Prudentius songs and *Loving*, but *The Geography of Eros*, the concluding aria of *Loving*, was already completed as an independent piece by December 1963 and performed the following year. Written in a free, athematic style, it employs voices pre-recorded on tape and contains sections of indeterminate pitch and rhythm.

In the second half of 1962, Schafer was occupied with two choral works, *Four Songs on Texts of Tagore* and *Opus One for Mixed Chorus*, and with his first commissioned work, *Divisions for Baroque Trio*. Of these, only the Tagore songs remain in circulation, and these have so far never been performed, perhaps on account of their difficulty. They are serial pieces for a cappella women's voices, demanding wide leaps and extremes of range, with the text fragmented into phrases, words, and

phonemes and distributed among the voices. The Tagore songs introduce no new techniques; *Opus One*, however, is Schafer's first compositional experiment with pre-recorded tape, a palindrome in which the
chorus sings its part against the same notes on tape played backwards.
The composer dismisses it with the comment, 'Definition of an experiment: that which does not work.'[12] *Divisions for Baroque Trio* is another
abortive experiment with tape in which flute, oboe, and harpsichord
play against separate parts pre-recorded. The resulting six-part texture
is muddy, and Schafer is strangely insensitive to antiphonal and
mirroring possibilities. Only in *The Geography of Eros* does his management of the tape medium become fully accomplished.

The following three years brought several minor instrumental pieces:
The two *Untitled Compositions* (1963) remain in circulation. *Festival
Music for Small Orchestra* (1966), a three-minute piece written for the
Charlottetown Festival, was soon withdrawn – Schafer's music is often
witty, but it is almost never festive. *Sonorities for Brass Sextet* (1966),
also withdrawn, mixes disparate styles uncomfortably, reverting at
times to the overworked vein of neo-classical syncopation last heard in
Partita for String Orchestra.

Most forward-looking of these works is *Invertible Material for
Orchestra* (1963), in which Schafer tried out aleatoric techniques in his
first composition for young students. The motivation for Schafer's
interest in chance was practical, resulting from his first contacts with
students in a classroom and a commission from Keith Bissell, then head
of music for the Scarborough (Ontario) Board of Education; but the
benefits of this experience point directly towards *The Geography of Eros*
and his subsequent development. *Invertible Material*, designated a
'practice piece,' assigns each player a single note to play according to
certain rhythmic and dynamic specifications; the parts are then
combined at will by the conductor. The piece met with enthusiastic
applause on its premiere at Cedarbrae Collegiate in Scarborough ('Mr.
Schafer will probably never again receive such an ovation,' reported
John Kraglund in the Toronto *Globe and Mail* – a prediction that the
composer copied for preservation in his private papers); but since then
Schafer has withdrawn *Invertible Material*, explaining that it was
'derivative of Earle Brown's *Available Forms*, but wholly without his
lambent touch.'[13]

Statement in Blue, however, remains one of Schafer's most often
heard pieces. The composer's first graphic score was written for an
orchestra of grade eight students who had been playing their instru-

ments for about one year; the graphic notation is simultaneously an imaginative stimulus and a practical way of bypassing difficulties. The score determines the overall textures of the piece (sustained clusters in the strings supporting solo wind instruments, with percussion in the background), orders the sequence of events, and gives verbal clues for the improvised solos. Duration is left to the conductor (calculating according to the abilities of each soloist to improvise), and pitches are left to the players. The composer adds that 'anything in this score may be omitted or changed if, in the opinion of the performers, it leads to an improvement.'

Yet even this disarming blank cheque, like all the improvisatory elements, is limited not only by the imaginations of the participants but also by their sense of what is fitting. For a composition like *Statement in Blue*, however indeterminate, is still contained within a tacit decorum, and it is still possible to judge different performances as better or worse. The performance heard on the Melbourne recording, says Schafer, is far from definitive, and he encourages student groups to improve on it rather than imitate it. Whatever choices and changes to the score are made, whatever solo instruments or percussion sounds are used, the leader's job is not just to give cues but to ensure that the piece has an appropriate general mood and form. 'Appropriateness' is partly suggested by the verbal cues to the soloists: 'Cool' or 'A bird climbs slowly into the sky ... then glides to earth again.' More fundamentally, it depends on the players' intuitive sense of sounds. As Schafer has advised one group of students,

Don't just doodle through the piece; try always to find arresting and beautiful effects as a group. If a section sounds dull or turgid, point it out to your teacher and change it. And don't forget to listen to your neighbours ... Sometimes during rehearsals I clap my hands and ask different people what note the flute or the trumpet has just played ... *Statement in Blue* is not a piece calculated to train you how to play your instrument better technically; it aims to train your ears, your feeling for expressive ensemble playing, and above all to help release whatever creative abilities you might have to make music of your own. In fact, it would be interesting after you have performed *Statement in Blue* if you tried to compose a piece of your own for your own class to perform.[14]

Such a score is a stimulus to discovery, not a prescription. Thus H.H. Stuckenschmidt's description of musical graphics as 'latter-day neumes'[15] is misleading because neumes were mnemonic in function, not imaginative stimuli. But some decorum must always operate.

The success of *Statement in Blue* has encouraged Schafer to compose other educational works in the same vein, like *Train*, or the choral pieces *Epitaph for Moonlight* and *Miniwanka*, which in turn have led to more ambitious graphic scores for voices – *In Search of Zoroaster* and *Apocalypsis*. The liberation of his talents as a graphic artist, latent since adolescence, points to the more floridly pictographic scores of *Lustro* and *Patria*. But his exploration of graphic notations and other devices of indeterminacy at this point in his career was important to redress the balance after a long preoccupation with serialism and counterpoint. Undoubtedly the confidence gained in these small-scale pieces bolstered the free, improvisatory style of *Loving*, the work in which Schafer consolidated his musical language.

Loving (1965)

'The Geography of Eros' (November 1963) was the first portion of *Loving* completed. Conceived as an independent composition, it was performed on 5 April of the following year by Mary Morrison, with a hint in the program notes that it might eventually form part of a larger work that would 'bear a remote similarity to opera.' The projected work remained vague, however, even when Schafer delivered a lecture on it at Memorial University, Newfoundland, on 3 January 1965.[1] Immediately afterwards the work assumed definite shape when Pierre Mercure secured a commission and a performance on television from the CBC French network. Ever since *Loving*, Schafer has continued to assemble his larger compositions like the *Patria* sequence and *Lustro* from shorter, independently conceived works. This practice enables him to arrange commissions and performances for his music while simultaneously working on large works more difficult and expensive to mount.

'The Geography of Eros' marks another of Schafer's stylistic leaps. Radically different from anything preceding it, it immediately established the idiom of *Loving* as a whole and brought the composer's technique to full maturity. Schafer himself regarded 'The Geography of Eros' as a reaction against the formalism of the Prudentius songs: '*Prudentius* was one of the strictest works I ever composed. By contrast, *Geography* is completely free and almost contrivedly athematic. The text for *Prudentius* was religious, narrative, and descriptive; the text for *Geography* is lyric, incantatory, and sexy. Both spiritually and musically, *Geography* was a necessary reaction to the rigorousness of *Prudentius*.'[2] 'Quite frankly,' Schafer told me, ' I don't really think there is any musical organization to it ... I think really what I was interested in doing there was accompanying a text which I had created, and trying to find those points at which the nervous systems of music and language touch.'[3] In *Loving*, then, words merge into music, music dissipates into words. Schafer's text is deliberately 'poetical,' even at times nonsensical, in order to ease the transitions. There is no chronological plot. The whole is a fluid 'audio-visual poem' performed without a break from beginning to end. (For a synopsis of *Loving*, see appendix 3.)

To realize this fluidity, Schafer combined several techniques already tested in smaller works. Here he benefits from the abortive experiments with tape in *Opus One* and the *Divisions for Baroque Trio*. Through much of 'The Geography of Eros,' the soprano sings in duo with her own pre-recorded voice, unmodified except for occasional reverberation. The tape, an important component in *Loving*, is used in this way frequently. Schafer also devises other textures of spoken and sung texts subjected to various tape manipulations and includes (very infrequently) some synthesized sounds, like the sine-tone crescendo in 'Air Ishtar' or the climactic passage of 'Phantasmagoria.' Schafer, in fact, seems to assume full confidence in his handling of tape during the composition of *Loving*, using it with restraint in 'The Geography of Eros,' the first section written, and relying on it for an effective if oddly placed climax in 'Air Ishtar' and 'Phantasmagoria,' the last sections written. One 'character,' the Voice of the Poet, is entirely pre-recorded. The skilful mix of live and recorded sounds and the functional ambiguity regarding the source and location of sounds within a quadraphonic situation contribute immensely to the fluid effect of *Loving*.

This fluidity also extends to rhythm and pitch. Schafer employs a wide range of indeterminate notations. He not only leaves formal organization of pitch quite random but writes glissandi of every conceivable range, duration, and shape, and he relies heavily on unpitched percussion. Most of the score is written in unmetered notations, with a few passages metered or given in stop-watch tempo. The singers are thus liberated, at least to a degree, from the demands of exact synchronization (Schafer had written a few years earlier in response to the notation of Pound's *Le Testament*, 'As long as singers remain poorly educated rhythmically, one can expect more discomfort than accuracy from finical scores, and this is especially true of opera where memory work and acting are factors of importance'[4]). There are passages of free improvisation, some of graphic suggestions, some (especially in Ishtar's aria) of given pitches. Schafer gives graphic notation for the events on tape, except where definite pitches are specified. He also offers a few tentative sketches for slide projections used in the 'Quartet' (though nothing like the elaborate notation later to appear in *Patria*), and in 'Phantasmagoria' he indicates general suggestions for the dancers – 'fast movements,' 'slow,' 'freeze.'

Apart from the dancers (marked optional), the whole of *Loving* requires only twenty-three performers, including four singers, two actors, and an electronic technician. Within the fairly small ensemble, however, Schafer's orchestration is unusual and varied. He eliminates brass and woodwinds altogether. The dominant sound comes from an enormous battery of percussion instruments needing six players. These are augmented by quasi-percussive and plucked instruments: harp, mandolin, guitar (also electric guitar and banjo), piano (also celesta and harpsichord). The only truly sustained sounds come from a quintet of strings, generally cast in a secondary role, and from a free-bass accordion, which the composer added in his 1978 revision of the score.[5] This ensemble generates a kaleidoscopic glitter of sound – fleeting, unpredictable, mercurial – a perfect foil for the singing voices. As in *The Judgement of Jael*, Schafer uses contrasting orchestration structurally, to characterize the arias of the four singers: strings for Modesty, percussion for Ishtar, plucked instruments for Vanity, and bells for Eros.

The most notable factor in the free style of *Loving*, however, is the vocal writing. Again, *Loving* perfects an experiment begun in *The Judgement of Jael*. Although much has been said about the difficulties of modern vocal music, the 'Webernesque line with its angular and ecstatic leaps,' Schafer remarks, is

little more than an elaboration of Wagner and represents but one of many traditions of vocal technique available ... For one thing, we have today two mutually exclusive traditions in the classical singer and the jazz or pops singer. The folk singing of numerous cultures shows us further techniques. Here we learn the effectiveness of such devices as the yodel, the glottal stop, the expressive use of quarter-tones, unusual forms of vibrato, and the production of whistling, clicking and other sounds. A whole new world of vocables remains to be explored by the classical composer. Mary Morrison's interest in jazz and pops music (her husband Harry Freedman began his musical career in jazz) made it possible for me to include in *Geography* a certain number of vocal embellishments characteristic of that field. My own study of certain forms of folk music, particularly that of the Balkan minstrels, has led to other incorporations which have by now, I think, become part of my own musical language.[6]

With these jazz, pop, and folk elements, combined with the vertiginous leaps and glissandi of the *avant-garde*, Schafer forges a modern equivalent for the erotic arabesques of bel canto style, where 'in the serpentine lines of the Italian aria with its affluence of embellishment we find a sensuousness that can be tasted with both the ear and the eye – for even the appearance of the notes on the page describes in voluptuous turns and passionate thrusts a true geography of eros.'[7]

Ultimately, however, the vocal style, like every other aspect of *Loving*, is tied to the text – to those points at which the nervous systems of music and language touch. Although Schafer had devised his own texts before (as early as *A Music Lesson*), *The Geography of Eros* is the first of his works to release a truly creative verbal and theatrical instinct together with his musical creation. Not that the libretto is 'literature' – the words themselves are mainly phrases taken from his own adolescent love poems: 'I transcribed these fragments to cards and then turned them up, seeking "le mot juste." This sounds more random than it is, and in any case I had a very strong feeling for the shape of the music of the particular aria before I began working with the text.'[8] The text itself is merely one component of a complex theatrical presentation.

Like many recent composers who have elaborated Schoenberg's *Sprechgesang* principle, Schafer treats his text largely as a source of abstract vocal sounds, often breaking words into isolated phonemes or otherwise allowing them to be obscured. In his published lecture on *Loving*, he draws up a scale of eight degrees ranging from pure sense to pure sound:

1 Stage speech (deliberate, articulate, projected);
2 Domestic speech (with no attempt to project; could include slang or deliberately free and sloppy speech);
3 Parlando (slightly intoned speech; sometimes used by clergymen);
4 Sprechgesang or sung speech (the moving curve of pitch, duration and intensity assumes relatively fixed positions. Schoenberg used both the 5 and the 3-line stave to indicate Sprechgesang);
5 Syllabic song (one note to each syllable, notated on the musical stave);
6 Melismatic song (more than one note to each syllable. Extremely melismatic writing can be found in Perotin or Machaut where one word of the text will be attenuated through an entire movement of music);
7 Vocables (pure sounds: vowels, consonants, noise aggregates, humming, whistling, screaming, etc.);
8 Electronically manipulated vocal sound (may transform or distort words completely).[9]

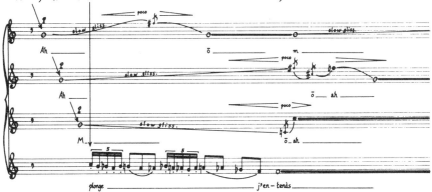

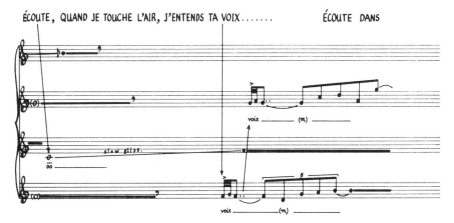

5.1 *Loving*: scene 2

Loving exhibits most of these (there is no 'domestic speech' or 'syllabic song'). The remarkable feature, in keeping with the fluid ideal, is the fusion or blurring of transitions from one category to the next, superimposing speech over music or overlapping arias with dialogue. Another passage early in the work ingeniously solves the problem of synchronizing a spoken text with a complex musical ensemble. Schafer writes unmetered lines, cueing them at specific points to words of the speaker (example 5.1). One other passage (example 5.2) is a strictly verbal text fitted with tempo indications and dynamics.

Still, Schafer's categories are really just an updated and more flexible equivalent for the dialogue, recitativo secco, arioso, and aria of

		LUI	ELLE		
large	pp	benedictine	thyme	acc.	pp
		petits fours	gloss with		
		menthes	eggyoke		
acc.	cres.	glace à l'oeuf	marjoram	acc.	cres.
		marjolaine, moelle	cough drops, marrow,		
		pâté d'amande	fudge, floc little	presto	ff
		Ishtar	Ishtar		
		une petite baise	in cinnamon		
		à la canelle			
mod.	mf	salpêtre	saltpepper	rit.	dim.
		butter brott	skin of bacon		
		peau de porc	butterbrott		
		petite Ishtar			
presto	ff	belle nourrice			
presto	mf	du vin rouge	red wine		
		pour ces messieurs	for men		
		du vin blanc	white wine		
		pour ces dames	for women		
		du vin rouge	red wine		

5.2 *Loving*: scene 10

traditional opera. Despite the composer's talk of a 'theatre of confluence' and his resistance to the word *opera*, *Loving* is perhaps not as
far removed from conventional opera as he would like to believe. The
work still has recognizable arias, so called by the composer, continuous,
and separable from their context; there is a quartet; there are (despite
denials) characters and a story line; the spoken dialogue moves the
action forward, while the arias and ensembles elaborate the emotions of
the dramatic situation. In a 1964 article called 'Opera and Reform,'
Schafer expressed his distaste for opera; but his objections are not new
(they are shared by many others, including Pound), nor are they
resolved in *Loving*. Schafer scoffs at the cult of the prima donna, yet his
arias are as exhibitionistic as anything in Strauss. 'Operatic music,' he
complains, must be 'simple, dramatic, and singable. Because of the
slower tempo of articulation in singing, the plot will have to be
elementary and its development dilatory, even static.' Schafer's aban-
donment of bar lines and commitment to unmetered notation, as he
admits, is partly a concession to the imprecision of stage singing. And
the story line of *Loving* is static indeed. Schafer goes on to attack the
mixture of 'realistic decor ... coupled with an unrealistic mode of
presentation'; yet operatic scenery is not typically realistic, and further-

more the romantic world of opera, particularly in its German strain from *Fidelio* through Wagner to *Die glückliche Hand*, rarely strays far from allegory.

Essentially, *Loving* is an allegory. In part, being a bilingual opera in English and French, it is a specifically Canadian allegory 'of the ambivalence of the two [sic] native peoples of my own country, each of whom detests the language of the other.'[10] That the lovers speak in different languages – the man in French, the woman in English – is also a comment on their problems of communication. Such themes obviously have their relevance beyond the borders of Canada.

Loving is even more centrally concerned with sexual psychology. It is 'a drama about love between the sexes' accomplished not 'by narrating a romance between lovers (à la Puccini),'[11] but rather 'by projecting faculties of the male and female psyches as allegorical figures in the manner of the medieval *Roman de la Rose* or the *Psychomachia* of Prudentius. In his published lecture on *Loving*, Schafer outlines his intention of representing both sexes equally in terms of a psychology entirely his own invention, involving three male and three female faculties. As completed, *Loving* fails to realise this scheme. The work is not a product of an 'androgynous' imagination (in Virginia Woolf's sense of the word) but instead dramatizes the female psyche from a decidedly male viewpoint. The man does not sing. He is represented only in the actor, as 'Lui' and by 'The Voice of the Poet,' presumably the interior voice of Lui, pre-recorded on tape. The woman is more complex; the actress, 'Elle,' is further represented by four singers who carry the burden of performance: Modesty, Ishtar, Vanity, and finally (symbolizing the three faculties in balance) Eros.

In the score, both verbally and pictorially, and in his lecture on *Loving*, Schafer has provided suggestions in some detail for stage production; yet, although up to 1981 it has received two major productions, neither has precisely realized the composer's intentions. The first was televised, the second a sketchily staged concert version. Still, being as successful as I think it is, *Loving* is a truly plastic theatre piece, adaptable to many conditions of performance – and posing some of the same problems in each. The principal problem is the static, processional quality of four lengthy arias in succession, a problem that springs from the original allegorical concept. The *Roman de la Rose*, after all, is not the kind of narrative that instantly seizes the twentieth-century imagination. Schafer evidently reached this same conclusion, for in *Patria* he writes shorter arias and merges them almost imperceptibly into the dramatic fabric. Consequently, *Patria* is both obscurer and more continuous, while *Loving* is more static but also more intelligible. This problem in *Loving*, however, is no more insuperable than it is in many operas in which singers are immobilized by long arias.

The two productions and Schafer's own proposals all have the common purpose of softening the edges of the straightforward procession and maintaining the otherwise fluid nature of the work. The singers are named in the printed program, perhaps, but not on stage, so the audience must infer their identities. The events, characters, and settings are generalized, free of specific period and location. The text is obscure deliberately; says Schafer, 'I wanted to create an aura in half-lights, allusions, confused vibrations and nocturnal thoughts.'[12] These effects smooth the transitions between speech and song, between actors, singers, and dancers, leaving the audience disoriented: 'Is there only one man and one woman or are there many men and many women? Are they meeting for the first time or the last time? Have they ever met? Which are real actions and which are fictions, myths, masks? What is dream and what is reality?'[13]

Television might seem the ideal medium for this concept, with its potential for blurred or abstract effects and rapidly shifting images; and *Loving*, being the first (so far the only) Canadian opera commissioned for television, has been called a 'television opera.'[14] But Schafer rejects this label. Aside from its inadequate sound, television, he remarks, 'is a *light* medium and totally unsuitable for the creation of mystery and nocturne.' The ideal production should have a 'neutral foundation of darkness,' just as the music has a foundation of silence.[15] This production would incorporate an elaborate system of films, still projections, lighting effects, and surrealistic sets, along with the forces already mentioned; but the chief advantage of live stage production, of course, is the live musicians themselves, whose effect no other medium (certainly not television) has ever been able to duplicate. Television, however, does contribute the seamless flow from one 'editing unit' to the next, a format later repeated in *Patria*.

6

Lustro (1969–72)

To survey Schafer's output since *Loving* by genre rather than chronologically does not mean that he ceased to develop. Since 1965 he has extended the spatial aspects of his music, he has developed the expressive capacity of graphic notation, he has continued to explore new vocal techniques, particularly in an impressive series of choral works, and he has tested ways of incorporating environmental concerns into his scores; he has also improved his electronic techniques, and he has proceeded from *Loving* to the greater complexities of *Patria*. Still, *Loving* is the watershed of his career and the wellspring of all his later development. Schafer has pursued so many developments simultaneously through the decade and a half since 1965 that it becomes nearly impossible to follow them in any linear order.

Before turning to his smaller pieces, instrumental and vocal, it is necessary to skip ahead a few years to *Lustro*, which falls conveniently into neither category. This monumental work is at least as imposing as the stage works – perhaps more so. *Lustro* is a triptych of three large compositions: *Divan i Shams i Tabriz*, *Music for the Morning of the World*, and *Beyond the Great Gate of Light*. The outer two are primarily orchestral but include seven or eight voices in their complex texture; the middle part is for mezzo-soprano accompanied only by tape. The whole is an evocation of mystical experience, certainly one of the most powerful attempts of its kind by any composer. If the *Patria* sequence at all resembles Wagner's *Ring*, then, says Schafer, '*Lustro* could be called my *Parsifal*.'[1] With its large orchestra dispersed through the concert hall and its masterful manipulation of four-track tape, the work compels in its hearers a 'sensation of wandering in sonic space.'[2]

Lustro was inspired by Schafer's visit to Turkey and Iran in 1969. There he became familiar with the writings of Jalal al-Din Rumi, the thirteenth-century Persian mystical poet who founded the Sufi sect known as the dervishes. Originally, Schafer planned two separate works based on Rumi. For one, he took the opportunity of a commission from the Vancouver Symphony Orchestra to compose *Divan i Shams i Tabriz*, by itself Schafer's longest and most complex orchestral work – so complex, in fact, that the Vancouver Symphony declined to attempt it, thus confirming Schafer's worst suspicions about symphony orchestras. Undaunted, he got the idea of combining *Divan i Shams* with *Music for the Morning of the World*, already in progress, and adding a third section for symmetry. *Beyond the Great Gate of Light* appeared in 1972, bringing the whole to seventy minutes. ('I feel that is about as long as an audience can be expected to listen to something without getting a desire to walk out. I hate intermissions. They take people into a completely different world.'³ This principle is also observed in the stage works.) *Lustro* had its first integral performance with Phyllis Mailing and the Toronto Symphony under Marius Constant on 31 May 1973.

Schafer says in the score that the poems in *Divan i Shams i Tabriz* describe 'a fusing of religious love with human love. Accordingly the piece is composed of disunited elements gradually growing together.' The solo voices, however, sing a different text, 'The Song of the Reed Flute,' the prelude to Rumi's most important poem, the *Mathnavi*. This prelude, says one scholar, 'is held in special reverence by the dervishes of the Mevlevi order and recited in their ritual.' The reed flute itself is used by Sufis 'as a means of rousing themselves into a state of fervor, from which the dance followed naturally.'⁴ In Schafer's piece, the native flute appears on tape near the end of parts I and II, dividing the sections, not wild but expressing 'the gentleness of the Sufi sect and the simplicity of their aspirations.'⁵ The text serves mainly a symbolic function, since it is sung in Rumi's Persian (or Tagore's Bengali in part III) and all but obliterated by the massive orchestration. Even the English version of Rumi in part II is sometimes difficult to make out because of the vocal fragmentation. The principal symbolism, however, relates to light. The word *lustro* itself is a Latin verb meaning 'I illuminate,' though the secondary meanings 'purify' or 'dance in a circle' are also relevant. The title of part I means 'poems of the sun of Tabriz,'⁶ so that all three sections deal with the sun, the traditional symbol of Oneness.

Schafer reinforces this symbolism with lighting. At the end of part I lights dim, and the whole of part II is sung in darkness illuminated only by a single candle; as part III begins, the lights slowly rise. This bit of theatre enacts the drama of the Self, with nothing but 'a little light, like a rushlight, to lead back to splendour.'[7] In a sense, then, *Lustro* contains a 'plot.' Beginning in a blare of chaos, the scattered forces around the auditorium (the external universe) gradually converge on a unison F♯ and move in a sweeping unison melody; in part II, the Self, isolated, sings out into the darkness; then, as the lights come up in part III, the forces of part I return, but this time dominated by a shimmering G major triad, with the transcendent solo voice rising over the massed sound, absorbed into the world of light.

Lustro is remarkable above all for its evocation of space. Space, of course, is a preoccupation of contemporary music – in Cage, Stockhausen, the experiments of Henry Brant, or Harry Somers' *Stereophony.* Schafer's essay 'The Philosophy of Stereophony' argues that while 'the composer of the past did not write for someone seated inside his piano or his orchestra, but for someone seated across the room,' with the new technology, 'a repertoire of new music may certainly come into existence.' This repertoire may bridge the gulf between the modern composer and his audience: 'Is it not possible that by placing the listener at the very centre of gravity of the music, stereophony may precipitate a new involvement?'[8] This is one way to revitalize the romantic orchestra.

Schafer's interest in stereophony, first evident in the Prudentius songs, had been spurred by experiments made possible by the new electronic studio at Simon Fraser. There he created *Kaleidoscope,* an electronic work for the Chemical Industries Limited Pavilion at Montreal's Expo 67. *Kaleidoscope* was quite a success with visitors passing through, but while Schafer does not regard it as an independent composition, it taught him an important lesson. The exhibition contained several booths, each with its own sound system not sealed off from the others; leakage from one area to another had to be considered part of the music. The audience, furthermore, was ambulatory, and thus not 'victims of an imposed point of view.'[9]

Neither the listeners nor the performers in *Lustro* are mobile; the spatial ideal is realized by breaking the orchestra into thirteen mixed quintets distributed around the auditorium: (example 6.1). The stage holds the remaining strings, the four percussionists, an organ, and a contra-bassoon (and later solo mezzo-soprano). The other singers belong to the quintets, their voices seeming to issue from indefinable distances. The tape sounds from the four corners. (The descriptive notation of the tape, with its flamboyant Persian-style arabesques,

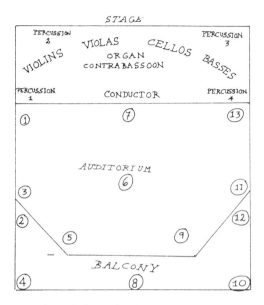

6.1 *Divan i Shams i Tabriz*: seating diagram (© Copyright 1977 Universal Edition (Canada) Ltd.)

makes this score a most beautiful thing to look at.) 'Such a situation,' Schafer remarks, 'devolves on the composer the necessity of creating music which makes complete aural sense on a great number of levels. Each sound source must make independent sense and be interesting by itself as well as make a coherent addition to any number of separate sound sources around it. Clearly a new form of counterpoint has emerged – a space counterpoint.'[10] *Lustro* thus differs both from Somers' *Stereophony*, which contrasts the different instrumental choirs in space, and from Stockhausen's *Gruppen*, which seems little more than homogenous, three-dimensional chaos. Schafer's groups echo each other's phrases, play in unison or consonant harmony, and generally respond to each other. The time-lag, of course, is part of the music. In performance, this creates problems of logistics necessitating stop-watches or transistorized earplugs for co-ordination, though the parts themselves are not difficult. *Lustro* is an ideal test for quadraphonic recording, met in the superb radio broadcast with an arsenal of technical equipment unprecedented in CBC history.[11]

The material for *Lustro* is nearly as remarkable as its acoustic effect.

6.2 *Divan i Shams i Tabriz*: series (notes in parentheses appear alternatively)

Schafer uses a series even longer than the seventy-six note subject of
Canzoni for Prisoners – 180 notes arranged in twenty groups of nine
(example 6.2). This long series remains audible through its internal
stucture. Each segment uses only two intervals alternating in a regular
pattern: down-up-up-down-down-up-up-down. Consequently, the first,
middle, and last notes of each segment are the same. The intervals,
however, shift from one segment to the next in a regular permutation,
moving from the smallest to the largest and back, covering every
possible pair except the tritone (there is no devil in *this* music).
Furthermore, the pivotal notes in each segment describe a sequential
pattern (example 6.3). The effect of this series is striking. Melodic
fragments are ever shifting, yet ever contrasting. Lines twist about
chromatically yet return to a momentary tonic, the most prominent

6.3 *Divan i Shams i Tabriz*: pitches of transpositions of segments of the series

being G. The parabolic ascent of the first segment resembles the 'Shepard glissandi' described near the end of part II (the illusion of the Shepard glissando is that while it rises constantly it never reaches the apex of its ascent). Melodic lines generated by this portion of the series seem at times to rise slowly into infinity. Throughout all, the first four notes of the series gradually assume greater importance, finally dominating part III.

Divan i Shams i Tabriz begins with a blare of instruments and electronic sound lasting over three minutes. Brass instruments sound fifteen segments of the series, clearly visible in the score (2′2″) but at this point scarcely audible. A string diminuendo (completing the last five segments) leads to an extended viola solo emanating from the rear left balcony, which leads in turn to a highly fragmented passage as the quintets gradually enter in crescendo. Within the confusion can be heard a few solo voices and snatches of G major consonant harmony. This mounts to a brief unison climax (8′34″), which yields to a section dominated by voices and outbursts of metallic percussion. As this passage gradually grows more frenetic, there is an indeterminate section resembling a similar passage from Ishtar's aria in *Loving*, in which all quintets play isolated chords at random (13′35″), followed by a tutti crescendo, all instruments playing notes of the series as fast as possible but eventually landing on a sustained F♯ (15′30″). Here, sustained tones begin ponderously to move through the series, connected at first by cascading multi-octave glissandi for full orchestra; a broad melody develops, reaching a climax on tone 168 (E♮ in segment S) over a tape crescendo. As the music subsides over a repeated percussion gesture, the last notes of the series (resembling the familiar opening notes) are heard, first in the voices, and finally on a native flute on tape, sounding as if from nowhere.

Where *Divan i Shams* overpowers with multiplicity of incident,

Music for the Morning of the World is minimal. If music were to be evaluated according to the quantity of 'information' it conveys, as Leonard B. Meyer proposes, this piece would score dismally; as John Kraglund complained, 'Our composer mystics seem to equate the degree of mysticism with the length of time they take to say nothing.'[12] When Schafer's music moves from outer to inner space, it moves from sonic saturation to sonic deprivation, evoking the half-heard distances between sounds. Such minimalism is always risky, demanding a participation that audiences may find disconcerting. 'Rumi sought to discover the world where "speaking is without letters or sounds,"' writes Schafer. 'Even today one may observe Bedouins sitting quietly in a circle saying nothing.'[13] The single candle amid total darkness is not just gimmickry – it is needed to induce receptivity to a special kind of music: 'By candlelight the powers of sight are sharply reduced; the ear is supersensitized.'[14] This is a music of hyperaesthesia.

The voice part is remarkable for the wide spaces between entries, stretching the listener's time sense. It ranges through wordless melismas, to intoned or sung verbal lines, to pure speech, and much of the line is improvisation around a single predominant pitch, as in the dervish flute melodies. The text covers the same ground as *Divan i Shams*, where some of the phrases are written in the score. Compiled from various works of Rumi, they describe the same fusion of human with divine love, this time from the viewpoint of the individual self. Out of the vocables of the opening phrase, 'love' is the first distinguishable word, and the voice goes on to describe a cosmic journey to love: 'We are drawn into a great whirlpool ... For a time I circled the nine heavens ... I am pure light.' At mid-point in the composition (16'20"), after the soloist unexpectedly pronounces the word 'beware,' a male whisper appears on tape (presumably the object of the mezzo-soprano's journey) saying, 'If you have seen me, tell no one you have seen ...' The remainder completes the singer's journey as a dying process: 'Die before you die ... Love is a fire in which all is consumed save the beloved ... I am love.' The long last gesture dwells on the words 'I,' 'I am,' as the individual ego is absorbed into the cosmos. The work closes with a spoken benediction: 'Keep silence like the points of the compass, for the King has erased thy name from the book of speech.'

Meanwhile, during this thirty-minute process of erasure, the points of the compass are depicted by the four-track tape. *Music for the Morning of the World* depends on electronic sound more than any of Schafer's other works. As in *Divan i Shams*, he continues to play with the spatial possibilities, unexpectedly shifting sounds from one corner of the room to another or moving a repeated note 'furtively around all speakers' (15'50"). Most of the sounds have high reverberation, and the many long diminuendos seem to recede physically into the darkness, pushing out the invisible walls of the auditorium. Schafer mixes concrete and synthesized sounds freely, but always with a strong sense of their symbolic connotations. He includes gong and cymbal sounds, as in most of his mystically inclined works, but he concentrates more on wind-like effects. These also evoke open space, but, even more specifically, wind is strongly associated with 'spirit' (as the origin of that word reveals). Schafer quotes Carl Jung on this subject: 'The breath of the spirit rushing over the dark water is uncanny, like everything whose cause we do not know – since it is not ourselves. It hints at an unseen presence, a numen to which neither human expectations nor the machinations of the will have given life. It lives of itself.'[15] The tape also includes magnified breath sounds – the sign of being and feeling – but the most extraordinary effect occurs in the 'whirlpool' (10'4"), a *tour de force* in which each track is transferred clockwise to the next, resulting in a slight delay. Reversals give counter-clockwise eddies. The material itself is scaled up and down, suggesting rapid wavelike motion, and the whole is combined with counter-clockwise buzzing sounds. Schafer's tape also contains some conventional music. Voices appear at times, seemingly disembodied. One passage quotes from a Bruckner adagio (22'30"), perhaps the music in Western tradition most deeply concerned with an expanded time sense. The dervish flute returns (17'32"), the symbol of the adept, 'burdened with a material body and longing to be freed... The soul, deprived of sympathy, seeks an ear that will listen to its lament and a mate who understands its woes.'[16] Wave sounds, archetypically associated with cleansing, purification, and rebirth,[17] bring the work to a close.

Beyond the Great Gate of Light serves so well as the resolution of *Lustro* that it is hard to imagine it by itself (it has never been so performed); but in its place, it creates a convincing, sonically luminescent Paradiso. The musical forces and thematic materials are exactly as in *Divan i Shams*, except that the soloist of part II remains on stage as the lights go up, her voice absorbed into the massed sound and at times rising above it. Where part I was concerned with disparate fragments eventually coming together, part III is concerned with surges of sound. The first four notes of the series become a motto in the tubular chimes, dominating the opening and echoed at various tempi in other instruments. As the quintets enter with motifs from part I, the sonorities mass in four slow, wave-like crescendos, each longer than the last, until, at the peak of the fourth (8′16″), the tape melts into a richly voiced G-major triad. It sustains this triad for the remaining six minutes of the piece.

Schafer is not the first composer to try the effect of a single sound prolonged interminably. Aside from contemporary examples, like Terry Riley's *In C*, Schafer may have recalled the opening bars of Wagner's *Rheingold*. But here the G triad brings to consummation intimations of tonality generated by the prominent first note and first segment of the series, which had already been reinforced by snatches of G major in part I. Schafer is not aiming at auditory fatigue. His compositional problem, of course, is to keep six minutes of G triad interesting, to give it grain.

The triad shifts from one tape track to another, and the operator has instructions to manipulate the volume ad libitum, only keeping the triad a constant presence. The triad is doubled from time to time in instrumental choirs, especially the strings, and in the Hammond organ. Towards the end of the piece, there is some grandiose harmonic movement. Superimposed are other sounds. The voices, hitherto silent, appear with the triad, led in by the mezzo-soprano. Other gestures, melodic fragments, tape sounds appear and at one point (12′15″) threaten to swamp the tonality completely. But the triad wins through, and while the mezzo-soprano finishes her solo line, the music fades in random bell sounds, as the conductor silences the thirteen instrumental groups, one by one.

Each section of *Lustro* is an imposing piece in its own right – most especially *Divan i Shams i Tabriz*. But if I had to choose Schafer's single greatest composition, it would be *Lustro* as a whole. Little else in music so well embodies the spirit of Walt Whitman's lines:

The orchestra whirls me wider than Uranus flies,
It wrenches such ardors from me I did not know I possess'd them,
It sails me, I dab with bare feet, they are lick'd by the indolent waves,
I am cut by bitter and angry hail, I lose my breath,
Steep'd amid honey'd morphine, my windpipe throttles in fakes of death,
At length let up again to feel the puzzle of puzzles,
And that we call Being.[18]

7

Instrumental works since 1965

Schafer's career as an orchestral composer has been a love-hate relationship with the central institution of musical romanticism. While
he has gone on record as believing the orchestra to have outlived its
usefulness, he has continued to write for it – if only on commission and
sometimes in subversive ways. Part of his animus arose from the
Vancouver Symphony Orchestra's refusal to perform *Divan i Shams i
Tabriz*; but his convictions have remained firm. Like the opera company, the symphony orchestra is bound up with a dead, or at least
dying, romantic tradition.

Romantic music has become institutionalized in conservatories, opera theatres,
and concert halls. This institutionalization has assured it a consistent place on
musical programs, perhaps more consistent than might otherwise have been the
case; for certainly other important musical styles have declined in popularity
today because they lack sufficient patronage to secure a continuity of tradition
in performance.[1]

Schafer's views are thus aesthetic, economic, and even political. In a
1967 interview for the *Vancouver Sun*, Schafer describes the orchestra as
a 'dinosaur' that feeds on quantities of green stuff and seems close to
extinction. Although the state 'has a responsibility to preserve our
antiquities' and ought to continue supporting orchestras, the medium is
dead as a means of expression: 'Schoenberg, Stravinsky, Debussy and
Mahler were the last of our great composers to add anything significant
to the orchestral repertoire – if we except Shostakovich – and Stravinsky
is the only survivor.' In addition, he repeats the familiar charge that 'the
symphony orchestra is still a dictatorship. One man is boss and the rest

are slaves,' and he looks forward to a time when musical ensembles will reflect the democratic ideals of society.[2]

Quite unexpectedly, not long after this interview, Schafer was offered a commission from the Montreal Symphony for a new work about ten minutes in length. He hesitated before accepting because it ran counter to his stated beliefs; but discussing the matter with Pierre Béique, manager of the Montreal Symphony, he met with a challenge: 'Why don't you guys ever write something our audiences will want to hear?' 'You mean like Strauss?' returned Schafer. The music of Richard Strauss had recently been the subject of some conversations with Jack Behrens in which both composers lamented that they would never experience the feeling of untrammelled ego that must have come from conducting a Strauss score. Given this train of thought, Schafer's mind gravitated towards *Ein Heldenleben*, the most egotistical of masterpieces, and *Son of Heldenleben* was conceived. The score is dedicated to Jack Behrens, but the piece, which stands with *Divan i Shams i Tabriz* as Schafer's finest orchestral music, strikes emotional roots back to his Vienna period and his deep-seated ambivalence towards romanticism.[3]

Son of Heldenleben is built on Strauss's swaggering first theme. In the score Schafer notes that the method of the piece 'rests on the identifica-tion of the memorable tune as it winds its way slowly, ever so slowly, through the combustions, clouds and constellations of sound which surround and adorn it'; the theme, he adds (foreshadowing *Patria*), is 'a melodious Ariadne's thread' winding its way through 'the labyrinthine corridors of this orchestral minotauromachy.' The Strauss theme thus becomes a kind of *cantus firmus*, a fixed line which the other parts embellish. Like an orthodox *cantus firmus*, the Strauss line determines the length and form of the composition, and it provides a faint rhythmic pulse, especially in its moving half-notes, against which the pulseless sonorities in the other parts are projected (see example 7.1). But a better term might be *cantus infirmus*, since the melody, sounded pianissimo throughout in interminable augmentation, certainly seems an emaci-ated shadow of Strauss's grandiloquent posturings. Still, as Schafer's title implies, heroes' sons rarely equal their fathers, nor do sequels often match the originals (one's mind runs perforce to films like *Son of Frankenstein*). Even Schafer's program note, appended to the score, is a parody both of Strauss's programs and of the reading matter customarily provided to concert audiences – a single monstrous 700-word sentence that says remarkably little about the music itself.

When Schafer presented his score to the Montreal Symphony in

September 1968, however, problems developed. The orchestra's conductor, Franz-Paul Decker, considered the work an insult to the reputation of a great composer and tried to persuade Schafer to alter at least the title. Schafer refused, explaining that his piece intended no disrespect: it is , he said, 'constructed as if it were groping its way little by little to the Strauss quotation towards its conclusion. It seemed to me inevitable that this quotation should form the climax of the piece, and as it finally asserts itself over the chaos of sound which comes before I want it to sound powerful, confident and tonic.'[4] Schafer somewhat disingenuously did not mention the screaming twelve-note chord that jolts the *Heldenleben* theme to a halt – a sound dominated by three piccolos in their highest register, anvil, suspended cymbal, and (significantly) police whistle. Elsewhere he speaks of the 'sentimental vagaries' of Strauss, which are 'perfectly consistent with the waning of the ... Austro-Hungarian Empire.'[5] So the piece has social and political implications, a depiction of the Viennese *Gemütlichkeit* in a state of terminal enervation. Schafer has come closest to defining his divided attitude in an interview with Gareth Jacobs:

The hero was not just Strauss himself, but it was man at the centre of the universe, dominating and driving his own ideas over and above the concerns of other living creatures. I saw *Heldenleben* as a typical piece of that 19th-century concept of progress and human imperialism, and so *Son of Heldenleben* is to some extent a send-up of Strauss' ideas. I say only to some extent because I have a lot of respect for Strauss's music; which is glorious and purple and very beautiful. So *Son of Heldenleben* is in a sense reflective of the more ecological times in which we live, in which man is no longer at the very centre of things, but is simply a participant.[6]

Schafer did not try to articulate these views to Franz-Paul Decker, but Decker eventually accepted the composer's assurances, conducted the premiere, and later recorded the work.

These conceptual aspects of the work are not extraneous: they are audible. Even a detail like the police whistle draws its symbolism not from the label in the score but from associations, natural or conditioned, with the sound itself. The *cantus firmus* line is discernible throughout, if intermittently. Other Strauss fragments emerge from the texture frequently. The gradual gathering of the full orchestra into the heroic moment of Strauss's recapitulation and then its sudden evaporation make the point unmistakably.

This generating idea in *Son of Heldenleben* is typical of Schafer's programmatic procedures through much of his music. For one thing, Schafer's 'subject-matter' is sonic. He is not interested in extra-musical narratives, nor does he, like Strauss, orchestrate the tableware. For another, Schafer's pieces often develop out of a single generating 'concept' that has some referential meaning; the musical lines and gestures, sometimes highly complex in themselves, are intelligible because of their common origin. This kind of conceptualism (an extension of orthodox serialism, where the generating idea is a sequence of twelve notes) is capable of infinite variation. Often, as in *Son of Heldenleben*, Schafer's greatest strength is his ability to invent a new and meaningful generating concept for a musical composition.

The notation of *Son of Heldenleben*, a large orchestral score, goes beyond the advances of *Loving*, which was mainly confined to smaller ensemble textures. Schafer uses a time log throughout and writes the whole score in 4/4 at stop-watch tempo, ♩ = 60; but only the augmentation of the Strauss line maintains any regular pulse, and that is barely palpable. The pulseless tape sounds are diagrammed at the foot of the page, and the orchestral parts are given sometimes in complex mensuration and sometimes in various free notations. Where synchronization of parts is necessary, Schafer joins the ligatures across the page, a device of great visual clarity, especially since empty bars in all parts are left as blank space. Schafer uses a greater variety of indeterminate notations here than in *Loving*, and he uses them more extensively, showing a confident command of the extended sonorities and random densities possible with a large orchestra.

The musical material of *Son of Heldenleben* is of three kinds: some borrowed from Strauss, some related to two tone rows derived from the Strauss theme, and some free. Furthermore, the orchestra tends to divide into pro-Strauss and anti-Strauss factions (though members often play both sides). The quoted material is assigned chiefly to instruments associated with Strauss – horn, solo woodwinds, solo violin. The free material uses aggressively contemporary sonorities. Thus Schafer's orchestra (which is not small) is smaller than Strauss's mammoth ensemble, but it calls for percussion requiring five or six players and some thirty-five different instruments (not counting piano), contrasted with the seven conventional idiophones in Strauss's score. The tape reinforces the futuristic sound. And players are required to produce unusual sounds on their instruments (rattled keys, reversed mouthpieces, woodwind multiphonics) as well as sing. Such effects may be taken as comment on Strauss's virtuoso orchestration.

The most important quoted material is of course the *cantus firmus* line, which consists of the first sixteen bars of *Heldenleben* rhythmically augmented (almost exactly) at the rate of ♩ for every ♪, as show in example 7.1. This accounts for the first 8½ minutes of music. The line is traded between the instruments, giving an effect of *Klangfarbenmelodie*. At times it threatens to dissipate entirely into glissandi and other forms of chromatic distortion. As the elongated Strauss period reaches its end, other *Heldenleben* themes appear, most noticeably the elegiac 'hero's withdrawal from the world' melody, in non-rhythmic notation. Strauss's final thirty-second note rush becomes a pyramiding E♭-major cluster in the strings building to the last sustained E♭, which releases a percussion explosion (notated graphically as a dense black smudge). Meanwhile, over the E♭ cluster, Schafer, recalling Strauss's self-quotation, suddenly introduces nine other themes as if to crowd them in as quickly as possible before the climax; for after the 8½-minute period is finished, Schafer cuts almost immediately to Strauss's climactic recapitulation, apparently omitting all the intervening material as irrelevant.

The Strauss material is tonal, of course, in the 'Eroica' key of E♭. This tonality, like the *cantus firmus* theme itself, is almost but not quite obliterated by the other material, and Schafer occasionally reinforces the E♭ – B♭ centre in the rest of the orchestra. At the same time, however, he occasionally blurs the E♭ feeling with E♮ (for example, the violin line at 8'36", or the E♭ – E♮ and B♭ – B♮ doublings in the twelve-note chord at 9'28", or the tuba motif at 3'36"). The curious analyst might also observe an emphasis on c that perhaps results from the prevalence of c in the Strauss theme (the third most frequent pitch, almost equalling E♭ and B♭).

Yet, without analysis of the score, the listener might be excused for not recognizing any key centre at all, because most of the notes in the piece have no reference to tonality, and these are generally projected at a louder dynamic level than the Strauss material. The two tone-rows are derived from the Strauss theme, one by augmenting, the other by diminishing the original intervals a semitone; also, the Strauss theme is itself sometimes treated serially, giving three rows in all (example 7.2). Certain inconsistencies appear, indicated by the bracketed notes in row A and the variant form of row D (D' – for example, the versions in glockenspiel and tubular chimes at 6'20"). Inconsistencies of detail in this kind of serialism call for no defence. The rows have two functions. Melodically, in rhythmic articulations, they suggest grotesquely distor-

7.1 *Son of Heldenleben*: Strauss theme and its augmentation, with approximate indications of instrumentation and timings (© Copyright 1976 Universal Edition (Canada) Ltd.)

7.2 *Son of Heldenleben*: series derived from the Strauss theme (S), from augmentation of the intervals (A), and from diminution of the intervals (D and D') (notes in parentheses in series A appear as options)

7.3 *Son of Heldenleben*: distortions of Strauss melodies, at 1'24" and 4'32" (© Copyright 1976 Universal Edition (Canada) Ltd.)

ted forms of the Strauss theme (example 7.3). More commonly, the rows are distributed in chords or other rhythms, so they simply supply a fund of self-consistent atonal pitch material loosely related to the central theme. In keeping with his usual practice, Schafer does not (I think) use inversions or transpositions of his rows, though a retrograde of row A appears in the full orchestral gesture at 7'24".

The rather unsystematic combination of this material appears in example 7.4. The *cantus firmus* (B♭ throughout) passes from horn to solo celli. The piccolo sounds the first twelve notes of row D' (the second two A's both substitute for F). Three solo violins play on all the rows: the first on row S, the second on row A, and the third jumping from row S (notes 9–15) to row A (notes 8–12). The two piano chords are based on row D' (notes 1–6) and row A (notes 1–6), but showing an anomalous

7.4 *Son of Heldenleben*: page 4 of score (percussion deleted) (© Copyright 1976 Universal Edition (Canada) Ltd.)

E♮ in the bass, illustrating the equivocal tonality mentioned above; this progression is reversed in the harp. Bass clarinet, bassoon, and tuba sustain a low three-note cluster unrelated to the tone rows. The pizzicato chords in the basses are based on row s (notes 1–6, then 11, 13–14). This passage is more easily susceptible to analysis than some others in the score, but it illustrates Schafer's free application of serial procedures.

Much of the material is free sonority, either instrumental or electronic. Besides the large percussion battery and special instrumental effects, Schafer also uses semitone clusters, often (as in the first bar) with some relation to the E♭ centre. The tape provides a running commentary. Its material bears no relationship to anything in Strauss.[7] Though important, it is used with discretion, dominating only at certain points and well integrated with the orchestra, so that the listener often cannot distinguish it from live sounds. Perfect synchronization is impossible, of course, and important only at the climactic *Heldenleben* quotation at 9′24″. The end of the *cantus firmus* phrase is reinforced by a gradual 57-second crescendo of white noise beginning at 8′00″; the rise is punctuated by jagged electronic sounds, like bombs detonating. The piece closes with an effect introduced earlier at 2′08″, a slowly oscillating tape band fading to nothing.

If *Son of Heldenleben* affectionately mocks the symphonic tradition, *No Longer than Ten (10) Minutes* is outright sabotage. Spurred by the success of *Son of Heldenleben*, or perhaps by a sense of rivalry with its Montreal counterpart, the Toronto Symphony offered Schafer a commission for a new work in 1970. Possibly it contemplated another piece like *Son of Heldenleben*, for an article on Schafer in *Time* magazine notes that the composer had received 'several requests for an encore – including a *Son of Beethoven*,' and Schafer's program note mentions an artist friend, Iain Baxter, who 'has for a long while tried to persuade me to write an "extension" to Beethoven's Fifth.'[8] But *Son of Beethoven* was not to be. Instead, Schafer seized on the wording of the Toronto Symphony's commission (standard for such contracts): 'It is agreed that the work shall have a minimum duration of approximately seven (7) minutes and no longer than ten (10) minutes.' Rightly or not, the implication seemed to be that, while the orchestra felt bound by duty (not to mention Canadian-content stipulations attached to government grants) to support Canadian music, no audience could be expected to sit through anything like a major work occupying a high-priority position on its concert program – especially after the extravagance of *Divan i Shams i Tabriz.*

Schafer retaliated with a piece that assaults the conventions of the standard subscription concert. The piece may start either half of a program, but it must start, for it begins imperceptibly while the orchestra is still tuning up, the players entering one by one, improvising chromatically within specified ranges. The conductor enters on page 2 of the score, at the peak of the crescendo, and begins beating; at the end of the piece, the full orchestra joins in an enormous improvised crescendo led by the percussion section, at the peak of which the conductor again leaves the stage, allowing the noise to subside gradually. (The conductor's movements are indicated by footsteps across the score.)

Then comes the real catch:

After the fadeout of the percussion, a few winds and strings continue with soft waves of sound as before, gradually diminishing. If there is applause the percussion is to begin another long crescendo and decrescendo. This is repeated each time the applause rises up, though each time with less duration and intensity (presumably like the applause). If there is no applause, those players who do not play in the following piece leave the stage; the piano is moved into position for the Brahms concerto etc. ... Gradually everyone stops playing as the conductor returns except for the string quartet of soloists holding the dominant seventh chord of the key of the piece following, very softly but definitely *audible.* They do not stop playing until after the downbeat of the following piece. If this piece has no tonic, they continue playing throughout it until the tonic of the piece after that has been reached.

At the premiere of this composition, conducted by Victor Feldbrill, Schafer achieved his closest approximation to the avant-gardist's dream: a *succès de scandale* (albeit on a Toronto scale) in the tradition of Stravinsky's *Le Sacre.* In the *Globe and Mail,* John Kraglund grumbled that the piece was longer than ten minutes; William Littler in the *Toronto Daily Star,* however, grasped the composer's purpose. His account of the event is worth quoting:

Finally, at the climax of a massive crescendo, Feldbrill retreated from the field, leaving the orchestra to continue on its own, buzzing as it had been doing at the outset.

The audience, somewhat taken aback by this breach of convention, reacted characteristically by applauding. This encouraged the orchestra to rise to another climax, which in turn led to another burst of applause, which in turn led to another climax, which in turn led to another burst of applause.

By this time the audience was beginning to divide into camps. The top balcony, heavily student-infested, was onto the game from the outset and apparently willing to keep the cycle of applause and orchestral response going indefinitely.

In the more expensive seats, confusion reigned. Some people kept applauding, some shook their heads, and others looked as though they would, on the whole, rather be in Philadelphia.

Then the lights came on and Victor Feldbrill peeked through the door he had recently closed behind him. This was enough to rouse the students to another burst of applause, which led to another orchestral climax and the cycle was in motion once more ...[9]

The contradictory responses of Kraglund and Littler are both accurate reflections on Schafer's piece, the effect of which lies largely in its breach of decorum. It depends on the conventions that it defies so wittily; in this respect, *No Longer Than Ten (10) Minutes* comes closer to being a sheerly conceptual work than anything else of Schafer's. To describe it in terms of ordinary analysis is of limited value.

The piece does have a form: apart from the blurred edges at the beginning and end, it is an orthodox ternary structure with repeatable coda. The final crescendo is balanced by the smaller one at the beginning, and by the still smaller one in lower strings before the general pause at the end of the A section. The A and C sections resemble each other, the strings (except double-bass) setting up a mass of improvised chromatic scurrying which becomes gradually clearer in section A, muddier in section C.

The contrasting middle section features a French horn solo (specially written for Eugene Rittich of the Toronto Symphony, who worked out a quarter-tone fingering for the instrument). The accompaniment uses mild sonorities – bell and gong sounds, whistling, and a sequence of consonant triads in the strings (almost like Vaughan Williams) mounting to a rich C-major chord, the calm centre of the piece.

But the main interest remains conceptual. Schafer's 'Afternote' cites Emile Durkheim's notion 'that in order to define the law the law must be broken, and therefore crime is necessary.' The public orchestra concert, a romantic invention, has evolved its own conventions, which Schafer's piece, by violating them, illuminates and challenges. Perhaps the best approach is to enumerate these conventions:

1 The concert hall provides a blank wall of silence to set off individual compositions one from another, but *No Longer Than Ten (10) Minutes* obliterates the frame, like one of those paintings whose contents spill out onto the gallery floor. It neither begins nor ends in silence; furthermore, it calls attention to the non-musical sounds of the concert hall, incorporating the tuning process into the composition.

2 John Cage has written that, with the point of disagreement between consonance and dissonance now past, 'it will be in the immediate future, between noise and so-called musical sounds.'[10] Schafer's piece, if it does not do away with the distinction, does obscure it, merging from one extreme to the other.

3 *No Longer Than Ten (10) Minutes* ridicules its own conductor. By including his movements in the score, it emphasizes his role as a performer in front of the music. He is not ineffectual, since he does cause things to happen, but the effect when he walks on stage is not immediately apparent. (The issue of the conductor's authority was challenged more directly at the premiere, for Victor Feldbrill, apprehensive, had instructed the percussionists to repeat the final crescendo only twice. Schafer, however, surreptitiously coaxed them to do the piece as written, thus placing the players at the center of a conflict between composer and conductor. Orchestral musicians are not wholly unfamiliar with this conflict, but normally the composer is at a disadvantage, being dead.)

4 Like *Son of Heldenleben*, this piece suggests an aura of slightly fractured romanticism, notably in the horn solo, which would not be far removed from *Oberon* but for the quarter tones.

5 Most romantic music is oriented towards a climax, but the notion of an infinitely repeatable climax is an aesthetic (not to mention biological) absurdity.

6 The audience, passive in relation to conventional music, in this piece determines both the outcome and duration of the piece. Moreover, the audience's applause, like the tune-up at the beginning, is incorporated into the composition as 'a cybernated wave-like motion' between the peaks of the repeated crescendo.

7 Most of Schafer's pieces since *Minnelieder* end quietly, but *No Longer Than Ten (10) Minutes* can hardly be said to end at all. After the crescendo-applause cycle has subsided. Schafer continues to prescribe various extraneous noises and furthermore insists on smudging into the next composition on the program. At a normal concert, pieces are

separated by silence, affecting each other only by juxtaposition; but this is another fiction of concert-going, since sound is continuous.

Curiously, Schafer at this same time was also writing his *String Quartet No. 1* (completed May 1970), a work similar in form but very different in concept. Although aesthetically the string quartet is just as conventional an institution as the orchestra, Schafer apparently felt no compulsion to undermine it, perhaps because it has never commanded the popular esteem of the orchestra or consumed the same quantities of government largesse. Given Schafer's work to this point, he might have seemed an unlikely candidate to compose a string quartet, but a commission from the Purcell Quartet drew from him one of his most successful and admired works.

The quartet belongs with the rugged tradition of modern quartet writing represented by Bartók, Carter, or Penderecki. It is written as a continuous movement in three clearly defined sections (fast, slow, fast) plus coda, using mostly definite pitches with occasional graphic notations; but, like other works of this period, it replaces bar lines with a time log, thus obviating rhythmic regularity. Schafer for the most part avoids cantabile and, as in his earlier works for strings, exploits massed sonorities, clusters, special glissando and pizzicato effects, and the like. The influence of electronic music is clear, though Schafer does not (like George Crumb) electrify the string quartet. Through most of the piece, except the middle section, all four instruments play all the time. The result (besides problems of page-turning) is a monolithic, block-like texture that threatens the kind of homophonic monotony that the early classical string quartet struggled to escape. But Schafer's textures are active internally, and they demand a responsiveness of the players to each other that creates an equivalent to the sophisticated give-and-take of the finest quartet writing. Consequently, the first string quartet is not only 'a veritable compendium of non-amplified sound generation techniques possible from the four stringed instruments,'[11] as Robert Skelton has remarked; but it evolves plausibly from the string quartet tradition. Schafer preserves the ideal of equal and interdependent parts within his stylistic framework of clusters, static sonorities, and unisons.

Like Schafer's best vocal works, the first string quartet is marked by a clear, though unprogrammatic, purpose. Each of the three sections expands a single gesture. The first (0″ to 4′00″) is a nearly uniform texture, sempre fortissimo, in the middle register from c down to F, developing out of the cluster of seven semitones contained in that

7.5 *String Quartet No. 1*: opening (in the composer's hand) (© 1973 by Universal Edition (Canada) Ltd., Toronto)

perfect fifth (example 7.5). This figure generates the entire first section. It is coloured by slow glissandi independently in the various parts, so that the cluster changes shape from within and effectively loses pitch identity. Other independent figures punctuate the general texture – chromatic fragments, accented appoggiaturas, savage *détaché* double stops, an abortive espressivo line in the first violin (*sul* G) – all helping to create, according to Schafer's note in the score, an 'impression of players locked together with each trying unsuccessfully to break away from the others.' This 'locked together' feeling is intensified by the prescribed uniform bowings (as much a visual as an aural effect), which from time to time become independent or, as the score says, 'ragged.'

The opening cluster recurs several times, but it also transforms itself into new but related sonorities. The passages of *détaché* and independent bowing become more frequent, accumulate, and finally overlap (after 2′20″), with all instruments accenting separate groupings furiously (example 7.6). Towards the end of this first section, these groupings grow calmer, and Schafer introduces metre signatures to draw the four instruments into a synchronized rhythmic pattern. The section closes with a passage of downward sliding double stops (triple stops in the cello), as if the opening cluster with its internal glissandi had expanded to the widest range of pitch.

Analysis of this section, as of the whole quartet, makes sense simply in terms of sonorities, but pitch organization is not irrelevant. A mere glance at the score will show that much of the material derives from the semitone cluster, which the composer apparently conceived in quasi-serial fashion. As he explained to Robert Skelton:

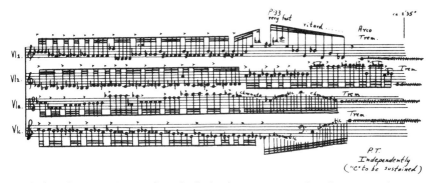

7.6 *String Quartet No. 1*: after 2'20" (in the composer's hand) (© 1973 by Universal Edition (Canada) Ltd., Toronto)

I always thought I needed some kind of row or serial procedure in this work ... The first 7 or 8 falling chromatic notes occur so often that they constitute a melodic grouping of some significance ... I know at the time I wrote the work I *wanted* to use a series though not necessarily a 12-tone series, and that I wanted to be very daring by taking as a starting point the unlikely material of the chromatic scale.[12]

This chromatic 'row' accounts for much of the material, but not all of it. Additional groups of notes appear together often enough to be called motifs, if not rows. Some are brief, like the four perfect fourths used chordally in the middle section and melodically elsewhere (these may derive from the perfect fifth of the opening cluster, or simply from the sound of open strings).

Another series is suggested in the second violin solo that begins the middle section. This solo, which marks the breakaway from the tight knot of dissonance that constitutes the first section, has 'a surprised quality gradually calming down.' It sets the tone of the middle section, using the higher registers and thinner textures, generally a solo line with accompanying pattern. It also states a version of the pitch series, which emphasizes semitones and minor thirds (example 7.7). The (*a*) group here derives from the semitone cluster. The (*c*) group reappears in several variants and also contains the (*b*) group, which becomes very prominent. The (*d*) group is the most frequently repeated elsewhere (example 7.8).

In the central section, Schafer devises two ingenious accompaniment effects. One applies his slow semitone glissando to a whole chord,

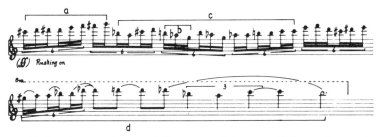

7.7 *String Quartet No. 1*: violin 2, transition to middle section at 4'10"
(© 1973 by Universal Edition (Canada) Ltd., Toronto)

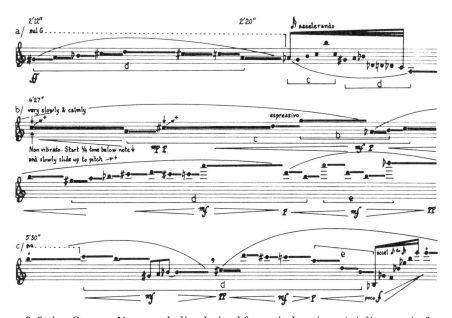

7.8 *String Quartet No. 1*: melodies derived from pitch series: a/ violin 1 at 2'12";
b/ violin 1 at 4'27"; c/ violin 1 at 5'30" (© 1973 by Universal Edition
(Canada) Ltd., Toronto)

sharped or flatted microtonally through several repetitions until it has
risen or fallen a semitone – an effect like an eerily prolonged Doppler
shift. Another works the gradual shift rhythmically: a pattern begins
with two instruments in unison; then one gradually speeds ahead of the
other and just as gradually slows down until the two instruments are

7.9 *String Quartet No. 1*: beginning of third section at 9'20" (in the composer's hand) (© 1973 by Universal Edition (Canada) Ltd., Toronto)

together again. Schafer notes the origin of this phase-shifting effect (explored exhaustively in several works by Steve Reich) in the machine, 'or more especially in the machine that employs belts as well as cogs. The cogged machine produces an unvarying clatter, but wherever belts are employed there is slippage giving rise to gradual rhythmic transformations.'[13]

In the last section, the four instruments are again locked together, not in a dissonant cluster but in a unison-octave line; the entire section consists of a gradual crescendo and accelerando over more than four pages of score. The overall gesture is varied, however, by rhythmic disruptions, by special effects assigned to one or two instruments only (pizzicato, tremolo, *col legno, sul ponticello,* glissando), and by breakaways parallel to those in the first section, forming moments of heterophony against the forward rushing octave line (example 7.9). At first the momentum is increased by larger and larger groupings in ligatures, from 2:1 to 8:1 (♩ to 𝄐); then, with a drop in dynamic level, the pattern is reversed from 8:1 to 2:1, although the accelerando continues unabated.

The pitches of this long passage in octaves are derived from all the groupings already introduced. In effect, the quartet begins with an amorphous semitone cluster, gradually evolves perceptible motifs through the middle section, and then proceeds to drive them into pandemonium. A fragment of the passage illustrates how the motifs are combined (example 7.10).

About in the middle of the long accelerando, the cello begins the first

7.10 *String Quartet No. 1*: violin II just before 13'00" (© 1973 by Universal Edition (Canada) Ltd., Toronto)

of four cadenzas passed up the ranks of the quartet, improvised within controls set by the composer's instructions:

The notes of the cadenzas are the same as those of the other players. The impression must be one of growing frenzy – in the end almost chaos ... The notes may be employed in any octave transposition, and the series should be repeated as often as necessary to fill the duration indicated. Special effects (pizz., ponticelli, multiple stops, dynamic contrasts, knocking effects, etc.) should be employed.

The accelerando continues in octaves after the wildly agitated first violin cadenza until all the instruments reach the fastest possible speed, intonation disintegrates, and the three upper instruments play very high notes ad libitum as fast as possible, while the cello puts on the brakes. Thus, like *No Longer Than Ten (10) Minutes*, the piece begins chaotically in a state of nearly indefinite pitch, progresses through a clearly defined slow middle section, and returns in the end to chaos.[14]

The quartet does not end here, however, but, returning to the opening semitone cluster, leads into a coda section that consists entirely of moments lifted out of context from earlier in the work, or, as the composer suggests, 'snapshots of previous events.' The 'snap' in each case is a sharp Bartók pizzicato from the cello, which intoduces each recollected event. Towards the end, the composer begins to separate each event with longer and longer spaces of silence in addition to the pizzicato. Previously, breathing spaces had been provided only in the midst of the middle section and leading into the third section; here, the silences suggest the final stages of exhaustion, or, in the metaphor of composer's notes, the 'camera' goes on snapping even though the 'film' has run out: 'Ergo, for the pauses between the final snaps the players should remain absolutely motionless.' The silences thus arouse anticipation, leaving the audience uncertain when the quartet is ended.

In 1973, Schafer produced two geographical works for orchestra, *North/White* and *East*, in contrasting moods, angry and contemplative. *North/White* grows directly out of the soundscape theory, as does the litte piece called *Train* (1976). Both were written with young people in mind, *North/White* for the National Youth Orchestra of Canada and *Train* for school orchestra. *North/White* is Schafer's most self-consciously Canadian work since *Brébeuf* (a hypothetical *West* by Schafer is imaginable, but a *South*, never): the whiteness and spaciousness of the Canadian Arctic, he writes, corresponds 'to a sense of purity ... Labrador is temptationless.'[15] But this mythic integrity is being destroyed by the industrialization of the North, and Schafer's program note voices his protest: 'When they chop into the North, they chop into [our] minds, blocking the awe-inspiring mysteries with gas stations and reducing legends to plastic dolls.'

Schafer's most spectacular expression of this 'rape of the Canadian North,' as he terms it, is his introduction of a snowmobile into the orchestra. Snowmobiles have 'now made deafness and ear disease the largest public health problem in the Canadian Arctic,' he writes. 'The Canadian winter used to be noted for its purity and serenity. It was part of the Canadian mythology. The snowmobile has bitched the myth. Without a myth the nation dies.'[16]

But the snowmobile is only one component in the sculpted sound mass that makes up the piece, which moves farther than ever in the direction of non-linear densities. The pitch material, as in the first string quartet, is a downward spreading cluster (F–B♭), but here Schafer packs the spaces with quarter-tones ('white' in the title refers to white noise as well as snow). More important to the overall effect, however, is the concentration of harsh metallic sounds, either sustained or in pounding reiterations. Brass instruments and metallic percussion predominate, with some unconventional effects: two suspended metal sheets, one tin (dull), one steel (bright); four suspended metal pipes; one corrugated metal surface; a large chain. And while the pitch of the composition stabilizes on B♭ and F, the violins insist on their steely open E.

The result is imposing, even terrifying; but whether it fulfils the composer's programmatic intentions is debatable. So much emphasis on quasi-technological sounds leaves the myth of purity too much in the background. True, it is not wholly obliterated: the quiet opening moments with two off-stage trumpets are effective. Another percussion novelty, two masonite boards flapped back and forth, evokes the menace of the Arctic wind, as do passages whistled by the players; a sung downward glissando closes the piece like a dying sigh. But the negative concept of purity requires more emphatic dramatization. Furthermore, the industrial sounds, though overpowering, do not in themselves relay Schafer's private attitudes. Even the snowmobile passage in the last few minutes recalls nothing so much as Alexander Mossolov's once-fashionable *Iron Foundry* – a piece intended to celebrate the triumphs of technology. As a composer, Schafer can only invite us to enter his biases in program notes; his music, however, can only present the sounds.

Curiously, *Train*, an unpretentious work, presents sharper contrasts. A *jeu d'esprit* tossed off lightly, it is the best of Schafer's shorter educational pieces. It also possesses the unusual virtue of being one of the funniest scores, visually, in music. Schafer feels more ambivalent about trains than about snowmobiles: 'Of all the sounds of the Industrial Revolution, those of trains seem across time to have taken on the most attractive sentimental associations.'[17] To a Canadian especially, trains have unifying rather than destructive connotations, the railway long being recognized as the spinal column of Confederation. The poet Earle Birney has exploited this feeling in his sound poem 'Trawna tuh Belvul by Knayjun Psifik,' a striking analogue to Schafer's piece.

Train was inspired, during a six-day train journey, by the CPR schedule. Schafer determined to translate the distance from Vancouver to Montreal (4633 km) into time, and the altitudes of the stations into pitch. Across this gridwork, he arranges three instrumental groups: the strings, forming the underlying mass of sound, rise and fall with the terrain of the land; brass and winds, off-stage, interject an E♭-minor triad (the sound of the CPR whistle); percussion marks the cities – louder for large cities, bells for night and wood for day, pleasant sounds for picturesque towns or dissonant clashes for the ugly (Winnipeg and Sudbury sound particularly horrendous). Notations for these sounds are delightfully coded into diagrams of train signals, and the pleasure of reading the score should not be reserved for the players (example 7.11). A performance might incorporate projections, maps, or other stage props.

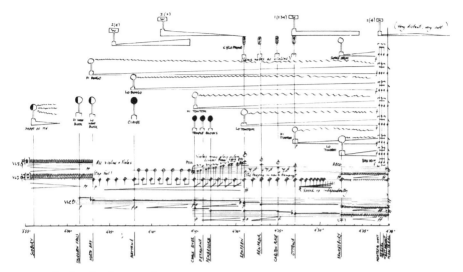

7.11 *Train*: final page of score

For all its flippancy, *Train* makes musical sense. The strings rise at once to quiet heights (Rocky Mountains), then gradually accumulate density. The train stops employ a wide range of contrasting sounds, from gentle bells to the heavy metal of industry, coming faster and faster as the train moves east. The Eb-minor whistle fixes tonality. 'This deep and haunting whistle,' writes Schafer, 'provides the unifying soundmark of the nation. More than any other sound it is uncounterfeitingly Canadian.'[18] He does not mention that Eb minor is the tonality of Wagner's *Götterdämmerung* – a fact that may or may not be symbolic.

Three remaining works – *East, String Quartet No. 2 ('Waves'),* and *Cortège* – all speak from the contemplative side of Schafer.

Related in subject to *Lustro, East* is a modest score for small orchestra with winds in pairs and strings muted throughout. It concentrates on soft, self-consciously beautiful sonorities, spinning out an almost uniform texture for eight minutes of hypnotic ritual. Five gongs plus tam-tam mark the progress of the piece, struck at ten-second intervals from smallest to largest; the cycle is repeated eight times. Gongs, like bells in the West, have acquired religious connotations, though the gong, Schafer notes, is 'more mellow, more diffused'; there is 'more aggression in the bell.' Both are sound equivalents of the Jungian mandala, symbol of wholeness or perfection.[19] The ten-second intervals are an extension of the ♩ = 60 conductor's beat of earlier works, but the slower pulse of the gong-strokes creates a sense of extreme slow motion. The one-second norm seems related to the human heartbeat (60 or 80 to the minute), but slower rhythm is found in breathing:

Normal breathing is said to vary between 12 and 20 cycles per minute, that is, 3 to 5 seconds per cycle. But breathing may be slowed down during relaxation or sleep to cycles lasting 6 to 8 seconds. Part of the sense of well-being we feel at the seashore undoubtedly has to do with the fact that the relaxed breathing pattern shows surprising correspondences with the rhythms of the breakers, which, while never regular, often produce an average cycle of 8 seconds.[20]

If so, then slower ten-second cycles may be related to the controlled breathing practised in yoga meditation. The relation of breath and wave rhythms also has implications for *String Quartet No. 2*.

In *East*, Schafer manipulates the spatial as well as the temporal dimension. As in *Lustro*, he separates groups of instruments from the main orchestra on stage – two trios of flute, trumpet, and horn, one stationed backstage and the other at the rear of the auditorium. These all have associations with outdoor space – the pastoral flute, the horn with its unlocatable woodland sound, the trumpet as an outdoor signal. Furthermore, Schafer directs the trumpet players to turn slowly while playing their notes, passing their bells across the audience and creating an uncanny sensation of movement in space. The gongs, too, are difficult sounds to localize, and they produce an elusive sense of pitch that Schafer exploits by instructing players to 'hum the pitch of the gong,' thus generating soft clusters around each gong stroke. Together with these devices, special effects from the orchestra, especially vocal effects – humming, singing, pronouncing phonemes, whispering, whistling – heighten uncertainty about the location and nature of the sound sources.

Except for these vocal effects, *East* is a purely instrumental composition; yet the pitches are all determined by an unheard and paradoxical Sanskrit text from the *Isha-Upanishad* translated in the score. As in the later *Arcana*, Schafer assigns a pitch to each letter of the text (example 7.12). The quarter-tones heighten the Oriental flavour, though the numbers (indicating frequency of occurrence) show that Schafer assigns the least frequent letters to the quarter-tones.

The cryptogram element of *East*, which injects a measure of

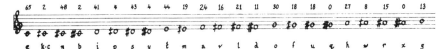

7.12 *East*: correlation of pitches and letters of the text (numbers indicate incidences of each letter)

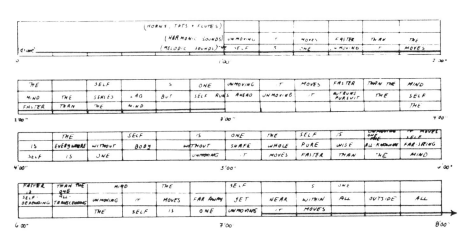

7.13 *East*: plan printed from score (© Copyright 1977 by Universal Edition (Canada) Ltd.)

composer-indeterminacy, may seem trivial or merely ingenious, but as in *Arcana* it ultimately makes musical sense. This emerges from the total plan of the work as printed in the score (example 7.13). The complete text appears only in the background of the piece, yielding the full complement of pitches. The foreground, dominated by prominent melodic motifs in the orchestra and the solo instruments, is limited solely to the first two sentences of the text: 'The self is one. Unmoving it moves faster than the mind.' Thus each pitch-encoded word appears several times, the solo instruments echoing motifs sounded in the orchestra. In each motif, the pitches (in whatever octave) are spaced evenly across the ten-second time interval, producing a stately, slow-motion melodic line (example 7.14). The word 'the' is most frequent, while 'unmoving' and 'moves' are linked by a common three-note cell. Although obscured by octave transpositions, these motifs are rhythmically stable and remain recognizable.

7.14 *East*: melodic motifs formed by words of the text

The *String Quartet No. 2 ('Waves')* is closely related to *East*. More than twice as long, it is tonally less complex but rhythmically more subtle. It too employs the long bars and justifies them programmatically on a basis of environmental rhythms. It too is a textural work, more daringly minimal in its materials than *East*, reaching a discernible but scarcely emphasized climactic area (too diffuse to be called a climax) at about 14'00". Musically simpler than the first, though a couple of minutes longer, the second quartet is Schafer's inventive response to the challenge of producing a fit mate for its predecessor without repeating its effects.

This work is Schafer's fullest attempt to translate into music the ocean sounds that inspired *Okeanos*. 'In the course of the World Soundscape Project,' he notes in the score, 'we recorded and analysed ocean waves on both the Atlantic and Pacific coasts of Canada. The recurrent pattern of waves is always asymmetrical but we have noted that the duration from crest to crest usually falls between 6 and 11 seconds.' Schafer, bending nature to art, rationalizes this asymmetry into an elastic rhythmic pattern with bar lengths of 6", 7", 8", 9", 10", 11", 11", 10", 9", 8", 7", 6", and so on. These bars, however, having no gongs to mark them, depend for recognition on the wave-like mounting density of texture at the bar lines, and on subtle shifts of pattern: 'I have sought to give the quartet a liquid quality in which everything is constantly dissolving and flowing into everything else. That is to say, the material of the work is not fixed, but is perpetually changing, and even though certain motivic figures are used repeatedly they undergo continual dynamic, rhythmic, and tempo variation.'

This fluidity of motif is almost wholly rhythmic, contained within a drastically attenuated supply of pitch patterns. Virtually the whole

7.15 *String Quartet No. 2*: pitch material

eighteen-minute composition is spun out of two ideas. The predominating idea is a seven-note scale containing an exotic-sounding augmented second. (This is the first time since *Brébeuf* that Schafer has leaned so heavily on a scale device.) The other deploys the remaining five chromatic notes in a sequence of unequal fourths (example 7.15). Of the three intervals found in the second motif, the tritone is prominent, emphasized through the quartet, as is the perfect fourth E–A, which Schafer describes as the call of the white-throated sparrow that he heard outside his rural Ontario home while writing the piece.[21] In the scale motif, the emphasis on D, particularly the E♭–D figure at the beginning, establishes a clear tonal reference which never becomes wholly obscured, even though attention shifts to other pitches later on. Almost every note of the piece is an articulation of one of these two patterns.

This description suggests that the second quartet moves in the direction of recent exercises in calculated monotony – Steve Reich's *Violin Phase* comes to mind, a piece that left its imprint on the first quartet. But any sacrifice of alertness to sound really runs counter to Schafer's thinking. The stationary pitch spectrum of *Waves* is animated by the unequal fluctuations of bar length, and within them the smaller rhythmic patterns alter and develop with great subtlety. The effect (though the procedures differ) is analogous to the Indian ragas, which sound monotonous to Western ears because of their static pitch arrangements but compensate with a rhythmic intricacy rare in Western music. This is a more profound Orientalism than the exotic scale or the quarter-tones that Schafer introduces about half-way through the piece; and, through its rhythmic correspondence with the natural world, the second quartet expresses a more persuasive Oriental spirit than works like *Gita* or *East*.

A couple of bars from the first page will illustrate (example 7.16). The notational device here elaborates ad libitum repetitions usually reserved for accompaniment figures; but Schafer's occupy the foreground, and he rings the changes on them most inventively (example 7.17). The metronome markings provide an important element of control by the composer over these free patterns, though of course there is no need to synchronize the four instruments within the bar unit. Later, between

7.16 *String Quartet No. 2*: at 0′13″

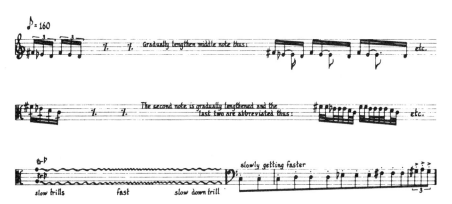

7.17 *String Quartet No. 2*: typical motifs: a/ violin 1 at 1′36″; b/ viola at 1′55″; c/ viola at 10′07″; d/ cello at 11′43″

9′16″ and 14′16″, Schafer introduces 'secondary wave motions … until each player is moving in an independent wave motion.' The texture there becomes so complex that Schafer drops the large bar units and resorts to bars of one second, returning after the climax to the simpler patterns of the opening.

Despite the climactic swell, the quartet is non-teleological, thus raising the issue of a suitable ending. Schafer returns full circle to the beginning. In addition, he specifies that the members of the quartet leave the stage one by one, moving out 'almost as if in a trance' – even though they continue playing from off-stage. The cellist, who cannot move while playing, is left alone. When the others are gone, Schafer instructs him to set down his bow, take up a spyglass, and look out slowly where they have left, then pan slowly across the audience.

Schafer does not intend this effect to be funny, but it inevitably provokes laughter, and after several performances he has had second thoughts and marked it optional. Personally, I suspect that this theatrical measure is out of keeping with an otherwise untheatrical atmosphere, and that the oceanography of the composition is not as literal as the effect attempts to make it. But the ending from off-stage does have a musical purpose. The piece ends as it began on the flatted supertonic (a favoured degree of the scale ever since *Minnelieder*), a sustained low E♭ in the cello.

Cortège (1977) is another of Schafer's efforts to subvert the concert ritual, but this time it is more constructive than parodic. It is really a piece of musical theatre, though it is wholly instrumental. The musicians are required to march in procession (hence the title), as well as perform various gestures, dance steps, and so on. The entire action takes place in slow motion, quietly, hypnotically. All the musicians are masked. They enter gradually; some of the action takes place on stage, some amid the audience; solo players enter and exit; at the end, all file out, playing the last notes from outside the hall. The score gives some indications for these movements, but since *Cortège* depends on them so heavily, they must be carefully choreographed either by the conductor or someone else (Schafer staged it himself at the premiere, which received a standing ovation).

Cortège is not complex music, but it focuses several of Schafer's earlier devices in a single work. The ritual element recalls the choral work *In Search of Zoroaster*, performed with action and costume, though such spectacle is much more startling in the context of a staid orchestral concert. (Theatre has been invading *avant-garde* music for two decades now, of course, as in a piece like George Crumb's *Echoes of Time and the River*, which also exhibits hieratic processions of musicians.) The masks and rigid movements underline the anonymity of orchestral players; balletic movements prescribed for the conductor in the score dramatize his quasi-mystical power over them. However, since the performers are mobile, as in *Zoroaster*, Schafer is obliged to keep the music itself fairly simple.

But there is more to the work than just visual spectacle. Extending the antiphonal effects of *Lustro* and the use of mobile musicians of *East*, the processions of *Cortège* make their point aurally as well as visually: winds call to each other across the auditorium, while the unwary listener may be startled by an oboe at his ear. The ostinato patterns that mainly constitute the piece (easily memorized by the musicians) shift and intermingle with a fluidity recalling the second quartet. The various patterns are sharply contrasted rather than uniform, as in the previous work, but the tonal material is limited mainly to the c major scale plus some admixture of F♯ and B♭, so that the scarcity of accidentals is surprising in a contemporary score. Consequently, the piece generates a soothing diatonic mesh of freely interweaving patterns. With its simple musical devices and its spectacular showmanship, *Cortège* is perhaps Schafer's most constructive solution to the problem of writing for the orchestral medium that he so often claims to dislike.

8

Vocal and choral works since 1965

Works related to *Patria*

Unquestionably, Schafer's most distinctive music has a theatrical flair. Four vocal works were chiefly responsible for establishing his international reputation in the years immediately after *Loving*, giving impetus to his most prolific decade. Two of these, *Threnody* and *Epitaph for Moonlight*, are educational pieces that accommodate Schafer's idiom to the understanding of young people. Two others, however, make no compromises: *Gita* won a *succès d'estime* at the Tanglewood Festival in 1967, though it has not been performed since; *Requiems for the Party-Girl*, on the other hand, is Schafer's most frequently heard work apart from *Epitaph*. It has been recorded three times; it received the Fromm Music Foundation Award in 1968; and it has been conducted in New York by Bruno Maderna and in England by Pierre Boulez.

The composition of *Requiems* repeated the pattern of *Loving*: in 1966, commissioned by the CBC to write a new work for Phyllis Mailing, Schafer seized the opportunity to sketch another stage work, eventually to become *Patria II*. Seven of his pieces over the next few years were subsequently written both as independent works and as portions of *Patria*. Most share a family likeness stemming from a common tone-row, and Schafer's sheerly musical inventiveness is nowhere more evident than in the variety of statements wrung from the same material.

Unlike the four arias of *Loving*, *Requiems for the Party-Girl* does not exist as a single block of music within *Patria II* but is distributed as arias through the piece. Altogether, the 'requiems' last about sixteen minutes of the ninety-minute stage work, and in so far as there is a narrative line at all, they encapsulate the whole up to and including the party girl's suicide, in effect outlining the drama in miniature.

Schafer's score describes the girl (Ariadne in the stage work) as 'gay-tragic,' one of those 'strange harlequinesque creatures one meets occasionally at parties.' Actually, neither the arias nor the stage work exhibit much gaiety (the grotesque party appears in *Patria 1*). Neither do the arias contain much hint of the asylum setting of the stage work, but the text unmistakably portrays an *Angst*-stricken soul *in extremis*, though simply enough that the sense can emerge through a rather complex musical setting. The text, Schafer's own, consists of ten brief fragments of contrasting character. Some contain nonsense concocted by a random disarrangement of English syllables ('mursing murvoice vocat con ingmur secon ...'). One is a trilingual sequence of words chosen more for connotation and vowel sound than for sense ('Allein alone âme soul seele moon mond lune allein – seul'). The last and longest is a straightforward six-sentence narrative of Ariadne's suicide. The first-person stance intensifies the situation, especially the girl's feeling of isolation, but the spectacle of the girl describing her own suicide and singing her own requiem in effect places the protagonist in a higher sphere, bringing an element of detachment to a subject that could otherwise have become overwrought.

The success of *Requiems for the Party-Girl* does not lie in the intensity of its evocation of insanity (this subject has been common property of nearly all serialists, probably because serialism conveys so well both the apparent irrationality and the concealed logic of madness); rather, as the composer Bruce Mather has noted, *Requiems* works through a rapid 'juxtaposition of diverse styles' ... 'The ridiculous and the tragic intermingle in order to create the frenetic atmosphere of nightmare and ambiguity that characterizes the life of the party-girl.'[1] The texts are short, sometimes haiku-like, and the settings are miniatures depending mainly on imitative sonorities. The danger of such a work, as Mather remarks, 'where every poetic nuance finds its reflection, where there is a mosaic of ideas and styles, is to fall into anecdotalism.' Whether Schafer avoids the danger is not, I suppose, susceptible to demonstration; the pieces are arranged for contrast, but in no necessary order, though beginning and ending are clearly defined. The sequence presents fragmented spots of time, irridescent glimpses into the party-girl's world, separated and objectified by breathing spaces of silence.

1 Aria 1 asserts the dramatic subject, 'I am about to commit suicide,' beginning quietly and building to a scream. It states only ten notes of the series, leaving it open-ended.

II 'Voices gossiping in other rooms' are heard in a pattering figure for harp and piano; they are interrupted suddenly, for 'no one listens,' then resume.

III Voice and instruments pulsate on stationary pitches (all twelve inclusive). The text ('Allein alone âme ...') suggests the murmuring of catatonic introspection.

IV The music subtly but audibly symbolizes the text: 'Everywhere I go I leave a part of myself. I am afraid that soon there will be nothing left of me.' The musical symbolism is ingenious: in the first sentence, an instrument sustains each successive pitch of the voice at the unison or octave; in the second, the voice returns in retrograde, while the instruments release.

V The setting is mainly declamatory, with sparse atmospheric effects and fragments imitating the one melodic gesture in the voice part (see example 8.4). The word 'visitors' perhaps suggests the triangle (doorbell?) and the tom-tom stroke (slamming door?). An ostinato pattern expresses repetitive action ('people are coming and going and ...'). At the end, instrumentalists are given lines of dialogue to speak, all simultaneously.

VI The word 'confused' elicits a vocal line of indefinite pitches linked by irregular curves, accompanied by sweeping harp glissandi (pedals changed ad libitum) and by Morse code drummed out loudly. The coded message is as enigmatic to the audience as it is, presumably, to the protagonist, but the rhythms are suitably jittery. (The message duplicates the vocal text.) In the middle, on 'life fades before fear of death,' there is a ritardando, the accompaniment evaporates, and the voice line becomes definite in pitch and almost tonal. The section concludes with a return to the nervous Morse-code rhythms now in the instruments, while the soloist hums quietly.

VII Here the text is mostly abstract, though the melodic intervals reflect the words 'grows' and 'diminishes.' The accompanying parts are chiefly pulsating pitches, as in III.

VIII The gradual rhythmic compression and panting manner of the opening line express fear; the grotesque line about 'a holiday in Florida' is set in exaggerated declamation, with wide intervals and fussy rhythms – in Mather's phrase, 'espèce d'expressionisme de faux Schoenberg' – leading to a fortissimo outburst in tam-tam and timpani.

IX To render 'voices of the world become fainter and fewer,' each note is separated from the next by a silence of several seconds. The music is almost immobile, catatonic.

X–XII After the attenuation of section IX, the suicide narrative is fast,

8.1 *Patria*: series

loud, and fully scored. The voice alternates rapidly between definite pitch, speech, a scream, and stylized laughter (repeated on one note and imitated in the instruments, sounding like machine-gun fire). The narrative subsides on the word 'death,' into a welcome espressivo passage, followed by the concluding 'Requiem' (see example 8.4c), dominated by the ecclesiastical associations of the tubular chimes.

The internal organization of *Requiems* is based on the same all-interval series that dominates the entire *Patria* sequence. This series has peculiar properties. Not only does it contain all the possible intervals, but its retrograde form is identical with the original transposed a tritone away, while the inversions are all but undistinguishable from the original (example 8.1). In *Requiems*, as through the entire sequence, Schafer characteristically confines himself (if not strictly) to the series in its untransposed form. As Bruce Mather has noted, 'it is remarkable that one never feels this as a limitation of material, such is the imagination with which he managed this series.' It is all the more remarkable in that Schafer projects this material through the whole of *Patria*. This is no less true, even allowing for the amount of non-serial matter – speech, percussion, indefinite pitch passages, and the like – that Schafer admits to his music. (Other composers have also used versions of this series – for example, Luigi Nono in *Canto Sospeso*, and André Prévost in his *Violin Sonata*.)

Melodically, the series generates clearly recognizable motifs of either expanding or contracting intervals, either a crescendo or diminuendo of intervallic tension. Schafer perhaps arrived at his series through such a melodic process, for his earliest series in *Minnelieder* is somewhat similar (see example 3.2), as is that of *Protest and Incarceration* (example 4.1b), and the whole turns up in Modesty's aria from *Loving* as a melodic gesture (example 5.6). More than most series, this one retains its *Gestalt* and provides a melodic principle readily apparent to the ear, even when subjected to unorthodox transformations. Fragments not infrequently appear in pure form (example 8.2). More often,

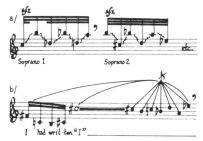

8.2 Voice lines based on *Patria* series: a/ *Gita*, page 28 of score; b/ *Requiems for the Party-Girl*, aria x (8.2a: © Copyright 1977 by Universal Edition (Canada) Ltd.)

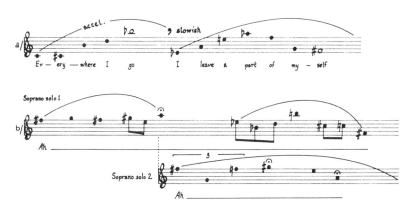

8.3 Voice lines based on *Patria* series: a/ *Requiems for the Party-Girl*, aria IV; b/ *Gita*, page 20 of score; (8.3b: © Copyright 1977 by Universal Edition (Canada) Ltd.)

the series is disguised by octave transposition – often enough for the melodic contours to become familiar (example 8.3). Other variants play freely on the semitone patterns and the fulcrum on C or F♯ (example 8.4).

Harmonically, the series as stated sequentially lacks any characteristic intervals for building chordal structures, and it resists triadic formations; but the semitone patterns, ascending and descending, remain audible. In *Gita*, they become the basis for a rugged brass fanfare, expressing wordly disorder, and also an expanding semitone cluster, expressing spiritual wholeness. Both are recurrent gestures throughout the piece (example 8.5).

8.4 Voice lines based on free expansion of *Patria* series: *Requiems for the Party-Girl*: a/ aria v; b/ aria VIII; c/ aria X; d/ *Hymn to Night*, page 39 of score (8.4d: © R. Murray Schafer, 1976)

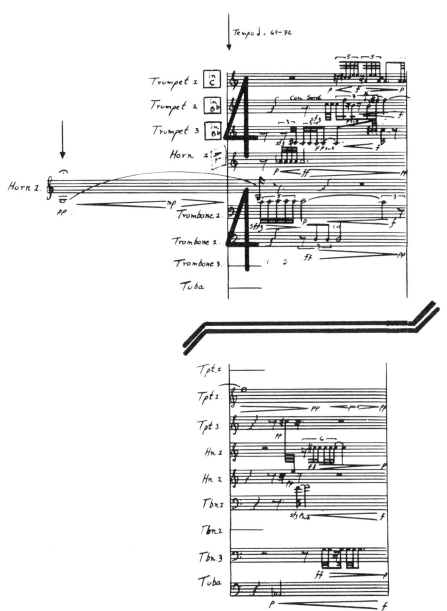

8.5a Chordal statements of *Patria* series: *Gita*, page 1 of score (in the composer's hand) (© Copyright 1977 by Universal Edition (Canada) Ltd.)

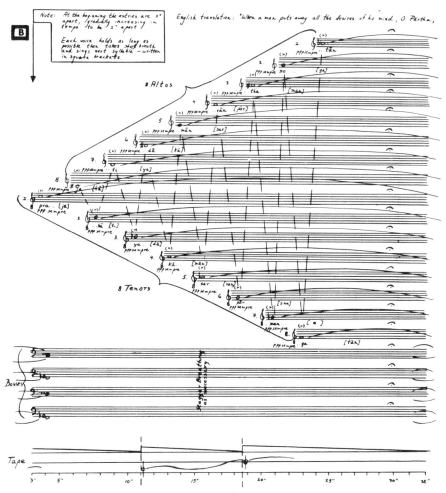

8.5b Chordal statement of *Patria* series: *Gita*, page 4 of score (in the composer's hand) (© Copyright 1977 by Universal Edition (Canada) Ltd.)

If *Requiems* retains its directness, *Gita* (written April–June 1967) remains arcane (although at the climax of *Patria I* it provides effective musical counterpoint for the stage events). *Gita* is nonetheless a moving piece of music undeservedly neglected since its Tanglewood premiere in 1967, when it was acclaimed by Irving Lowens: 'With his *Gita* ... Schafer ran away from the field ... *Gita* was the high point of the Fromm Festival.'[2] In the context of a contemporary music festival, *Gita* perhaps benefited from the mist of obscurantism that composers sometimes use to make their objects appear larger than they are; but the esoteric aura of the Sanskrit text (paraphrased for convenience in the score) if anything blunts the impact of the piece, which, like *Requiems*, depicts text-inspired effects. Also, Schafer's fragmentation of the words would give even a Sanskrit-speaking audience difficulty. Such treatment of words has its musical justification, but it still necessitates a written explanation. *Gita* is thus 'programmatic' in a way that *Requiems* is not. It must remain a piece for the initiate.

Schafer draws his text from the Hindu *Bhagavad Gita* (II 55–64). This source need not be considered esoteric, for the *Bhagavad Gita*, which T.S. Eliot called 'the next greatest philosophical poem to the *Divine Comedy*,'[3] long ago entered Western consciousness through the romanticism of the Schlegels in Germany and Emerson in the United States. The ten verses set by Schafer, which sum up one of the central doctrines of the poem, are spoken by the deity Krishna to the mortal prince Arjuna, who is seeking spiritual enlightenment in the midst of warfare. 'The soul that moves in the world of the senses,' Krishna advises, 'yet keeps the senses in harmony, free from attraction and aversion, finds rest in quietness' (II 64). In other words, Krishna counsels disinterestedness – participation in the warfare of the sensuous world but spiritual detachment from it. Such a course breeds conflicts, which the musical polarities of Schafer's piece dramatize.

This conflict is the crux of Schafer's program note: 'The text describes how one should proceed in attaining serenity of spirit and details the dangers of egoism and passion. Breaking through the mysterious and omnipresent sounds of the choir and tape are occasional harsh intrusions from brass instruments. Their brutal interference with the mystical exercise really constitutes a second piece of music and certainly a different philosophy.' Schafer enumerates his musical forces – four-part mixed choir (thirty-two voices), nine brass instruments, and tape – but their functions in the piece are not quite so well defined. The brass provide disruptions – but so does the tape, loudly, even though softer bell and gong sounds prevail most of the time. And the choir, enacting the part of the soul, represents both the search for serenity and the contrary pull of the senses. Furthermore, while the brass entrances may sound like a second piece of music in character, they are of course based on the same series. In the passage cited above in example 8.5a, no two beats are subdivided alike and no two figures contain the same number of notes in anacrusis; dynamics are contradictory, and only one instrument is muted. The symbolic suggestion is of worldly multiplicity; as a fanfare, it recalls the warlike context of the *Bhagavad Gita*.

The choral writing in *Gita* bridges the transition between the conventional serialism of the Tagore songs and the almost wholly graphic scores that follow. For the most part, Schafer writes definite pitches, making stiff demands on the accuracy of the choristers, but he also includes sections of indeterminate pitch and rhythm.

Formally, *Gita*, like *Requiems for the Party-Girl*, is a sequence of events determined by the ten verses of the text, punctuated by the brass. In the first five verses, where spiritual character dominates, choir and tape remain subdued while the brass intrusions progressively weaken. In the next four, where Krishna warns against temptations of the senses, the brass gain strength again while the chorus and tape become more agitated, building to a climax on the ninth verse. In the last, calm is restored.

1 'When a man puts away all the desires of his mind, O Partha, and when his spirit is stable in itself, then he is called stable in intelligence.' The opening fanfare is sounded twice, separated by long, measured pauses. The basses intone the sacred syllable 'Om' on two deep tritones a semitone apart (B–F, C–F♯), as the middle voices softly expand from c through the row into a semitone cluster, varied by gentle internal movement before dissolving in soft whistles (see example 8.5b).

2 'He whose mind is untroubled in the midst of sorrows and is free from eager desire amid pleasures, he from whom passion, fear and rage have passed away, he is called a sage of settled intelligence.' The brass figure again introduces an expanding cluster with internal movement, converging finally on F♯. At the end the brass interrupt briefly, urging the voices to sweep into a thirty-two part cluster, fortissimo, followed by an outburst from the tape.

3 Here the attenuated texture reflects the text: 'He who draws away the senses from the objects of sense on every side as a tortoise draws in his limbs, his intelligence is firmly set in wisdom.'⁴ At the end, after brief brass comment, the women's voices rise in a rippling pattern, forte, before dissolving, subito pianissimo, into free glissandi and soft whistles.

4 'His intelligence is firmly set who is without affection on any side, who does not rejoice or loathe as he obtains good or evil.' For the first time, a melodic line emerges, unaccompanied (the series, thinly disguised by octave displacement), only to fragment into spoken bits rising in volume over mutterings from the brass.

5 'The objects of sense turn away from the embodied soul, who abstains from feeding on them, but the taste for them remains. Even the taste

turns away when the supreme is seen.' Here, as in the first two verses, the voices enter on the notes of the series, but arranged differently, not sustaining a cluster but growing in volume; when they reach the final F♯, fortissimo, a tape outburst heightens the gathering climax. Two solo sopranos (see example 8.3b), then a tenor, sing brief lines based on the retrograde.

6 'Even though a man may strive for perfection and be ever so discerning, his impetuous senses will carry off his mind by force.' A *Sprechgesang* roulade ushers in the brass, absent from the previous section, and leads to a louder tape outburst than before. Over this, the choir rises to a measure containing sixteen conflicting rhythmic patterns in the upper voices.

7 'Having brought all the senses under control, he should remain firm in yoga, intent on me; for he whose senses are under control, his intelligence is firmly set.' This verse is a calm before the major climax, with the choir again evolving a near cluster and even moving into something like block harmony, as brass and tape continue to threaten.

8 'When a man dwells in his mind on the objects of sense, attachment to them is produced. From attachment to them springs desire, and from desire comes anger.' A bass solo (marked 'dramatic') begins a passage of speaking, shouting, and forced breathing noises from the choir. The spiritual character is maintained in the tape, where an Oriental priest is heard reciting, and moments later, the recorded voice of Rabindranath Tagore, almost drowned by the clamour; the tape also produces loud echoing shouts and synthesized sounds.

9 'From anger arises bewilderment, from bewilderment loss of memory, and from loss of memory the destruction of intelligence, and from the destruction of intelligence he perishes.' The brass, restrained during the last verse, grow into their loudest, most sustained passage, supported by a swell of white noise on the tape; the choir merges from a chaotic passage of random pitch into a unison (or near unison) line based on the series, which rises to a slow, wailing oscillation, almost like a wide vibrato over the interval of a minor third. The brass crescendo to the end of the section, a fortissimo G-major cluster over the lowest C of the tuba, while sopranos sustain F♯ above it, almost inaudibly.

10 'But a man of disciplined mind who moves among objects of sense with the senses under control and free from attachment and aversion, he attains purity of spirit.' Schafer's most dramatic stroke occurs here, as the brass chord suddenly cuts off, resolving magically into a choral passage by Heinrich Schütz on the tape, while the live sopranos move

from their F♯ (dissonant against the D♭-major Schütz passage) into a quiet lyrical sequence that seems to echo the archaic part-writing texture dying away on the tape. The Schütz passage (in which Christ is mentioned) evokes the Western equivalent of Krishna's 'purity of mind.' At the end, a unison C slides into the same cluster heard earlier (letter G), and the basses close with their double tritone chord on the syllable 'Om.'

From the Tibetan Book of the Dead (1968) strikes a vein very like that of *Gita*, not surprisingly, since it is the major chorus of *Patria II*. Again, Schafer sets an esoteric language, Tibetan (using the International Phonetic Alphabet in the score), thus requiring certain explication. The *Bardo Thödol*, or *Tibetan Book of the Dead*, is not merely a Buddhist funeral rite but a set of instructions to the dying person preparing him for his stay in the Bardo, or after-death, state.[5] Great importance is attached to the person's mental state at the exact moment of dying, since this determines the form of his reincarnation, so particular messages are whispered into the person's ear during the last minutes in order to focus the consciousness properly. Schafer's portion of the *Bardo Thödol* (literally, 'Liberation by Hearing on the After-Death Plane') is such a whispered message, appearing near the beginning of the work, and his piece enacts the death of Ariadne and her entrance into after-life; there she will first experience perfect enlightenment, and then through a series of experiences lasting forty-nine days will descend to the earthly womb for rebirth. Schafer's piece, then, is more strictly other-worldly than *Gita*, not a dramatization of tensions but a dreamlike ritual. It has none of *Gita's* aggressive brassiness, and the whole seems to proceed in ultra-slow motion.

From the Tibetan Book of the Dead is scored for flute (alto flute and piccolo), clarinet, soprano, chorus, and tape. The soloist is Ariadne, the chorus her spiritual adviser in attendance. The text is not sub-divided; the music is more or less continuous but seems roughly to fall into three sections. In the first ('O nobly born, the time hath now come for thee to seek the path. Thy breathing is about to cease. Thy guru hath set thee, O Ariadne, face to face before the clear light'), the chorus murmurs the Tibetan incantation over a background of woodwind multiphonics and tape. Upper voices introduce a descending cluster figure (much like the first string quartet), and the music crescendos on 'O Ariadne,' where the all-interval series first appears, representing (as in the *Gita* fanfares) worldly disorder. In the second section ('Thou art now in the Bardo state, where all things are like a cloudless sky, a void, and the naked intellect is like unto a transparent vacuum without circumference or centre'), the moment of death is signalled by a choral gesture (*shshsh* and clucked tongues) plus strokes on finger cymbals, while a French-speaking voice appears on tape.[6] Having entered the Bardo state, Ariadne begins humming freely, while the chorus begins a stately passage based on the series (transposed to E) through a slow, measured accelerando rising to a fortissimo twelve-note chord dominated by the soloist's high B♭ on the expressive syllable *toŋ* ('void'). As the climax subsides, the chorus repeats the word on a C-minor triad, sounding 'like a deep gong.' In the final section ('At this moment know thou thyself, and abide in that state'), the music again swells in crescendo, but only to forte, in a passage of two-part counterpoint loosely based on the series – Ariadne doubled by choral sopranos against the other voices in unison. At the peak of the crescendo, Ariadne's voice appears on tape, and the two voices sing a closely echoing canon as the music fades slowly. (The voice in canon with itself recalls 'The Geography of Eros' and looks forward to *Hymn to Night*; all three works deal with a healed and reintegrated psyche.) At the very end, a voice on tape speaks a benediction in Arabic.

Arcana (1972) belongs with the *Patria* pieces only because, since writing it, Schafer has decided to include it in part of the sequence yet unwritten; it is the only one of these works that makes no use of the all-interval series. It does, however, explore yet another esoteric language and adds another to an impressive series of works for solo voice and chamber ensemble, a form congenial to Schafer ever since *Minnelieder*. (He has also prepared a version of *Arcana* with full orchestra.) When the Montreal International Competition commissioned a work for its *pièce imposé*, it stipulated that the text should not be in a modern language that might give any contestant an advantage; presumably expecting, say, Latin, the competition officials could hardly have bargained for ancient Middle Egyptian. *Arcana* is possibly the only musical setting of Egyptian hieroglyphics.

Schafer usually offers helpful information in his scores about his sources and general aims; in *Arcana*, however, he is guilty of leg-pulling. His text was not 'discovered near Memphis by the Arabian explorer Al Mamun' but written by himself, in English, and then rendered into hieroglyphics by the Toronto Egyptologist D.B. Redford. It consists of some fourteen gnomic utterances vaguely mystical, or else vaguely parodic in character, really bearing less resemblance to real

Egyptian texts (as several of the contestants discovered when they sought scholarly advice) than to Schafer's customary preoccupations, with references to labyrinths, secret formulas, sacred fires, and the like. Furthermore, since the sounds of Middle Egyptian are sheer guesswork, the whole seems yet more arbitrary.

Still, despite the hoaxing (Mary Morrison once performed *Arcana* in full Egyptian regalia), there is nothing tongue-in-cheek about the music. *Arcana* turns out to be a surprisingly expressive piece which, though lacking the dramatic impact of *Requiems for the Party-Girl*, discovers instead a vein of restrained vocal lyricism, Oriental-sounding without hackneyed exoticism.

With a text suggesting no narrative incident and relatively little imagery, Schafer indulges less in word painting and turns to a more cantabile vocal style. Furthermore, since *Arcana* had to be performed by singers of all voice types, male and female, Schafer was obliged to maintain a middle tessitura and avoid large operatic gestures in extreme registers. *Arcana*, then, consists of a sequence of brief, inventively contrasted lyrical statements treating the voice in a chamber-music manner and at the same time exploiting unusual glottal and guttural sounds in the language.

The compositional procedure in *Arcana* extends the system of phonemic correspondences already tried in *East*. As Schafer explains in the score,

Each phoneme of the text was given two notes within a range of two octaves, including a few quartertones. Thus each phonemic element always has the same note or notes associated with it. Often the singer sings one of these notes while the instruments play the other. The frequency with which each phoneme occurs in the text thus gives the melodic line its character, even a sense of tonality. Motives result from frequently repeated digraphs and trigraphs. This helps to give the songs a melodic and harmonic unity which can easily be sensed, even if it cannot be followed analytically. The accompaniment is never free but forms 'words' on its own.

Schafer handles this method freely, admitting many anomalies, particularly in the supporting parts. Analysis, a process of cryptographic decipherment, is complicated because pitches are often near the phoneme, not on it, and because several phonemes may be assigned to one pitch, while two pitches are assigned to each phoneme. The voice line, nevertheless, is usually easily decipherable. Following the 'text' in

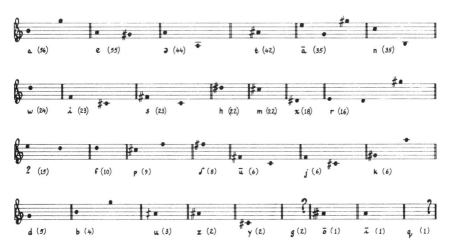

8.6 *Arcana*: correlation of pitches with phonemes in the text (numbers indicate incidences of phonemes in the complete text)

the instrumental parts, however, is far more problematical because of octave transpositions outside the vocal compass. In example 8.6 allowance should be made for the less frequent pitches and phonemes, where correspondence is hard to determine with certainty. Nevertheless, given all these qualifications, melodic fragments do recur, as Schafer claims, and these pitches tend to be prepared and supported in accompaniment. Schafer's rationale for the musical unity of *Arcana*, however, depends on a pre-analytical recognition of recurrently associated pitches – the same principle that Schafer questions as a justification for conventional serialism.[7] If *Arcana* makes a satisfying whole, as I think it does, it succeeds without a clearly audible thematic *Gestalt*.

But recurrent digraphs and trigraphs do appear, as in example 8.7, where the letter *t* (B♭) is most commonly associated with *e* (A♭), and often with *w* in the syllable *wet*. The same excerpts show, though less clearly, the relationship of *saʃte* with the words *waʃteu* and *sajset*, developing an F♯'–B'–F♯" nexus. Other syllables (*an* or *na, eu, hi*) recur elsewhere, so that the music, on this microcosmic level at least, is a tissue of cross-references. The quarter-tone on long *o*, however, is its only occurrence in the piece (example 8.7a).

In *Hymn to Night*, Schafer turns for text to the romantic German poet Novalis. The composer's interest in the high romantics, rekindled by the

8.7 *Arcana*: voice lines showing recurrent pitch groupings associated with recurrent groups of phonemes: a/ No. 2, page 3; b/ No. 8, page 13; c/ No. 12, pages 21–2 (© Copyright 1977 by Universal Edition (Canada) Ltd.)

task of revising his Hoffmann book, emerges in a more unabashed lyricism than ever before, both in this work and in *Adieu, Robert Schumann*. There the lyricism is borrowed for collage; here it is Schafer's own, spun throughout from the recurrent *Patria* series. Writing for the coloratura Riki Turofsky, Schafer creates some of his most challenging vocal bravura, a surge of intricately bounding lines employing extremes of range and soaring tessitura (example 8.4d).

Schafer handles the *Hymnen an die Nacht*, which is too long to be set in its entirety, with a freedom rather daring in the case of a celebrated classic. He sets a composite of lines from several parts of the six-part sequence, selecting mainly from the first poem but including lines from Parts II, IV, and VI. He prunes unwanted phrases and adjusts syntax at will, omitting all references to Christianity, but he preserves the basic thematic shape of Novalis' opening poem. Starting, rather unexpectedly, with a paean to Light, the spirit breathed through all of Nature, the poem turns to Night, tentatively at first, then ardently embracing the *Weltkönigin*, keeper of mystery, the subconscious, healing sleep, dreams, death. Within the *Patria* sequence, then, *Hymn to Night* will apparently stand as a kind of *Liebestod*, expressing a comparable kind of ecstasy and spent passion.

These two feelings emerge in alternation. The piece opens abruptly with the soprano's intricate melisma echoed and supported by the smallish orchestra (single winds with harp, keyboard, substantial percussion, a tape, and strings). Here Schafer gives the strings more linear warmth than he usually allows. Then in the slower middle section the voice becomes more declamatory in the middle register, bringing the text to the fore. The sparse accompaniment here includes Aeolian harp on tape. The Aeolian harp, an obsession among the romantics for its ability to reveal the music of natural sounds, seems almost an inevitable symbol for Schafer: it couples 'the soul with the transcendental breath of the pneuma,' he writes; but it has also a sinister 'wailing quality which Berlioz likened to "a sharp attack of spleen linked to a temptation toward suicide." '[8] Even more haunting, however, is Schafer's use of tape-delay; the soprano's voice is not pre-recorded but recorded on the spot and played back almost immediately – not once but in a cavernous twofold echo from the rear corners of the hall. *Hymn to Night* closes with the voice echoing and re-echoing itself in a slow fade-out, until nothing is left but the faint wailing of the Aeolian harp.

A slighter work than *Hymn to Night*, *La Testa d'Adriane* is more than a musical excerpt: it is a self-contained dramatic scene relying for its effect on stage illusion. After Ariadne's suicide in *Patria II*, *Patria III* will open on a dishevelled side-show barker who plays an accordion. Announcing that the head of Ariadne has been preserved alive, 'suspended between this world and the next,' he whips aside a curtain to reveal a table holding the disembodied head of the soprano, which proceeds to sing the remainder of the work to the accordion accompaniment. (The trick needed to achieve this illusion is described in the score.) The music, again based on the *Patria* series, reinforces the grotesquerie of the scene. Ariadne's head sings a wordless text in an apparently desperate and unsuccessful effort to communicate – isolated phonemes, giggling, gurgling, hissing – while at the same time miming all the gestures of which a disembodied head is capable, mainly movements of the mouth and eyes.

Like *Patria* as a whole, *La Testa d'Adriane* does not exist as a piece of music separate from its drama; there is no audition without spectacle. The choice of free-bass accordion owes as much to the carnival setting, then, as to the persuasiveness of Joseph Macerollo, the principal virtuoso and commissioner of works for the instrument in Canada.

Rather than disguise the vernacular connotations of the instrument, Schafer exploits them, particularly in a mock-serious ritornello written in block harmonies; but he exploits as well the special capabilities of the accordion, which is really a small, portable organ with several registrations, plus a control over dynamics – sforzando, crescendo, diminuendo – plus a few special effects like the bellows shake. *La Testa d'Adriane* is the most startling of the *Patria*-related works, perhaps, but it will not be the last, for unwritten portions of the sequence seem likely to occupy Schafer for many years to come.

Threnody and other works

Threnody is unique in Schafer's work both in style and in concept. The notion of an anti-war composition dealing with the atom bombs dropped on Japan had been simmering in his mind for many years before a commission in 1967 on behalf of the Vancouver Junior Symphony Orchestra brought a suitable occasion to attempt it. *Threnody* is scored for youth orchestra and choir, five speakers between the ages of eight and eighteen, and tape. The youth of the performers is integral to the nature of the piece, which depends on the contrast between the adult aggressions that caused the war and the innocent that suffered. The piece really stands third in the series of 'educational pieces' after *Invertible Material* and *Statement in Blue*; but while it fulfils its educational function admirably, its ambitions reach far beyond his other pieces for young people.

H.H. Stuckenschmidt has traced a tradition of politically committed compositions produced almost entirely in this century. It derives, he argues, from secularized religious impulses:

Music cannot expound beliefs. It can, however, reinforce the expression of a belief and make it more emphatic and persuasive. This should be remembered in any discussion of the use of music with texts whose authors seek to change the world. The desire to change mankind, the world, or preferably both, has always been the aim of founders of religions and of their modern counterparts, politicians and social theorists. Such men have always been aware that music can be as effective as the spoken or written word.[9]

Schafer himself calls *Threnody* 'a religious piece for our time,' and his concept draws ideas from some of the key works in this tradition: from Schoenberg's *Survivor from Warsaw*, the narration; from Britten's *War*

Requiem, the children's voices and perhaps the 'Ora pro nobis' at the end; from Penderecki's *Threnody for the Victims of Hiroshima*, not only the subject and title but also several orchestral effects. Stuckenschmidt traces this tradition to Wagner, whose 'vision of the *Gesamtkunstwerk*,' he notes, 'went right against the doctrine of *l'art pour l'art*.'¹⁰ Hence the mixed-media format of *Threnody* (which links it to the stage works *Loving* and *Patria*), as well as the anti-aestheticism of Schafer's remarks: '*Threnody*,' he says, 'has two main purposes in performance and only one is musical ... Of all my works I hope it will travel the most, the farthest and deepest. I literally want it to be performed to death. I want it to be performed until it is no longer necessary. Then I will burn the score.'¹¹ Given this avowal, perhaps the remarkable fact about *Threnody* is that it manages to avoid direct preachment, working instead through description and evocation.

Of all Schafer's works, *Threnody* leans most heavily on its subject. This is either its strength or its weakness. Most of the text – that spoken by the young narrators – is drawn from eye-witness accounts by young people who witnessed the bombing of Nagasaki. These are flat, factual, horrific: 'As I came near to Urakami I began to meet many injured people. They were stumbling along, weeping crazily. Their faces, necks and hands were blistered and on some of them I could see sheets of skin that peeled right off and hung down flapping.' Orchestra and chorus underscore these comments, though the orchestration is surprisingly restrained. Schafer depends greatly on 'thoughtful improvisations' notated like those in *Statement in Blue*: they are 'thoughtful rather than spontaneous,' he says, because they must illuminate the narration. 'To perform *Threnody* properly one must take up an ethical position on the subject matter.'¹² Also, the tape contains one passage of detached adult comment as ironic counterpoint ('The test was successful beyond the most optimistic expectations of everyone'). In addition, the choir contributes the 'Ora pro nobis' at the end, plus a number of shouts, screams, and other vocal effects.

But Schafer underplays the blast itself, perhaps because it necessarily comes near the beginning and must not overshadow the remainder of the piece. The emphasis is not on violent death but on conscious suffering. Most of the piece is subdued and elegiac. There is a not too blatant effort to suggest the Japanese context in the opening piccolo and flute solos, which should be extended to later improvisations, and Schafer supports these with Japanese-sounding strokes on harp, xylophone, chimes, and temple blocks, as well as by spacing his musical gestures widely with silences. Despite his large forces, he avoids tutti altogether. *Threnody* closes quietly: 'There was a faint smell of chrysanthemum. Alongside my cheek ... stood ... a ... torn ... flower-less ... stem ...'

Threnody has been much performed and discussed. For the most part, it has met with approval from audiences and critics. 'Overwhelming emotional experiences at concerts are rare,' wrote John Kraglund; 'it is difficult to recall more than one or two occasions in three decades of concert going when a new work in a totally modern idiom has achieved this sort of effect.' In Ottawa, Geoffrey Thomson agreed: *Threnody* proves that 'avant garde music and gimmickry can be made almost unbearably moving in the hands of a composer who really has something to say.'[13]

Yet underneath all runs a current of suspicion. Does the impact of the work derive from the music or merely from the subject? Pre-conditioned responses may work for or against the piece. The feelings lie too close to the surface; they are too easy and, sadly, too familiar. Robert Sunter felt that Schafer's text, aiming at poignant simplicity, 'sometimes crossed the boundary of banality.' Jacob Siskind, after playing the recording to a group of teen-agers, reported 'only mild interest' mixed mainly with embarrassment.[14] Perhaps the bomb itself has become an artistic cliché. Or perhaps the reason is a resistance to extreme emotions, particularly those that touch our gravest anxieties. Schafer is right in insisting that '*Threnody* is an uncomfortable work.'[15] It aims to provoke, even (worst of sins) embarrass, in order to focus for fourteen minutes on the experience of incineration.

The most articulate dissenting voice, however, has come from Kenneth Winters, who insists – rightly – on the primacy of aesthetic values. The piece, he says, depends 'more heavily on its subject than on its art ... [It] holds me at musical arm's length.'[16] As a listener, I can only disagree, for no analysis can settle this kind of argument. But Winters raises the question 'whether music can express ... the kind of thing Schafer is dealing with in this work' and, implying that it cannot, faces the central issue that *Threnody* provokes about the limits of art. Two hundred years ago, Samuel Johnson voiced a similar opinion, arguing that religious meditation is an impossible subject for poetry: the praying mind 'is already in a higher state than poetry can confer.'[17] This parallel reinforces the point that *Threnody* deals with a surrogate religious experience: the Bomb has supplanted God as the subject beyond the reach of art. But really *Threnody* deserves the same

8.8 *Threnody*: page 13 of score

consideration as any religious music. As an aid to meditation, it will always be rejected by fundamentalists like Winters, while others will accept it as a suitable musical ritual for bringing the mind to bear on the Unthinkable. *Threnody* accomplishes this aim more directly, more austerely, and with less irrelevant ornament than any other musical treatment that I know. In so doing, it forces more searching aesthetic questions than many a more complex score.

For musically *Threnody* is not complex. Although its idiom is thoroughly contemporary, Schafer points out that 'it is always conceived for the age group for which it was intended.'[18] As in all his educational pieces, he abandons serial procedures. Instead, he concentrates on intervals announced in the first chord (c–g–b): perfect fifth, major seventh, and their inversions. The pitch determinants are hardly novel, but they are more than onomatopoeic sound effects; they generate motifs, which may expand into lyrical lines, and they establish a harmonically consistent texture. Thus the trumpets sound a semitone cluster that is followed by a chord of fourths in the lower brass; this is repeated as a whole-tone cluster followed by a chord of fifths (the whole tone never becomes prominent, but here it is understood as an expansion of the semitones). This sequence is extended in full orchestra while the tape depicts the bomb explosion (example 8.8). The opening piccolo solo extends the c–b relationship. Quartal harmonies dominate the choral writing. Semitone clusters colour several other passages (pages 4, 8, 25, 27, 28, 32). Elsewhere, pairs of major sevenths enter a fourth or fifth apart (pages 9, 15, 28). In general, the semitones provide the dissonant bite, and the perfect intervals evoke a sense of blankness; but these recurrent patterns are less important for themselves than for creating a unified substructure supporting the larger dramatic gestures of the piece.

Since 1965, Schafer has written many pieces for solo voice but only three not related to *Patria* or *Lustro*. Two of these set the same ancient Greek text. *Sappho* was commissioned by the Coolidge Foundation and premiered at its festival in 1970. It was a failure, described by Irving Lowens, a sympathetic critic, as 'far more dessicated than other Schafer music I have heard.'[19] Schafer withdrew it and in the following year essayed another setting of the same words. *Enchantress*, written for soprano, exotic flute, and eight cellos, is a relatively subdued piece that makes no reference (surprisingly) to the legend of Sappho's suicide. The text stitches together several fragments dealing with passionate love. The phalanx of cellos surrounding the humming soprano recalls Villa-Lobos, but distantly, for Schafer's string writing is his own – unmetered, improvisatory, and reliant on colouristic effects.

Adieu, Robert Schumann (1976) is one of the best illustrations of Schafer's ability to communicate with audiences through a contemporary idiom. John Roberts and the CBC had commissioned a work to be performed by Maureen Forrester, the Canadian contralto who is celebrated internationally – but not particularly for her singing of *avant-garde* music. Schafer's problem was to write without compromising his own style a piece that Maureen Forrester not only would sing, but might want to continue singing.[20] He found his subject in Schumann, whose *Lieder* stand near the heart of Maureen Forrester's repertoire and whose biography fits prefectly the model of the unworldly, alienated artist. The work deals with Schumann's last days from the time of his first hallucinations until his death in an asylum in 1856. The contralto portrays Clara Schumann, singing a text freely adapted from her diaries. Robert Schumann, then, appears as another of the insane or suicidal idealists that populate Schafer's work, and he is seen with the same mixture of affection and detachment that has been noted elsewhere. Here, however, the affection is more on the surface because the adopted point of view is Clara's, and because Schafer's piece relies unabashedly on the *Innigkeit* of Schumann's music.

Though the subject is familar, the technique is not, for nowhere else does Schafer rely so heavily on collage. Through his piece drift Schumann's phrases, and the proportion of notes 'by Schafer' is low enough that even in the context of *Patria*, where collage appears *Adieu, Robert Schumann* would seem out of place. The piece is evidence of a revival of interest in romantic music not only on the part of Schafer but among other contemporaries. However, unlike, say, George Rochberg, Schafer does not compose original music in a nineteenth-century style mixed with a modern texture; nor does he resort to electronic manipulation, like the homages to Beethoven by Stockhausen and Kagel. A closer analogue is the great Mahler movement of Berio's *Sinfonia*, which also superimposes romantic collage over modern textures and a narrative, and which shares Schafer's nostalgic yet critical attitude. But like Berio, Schafer combines his materials in a way that makes the work all his own.

The Schumann components are chosen either for their biographical appropriateness (one of the last songs; the piano piece 'dictated' by angels) or for their familiarity, though these too have an ironic relevance. Heine's text for 'Dein Angesicht' could hardly be more prophetic:

Dein Angesicht, so lieb und schön,
Das hab ich jüngst in Traum gesehn,
Es ist so mild und engelgleich,
und doch so bleich, so schmerzensreich.

Und nur die Lippen, die sind rot;
Bald aber Küsst sie bleich der Tod.
Erlöschen wird das Himmelslicht,
Das aus den frommen Augen bricht.[21]

The *Kreisleriana* fragments carry associations of Hoffmann's mad hero. From *Carnaval*, Schafer selects the dashing, half-manic 'Florestan' motif and the defiant 'March of the Band of David against the Philistines,' and from *Kinderscenen* the 'Important Event' – all with ironic effect. The Schumannesque signature device (A–C for Clara, B♭–E for Robert) is easy enough to spot in the voice line.

Schafer's chief compositional problem, working with no tape to help obscure the metre and everywhere avoiding the protection of an Ivesian muddle, is to move convincingly between disparate styles. For this reason, Schafer handles his usual devices with great restraint. The orchestra is Schumann-sized, with all winds in pairs and only two percussionists. Flutter-tonguing, assorted brass mutes, and glissandi all appear but do not dominate; percussion extends to guiro, bongos, and xylophone but centres on bass drum and timpani; the romantic solo piano (often avoided by Schafer) is a constant presence. Unlike much of his recent work, most of the piece is metred conventionally but uses extremely flexible tempi and alternates between strict and parlando passages. At times, the piano moves at its own tempo, sometimes taking the solo voice with it. Occasionally, different Schumann fragments are superimposed in different rhythms. All these procedures are effective without being radical. Like many of Schafer's pieces, this one rests on a stroke of invention that seems easy – once it has been conceived and brought to birth. The result is one of his most deeply moving compositions.

From *Epitaph* to *Apocalypsis*: The later choral works

The choral writing of *Threnody* and *Gita* is still relatively conventional, with just a few passages in graphic notation. But with *Epitaph for Moonlight* (3–10 March 1968) Schafer embraced what has been termed 'the new choralism,'[22] initiating a series of choral works written largely for amateur groups and using scarcely any ordinary notes. *Epitaph for Moonlight* proved an even more successful experiment in graphic notation than *Statement in Blue*; Schafer followed with the even more indeterminate *Minimusic* (for instruments or voices), *Miniwanka* (another descriptive work), *Yeow and Pax* (two sacred anthems suitable for Christian worship), and the more ambitious anthem *Psalm*. But already before *Psalm* Schafer had completed a large, semi-dramatic choral piece, *In Search of Zoroaster*, and more recently he has written the monumental *Apocalypsis*. The line of development connecting these works is clear.

Epitaph for Moonlight is Schafer's C♯-minor prelude – probably his best-known composition. Written as a modest 'study piece for youth choir,' it has entered the repertoires of choral groups across Canada and elsewhere. Its success is well deserved, for its combination of new choralism with a charming programmatic text speaks even to the most unsophisticated audience.[23] *Miniwanka, or Moments of Water*, a companion piece added in August 1971, is equally effective and almost as well known. It would be wrong to make too much of these pieces on account of their popularity: they are uncomplicated, naïvely representational works in a choral tradition extending back to Janequin; but it would be equally wrong to discount them, for the appeal of the genre is indelible, and the number of crowd-pleasing *avant-garde* pieces is not large.

Onomatopoeia in both works starts with the texts. *Miniwanka* directly imitates water sounds, exploiting several words related to water from ten North American Indian languages. If this is an environmental work, so too is *Epitaph*, for moonlight required an epitaph only when its symbolic properties died in 1969 at the hands of the US space program. It is another of Schafer's elegies for a lost romanticism. Here, onomatopoeia involves a transference of visual into aural terms. Schafer tells in his score how the piece grew out of an exercise in synaesthesia, an assignment given a grade seven class to invent synonyms for 'moonlight' in a private language: the results run from the pseudo-etymological ('lunious') to the silly ('sloofulp'). The best commentary on this piece, which need not be repeated here, is the whole of the pamphlet *When Words Sing*, which includes the complete score. There, Schafer traces the process from the appreciation of words as sounds to the realization of onomatopoeic word sounds in choral textures. He suggests further possibilities for classroom experiment and even usefully categorizes some of the principal graphic symbols.[24]

Schafer's didactic intention permeates every aspect of these pieces, from composition to rehearsal to performance. Labelled an 'ear-training exercise,' *Epitaph* is notated in relative rather than absolute pitch. At seven different points pitch is ad libitum, but the pitch chosen then determines the subsequent section, notated with interval signs ($+3$, -7, and so on). But since choral singing demands interval recognition anyway, the experience of singing *Epitaph* is not as strange in this respect as it first might seem. There is no supporting tonality, but the piece still moves in the chromatic scale and it contains no effect not obtainable through conventional notation. Yet a random effect like the 'constellation' sonority just after the opening, executed effortlessly as written, would place impossible demands on pitch and rhythm if written any more exactly (example 8.9). Schafer's graphics are really more accurate than conventional notation. They allow the singers to ignore meaningless exactitudes and concentrate on the quality of the sound.

Graphic notations, placing the performer in a position of collaboration with the composer, cause some consternation, especially among musicians used to being told what to do. Schafer's ear-training intention does not abandon ordinary practices: the semitone cluster at the beginning, for example (nearly identical with the choral entrance in *Gita*), and the whole-tone cluster provide valuable experience for any choir. *Miniwanka* contains some 'real' notes. But the real ear-training applies above all to timbres. Vocal sounds in *Epitaph* must be fitted sensitively to the liquid, nasal, and sibillant onomatopoeia of the moonlight synonyms. So must the percussion, if used. In *Miniwanka*, the program is stated: 'to chronicle the transformations of water, from

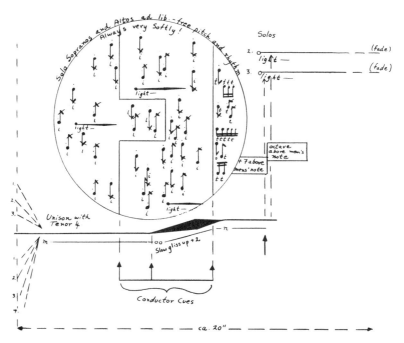

8.9 *Epitaph for Moonlight* (vertical lines indicate conductor's cues)

rain, to streams, to quiet lakes, to broad rivers, to the ocean.' This effect must be created imaginatively within the sequence of events and visual cues set by the composer. The piece is a little dramatic picture created by voices alone. The danger with performers unused to indeterminate notations is an attitude that just anything will do.

This dangerous insouciance is also liable to threaten rhythm in performance. The sonic events unfold slowly, so with no bar lines and no regular pulse inexperienced performers may conclude that rhythm is negligible. But for pieces like *Epitaph* and *Miniwanka* and their larger successors, a better word than 'rhythm' would perhaps be 'timing,' for the unfolding of such pieces is as closely related to the timing of an actor as to the exacting rhythms of a musician. An actor's timing, while it may seem impossibly loose to the musician, is nonetheless an essential quality of his performance.

After the success of *Epitaph for Moonlight*, no one would have blamed Schafer for producing a dozen other pieces depicting birds, battles, or windstorms. But the limitations are obvious. Instead, *Minimusic*, a kind of musical game, is Schafer's farthest excursion into chance. *Minimusic* is designed for any practicable number of voices or instruments of any type. The score consists of thirty-six boxes containing instructions or graphic notations; all players start from box 1 but proceed in any direction from there. Most of the boxes have three or four different exits, and the possibilities are multiplied by cutting the pages of the score along dotted lines indicated, so that no linear sequence of events is likely to happen. Box 18, a special exception, instructs the player to 'play' Paul Klee's well-known painting 'The Twittering Machine' (reproduced with the score); whenever this happens, all the others join in.[25] With so much left to chance, *Minimusic* is more chaotic than most of Schafer's work and lacks the broad audience appeal of *Epitaph for Moonlight* or *Miniwanka*. Like many games, it is more satisfying to the participants than to the onlookers, a kind of *avant-garde* madrigal for children.

Since Schafer's instinct for choral textures stems from his days as an Anglican choirboy, it seems surprising that he has not turned more often to church music. He has written only two pieces for liturgical use, and these have never won the popularity of his educational pieces. While Schafer is committed to no orthodoxy, he shows sympathy for many expressions of religious feeling. Moreover, he has remarked on the need for a truly contemporary church music. Once the strongest patron of music, the church has lost its position and instead of vital new music offers only 'flabby substitutes.' 'God's taste seems to have deteriorated in recent years.'[26] This failure is only one part of the widening gulf between composer and audience, of course, but, given the appeal of *Epitaph for Moonlight*, Schafer might seem capable of bridging it again. Audience resistance in this case, however, is aggravated by the traditional conservatism of church music through the centuries. So, perhaps regrettably, Schafer exhibits little desire to become the Healey Willan of the *avant-garde*.

The title *Yeow and Pax* (1969) combines the Hebrew word for 'howl' (from the same text in Isaiah that inspired Allen Ginsberg's 'Howl') with the Latin for 'peace.' Like *Protest and Incarceration* or *Apocalypsis*, these two anthems with organ and electronic sound balance the aggressive and quietist strains of Schafer's temperament. (The 'howl' passage reappears in the introduction to *Apocalypsis*.) *Yeow and Pax* gain from being performed together, since both are fairly slight and the chanting of *Pax* helps restore liturgical solemnity after Isaiah's vociferous prophecy of Doomsday.

Psalm (1972), formerly called *Tehillah*,[27] is a cappella except for percussion. This setting of Psalm 148, which describes the praise of God in music, is a favourite of the composer's (he includes it as part of *Apocalypsis*); but it too has failed to win many performances. The choral writing in *Psalm* uses most of the earlier devices – indefinite notations, whistles, shouts – but it includes more orthodox notation, with several triads and conventional chords. These are treated more as stationary, block-like sonorities than as functional chords, and they are mixed freely with dissonant complexes. *Psalm* is distinctive as well for its strong pulse, most of it governed by time signature and accentuated by percussion, although neither rhythm nor harmony functions to unify the piece. Momentum is beside the point: tempo changes occur frequently and alternate with pulseless passages. The effect is rather a shifting mosaic of sounds that close with a particularly effective section combining clapping, stamping, finger-snapping, and shouting in rhythm and cross-rhythm.

Schafer's private religious views have found expression more completely in two large choral works expanding from the idiom of the earlier pieces: *In Search of Zoroaster* (1971, antedating *Psalm*) and *Apocalypsis* (1977). Both are long works employing large forces with percussion support and conceived theatrically. Both, dealing with final things, are in this sense sequels to *Threnody*.

In Search of Zoroaster, inspired by Schafer's visit to Iran in 1968, is not so much a musical composition as a newly invented ritual for a non-existent religion, involving costumes, masks, movement, and a play of light amid total darkness. It is 'not so much a performance as a perpetual celebration' intended more for the benefit of the singers than the audience: 'In addition to the performers an audience may also be present but is not obligatory.'[28]

Zoroaster is a lesser work than the monumental *Apocalypsis*, but also more manageable in production; its theatricality provides one of the most intriguing audience experiences in all of Schafer's work, as well as an unusual performing experience for a choral group. Like the shorter choral works, *Zoroaster* was written for amateur singers, in this case the Dartmouth College Glee Club, who must perform widely separated in a large space while moving about and handling the percussion, and all in near darkness. Consequently, musical demands are kept simple, throwing the ritual elements into high relief.

This ritual is mysterious. Reviewing the second performance, John Fraser, adopting a quizzical tone, concluded that the piece was 'sometimes moving, and elsewhere a big giggle.'[29] Schafer's intentions are not openly comic, but he is aware that a true liturgy cannot be invented in isolation. Choristers draped in sheets and performing portentous but incomprehensible gestures risk looking like a fraternity initiation or a new California cult. They thus alienate the audience, insisting on critical detachment, but at the same time draw on the communal, archetypal symbolism of ritual. The priest's incantation 'Search for the secret formula of the fire in the water' suggests the symbolism that lends charm to Mozart's *Zauberflöte*, but, as in Mozart, the uneasy balance between religious and theatrical rhetoric recalls the origins of all drama in religious ritual. Schafer's notes also mention another kind of ritual: 'Today concert giving has been deflected and twisted from its true purpose. It is becoming almost impossible, given this format, to prepare a climate of attentiveness and clair-audience into which the musical and the religious experience can come.' Schafer's piece is then, like *Apocalypsis*, a personal fusion of religious and aesthetic perception, inviting the not uncritical involvement of the audience.

Accordingly, Schafer chooses for the leader of his ceremony the Persian divinty Srosh. the 'genius of hearing,' a solo baritone. Schafer adapts the Zoroastrian Srosh, who represents something closer to 'the listening obedience,'[30] but according to Schafer he 'stands between man and the pantheon of the gods, listening for the divine messages, which he transmits to humanity.'[31] This genius of hearing emphasizes the composer's aesthetic concerns, affirming that the experience of religion – Western religion too – is chiefly acoustic: the hymns, the choir and organ, the prayers and congregational responses, even the bare sermon of Protestantism, all are acoustic experience. The object of worship is invisible, it surrounds and enters us, and it is highly emotive – all properties of sound. Hence the resonance of European cathedrals, an enveloping communal sonic environment. Muslim equivalents are the 'towers of silence' and the perfect seven-fold echo of the Shah Mosque at Isfahan.[32]

In Search of Zoroaster benefits from an acquaintance with Persian cosmology, and the score refers the students to appropriate volumes in Max Müller's monumental *Sacred Books of the East*.[33] A brief summary of this recondite lore seems useful here. Zoroaster founded his religion in the sixth century BC on monotheistic principles not quite as rigorous as those of Judaism. The highest god is Ahura Mazda, who alone is worthy of worship; he is creative principle, lawgiver, order in nature, and source of alternation between light and dark. This alternation is the source of the Zoroastrian dualism, which conceives the world as a struggle between good and evil. Ahura Mazda's evil counterpart is Ahriman: every man must dedicate himself to one or the other. Ahura Mazda is surrounded by six or seven (the number varies) other figures called the *amesha spentas*, or beneficent immortals. These differ in exact name and function from one account to another, but Schafer's labels in the score accord well enough with the sources. In addition, Mithra (a survival from the earlier Iranian religion) is evoked as god of the heavenly light and a creature of Ahura Mazda. All these subsidiary beings, really personifications of abstract concepts, have evil counterparts, which, however, do not figure in Schafer's piece. Only the battle with Ahriman appears. Srosh is a divine mediator between Ahura Mazda and man. In Persian myth, he offered the first sacrifices and the first hymns. Thrice daily and thrice nightly he engages in battle with the demons of Ahriman. He protects mankind from the evils of night and from the terrors of death. At the end of time, through a joint effort of Ahura Mazda and Srosh, Ahriman will be vanquished utterly. The instrument of this ultimate victory will be a son born to a mortal virgin by a reincarnated Zoroaster, the deified founder of the faith who has already brought the revealed Word of Ahura Mazda. Thus the search for Zoroaster is a search for a Second Coming at the end of time.

Such a summary cannot convey the richness of one of the great world religions, but in this context the outlines of Schafer's piece begin to emerge. Still, *In Search of Zoroaster* is written for Western audiences who can only perceive its matter as exotic and nearly incomprehensible and will grasp at anything familiar. Nietzsche's Zarathustra may linger in the background, but Schafer's piece has little to do with Nietzsche's *Übermensch*, still less with Strauss's musical portrait. More relevant, I think, are the Christian analogues. Persian mythology is often considered the source for a number of familiar Christian concepts: the *amesha spentas*, the embodiments of good and evil as angels and demons; Ahriman as Satan, Prince of Darkness; and most notably, the notion of the Second Coming of a Messiah pronounced by the prophet Isaiah and fulfilled in Jesus Christ. So even though Schafer's notes declare that this text 'suggests the history of the Zoroastrian religion, originally a proud monotheism, which later broke into a confused polytheism, full of magic formulas and practices,' his piece depicts not just the decline of a religion, but a world's fall and restoration through divine intervention in the form of an earthly saviour. The story is unfamiliar in its vocabulary and arrangement, but not in its component parts.

In Search of Zoroaster divides into three parts with a prologue, each part announced by twelve strokes on the wood block. The participants, humming the 'cosmic sound' (B♮), proceed into the totally darkened hall.

The first section suggests a creation *ex nihilo*, proceeding from silence and darkness to the lighting of myriads of candles. As the light is passed among the choirs, a tutti passage begins, elaborating a richly sonorous E-major triad with embellishments of definite and indefinite pitch; this emergence of E major (with G♮ prominent) gains some of its satisfying effect from memories of the B♮ 'cosmic sound.'

The second and shortest section deals with the coming of Ahura Mazda's son, described as 'the holy one who is both heavenly and earthly.' Here for the first time melodic fragments emerge, a melodic line in canon with its inversion, then a unison phrase for all voices, which is repeated several times. At irregular intervals, terrified outbursts represent the corruption of the religion into 'confused polytheism' and magic, as the composer's notes declare; theologically, it appears that the corruption is a direct consequence of the incarnation of Ahura Mazda's son, which seems an uneasy compromise between divine and human nature. In effect, his very coming is a fall from purity. Schafer thus emphasizes the Manichean tendency of the Persian dualism, unable to conceive of an incarnate yet uncorrupted being.

The third section, the longest and most theatrical, moves from fragmentation of the faith through the struggle with Ahriman and into a final apocalyptic harmony. Srosh and the male quartet put on animal masks, Srosh falls prostrate on the floor (a kind of crucifixion?), occasionally squealing out the name of Ahriman, while the male quartet performs a mystifying ritual over his body. The remaining five groups, meanwhile, circulate among the audience pronouncing nonsensical rules of purity to hapless individuals selected at random ('When a dead pregnant woman is to be carried by two men, both are to be cleansed ...'). These tasks completed, the performers begin to chant 'Ahriman' and continue in an enormous crescendo until Srosh rises and signals for silence. In the final sequence, all six groups continue independently, until the sounds finally merge into one sustained sound mass centering on C but fluctuating to other pitches. As in the final part of *Lustro*, Schafer is less interested in mere volume than in 'shifting waves of sound' achieved by exaggerated dynamic changes in all the six groups. All voices combine in unison praise of Ahura Mazda (the same unison melody heard earlier), then merge on the 'cosmic sound'; the singers extinguish their candles and file out slowly.

The summit of these choral works – Schafer's longest composition – is

Apocalypsis, a commentary on the Revelation of St John (a synopsis of which appears in appendix 4). With its quasi-ritualistic pageantry, its ecclesiastical setting, and its massed sonic effects, it evolves clearly enough from *In Search of Zoroaster*, though it is more intricate both musically and theatrically, and it has the advantages of a familiar mythology.

Given the state of the world in 1976, Schafer's decision to compose an Apocalypse needs no explanation; his meditations on the subject extend back to the song 'Protest' and emerge again in the Prudentius songs and *Threnody*. St John's unveiling of God's purpose. with its indelible imagery, would seem to beg for full-scale musical treatment, but it has held strangely little interest for composers.[34] Schafer's dramatization represents scenes chosen from John's narrative (plus Psalm 148) with an orthodoxy untypical of the composer. Consistent with his Manichean leanings in *Zoroaster*, however, his Christian pageant sets the damned against the elect starkly enough (a tinge of Upper Canada Calvinism probably shows here as well). But more important, Schafer's identification with St John the man seems complete: John, the prophet seer who in the face of imminent crisis reaffirmed spiritual truth, was also an artist of the highest order, conscious of speaking for a tiny band of faithful against a hostile society. But while Schafer embraces John's vision of destruction, he replaces the heavenly Jerusalem (the city metaphor is unattractive to him) with a pantheistic Credo freely adapted from Giordano Bruno, the mystically inclined heretic burned at the stake in 1600.

The two parts of *Apocalypsis*, 'John's Vision' and 'Credo,' juxtapose (like *Yeow and Pax*) the violent with the motionless. So widely contrasted are they, in fact, that they make sense performed separately. 'John's Vision,' lasting seventy-five minutes, makes immense logistical demands in production, requiring multitudes of choristers, speakers, dancers, and instrumentalists, not to mention technicians, all co-ordinated by several conductors. Like *Zoroaster*, it works more through threatrical than strictly musical expression. As often before, Schafer's inspiration is medieval: the pageantry performed in medieval cathedrals. Here, he notes in the score, 'musicians, actors, dancers, guilds, and townspeople participated ... Such events broke down distinctions between sacred and secular, clergy and guild, church and marketplace. They also brought artists and public into firm unity of purpose.' The premiere at the University of Western Ontario was described by William Littler as 'one of the most spectacular events in the history of Canadian music. Not only St. John the Divine but Cecil B. DeMille would have been impressed.'[35] While 'John's Vision' is dominated by noisy, milling crowds, 'Credo' is daringly, defiantly static. It is sung by the choristers, immobile for forty-six minutes and supported only by quiet electronic sound (at the premiere their parts were doubled by strings). The music slowly unfolds a series through the circle of fifths.

Serialism is signally appropriate to *Apocalypsis*, of course, because John's narrative is itself constructed in numerical cycles. John's mystical numbers, furthermore – seven for earth, twelve for heaven – correspond to the notes of the diatonic and chromatic scales. The possibilities of this circumstance seem enormous, and Schafer incorporates too many of them into his structure to enumerate; but in general they apply in 'John's Vision' to time and massed groups and in 'Credo' to rhythm and pitch. In 'John's Vision,' for example, there are seven scenes lasting (exactly or approximately) seven minutes each; these are preceded by introductory speeches and followed by a longish epilogue (twelve minutes). This attention to time is symbolically apt in a work describing the end of time; but Schafer's emphasis on clock time as opposed to musical (or 'virtual') time suggests that *Apocalypsis*, despite all its activity, is pageant rather than drama. Like *Loving* – and like John's narrative itself – it possesses the processional quality of allegory, with strangely little impetus towards climax.

Schafer's numerology applies as well to some, though not all, of the performing groups. There are seven leading parts (Schafer specifies 'sound poets,' thinking of his friends b.p. Nichol and the group 'The Four Horsemen'): three speakers – St John, Archangel Michael, and Antichrist – and the four Living Creatures. (Three and four are also significant: added, they equal seven; multiplied, they equal twelve). Seven mimes represent Angels. Four dancers are the four Horsemen. In addition, there is another singing role (Old Woman) plus other dancers and mimes. The choral groups (men's, women's, two mixed, speech chorus, and boys' choir) do not follow the numbering scheme until the 'Credo,' where they are regrouped as twelve four-part mixed choirs set around the circumference of the hall. There are four instrumental groups; high instruments, containing a minimum of twelve recorders, flutes, piccolos, violins, etc; brass instruments, containing a minimum of twelve trombones, tubas, or trumpets; Middle-Eastern instruments, number unspecified; and percussion, further subdivided into four groups – drums and xylophones (seven players), gongs and tam-tams (seven players), snare and tenor drums (six players), plus seven anvils and seven varieties of specially constructed instruments (seven players). The specially constructed instruments (described in appendix 4) form one of the most essential features of *Apocalypsis*, intended as much for visual as for audible effect. The remaining instruments include organ, used mainly for sustained pedals, and electronic tape, used in 'John's Vision' (with a modicum of restraint) only at beginning and end.

Pitch, though of secondary importance in 'John's Vision,' also repeats the sevenfold scheme; a seven-note exotic scale on F, sustained on the organ in the opening scene, underlies much of the piece. The second scene uses the remaining five chromatic notes, which are associated particularly with a recurrent benediction for boys' choir. These two note-groups alternate from scene to scene without mixing, except for the keynote F, often sustained as a pedal. Near the end of 'John's Vision,' the exotic scale sounds clearly once more before the choirs in their recessional repeat over and over a modal cadence. The 'Credo' that follows then pivots around C, so that the whole of *Apocalypsis* may be heard as one gigantic plagal cadence of Amen.

The 'Credo' protracts the near immobility of this recessional to extravagant lengths. Schafer's Jerusalem is surely a heaven for the faithful only, for others would find it intolerable – a forty-six minute expanse of nearly featureless, inwoven choral sound. Sheer sonorous beauty is the most immediate quality of this music, but as in *Music for the Morning of the World*, its effectiveness depends finally on hyperesthesia. The choral texture ranges from a minimum of twelve parts to a forty-eight-part tutti at the end, surpassing in its intricacy even the celebrated forty-part 'Spem in alium' of Thomas Tallis, while Schafer's harmonies, based (as in *Cortège*) on sweet, shifting diatonic clusters, slowly unfold lines, each independent but each bound into the massive sostenuto. The concentration required of the choristers and the vertiginous soprano tessitura (sustained C and even C♯) approach the superhuman.

If 'slowness is beauty,' as Ezra Pound has told us, then this 'Credo' is surely beautiful. And its beauty is that it touches the outer limits of the possible. After the line of development leading to *Apocalypsis* from the modest beginning of *Epitaph for Moonlight*, no further expansion would seem likely. If Schafer's present projects are realized, however, his audience will have ever more reason for admiration. Schafer's capacity for surprise is not to be underestimated.

9

The *Patria* sequence (1966–)

'*Patria* needs to be deciphered like a cryptogram. All solutions are correct. There are thousands of messages on different frequency bands. No one can hope to decipher them all. For there are millions of universes, as many as there are human intelligences.' This particular message is conveyed on one of the less accessible frequency bands: Morse code sounded by woodwinds near the beginning of *Patria I*. But it is perhaps the best summation of Schafer's still unfinished *magnum opus*. *Patria* creates a universe so saturated with information that information becomes a blur, so full of communication that communication withers. Yet its bewildering textures, if sometimes diffuse, are not formless, even though they project a world in which form disappears. Patria communicates as well as bewilders because the condition that it portrays is so instantly recognizable.

Schafer's success in at least one segment of *Patria* was tested at the Stratford Festival in 1972. This production, a *tour de force* by the director Michael Bawtree, realized Schafer's intentions minutely, validating both his daring stagecraft and his ability to reach a general audience without compromising his musical idiom. Critics, whatever their reservations, agreed unanimously that *Patria II* at Stratford was moving and important: 'a powerhouse of a piece'; 'a haunting work written with extraordinary sensitivity and theatrical power'; 'as skilful a mating of subject and treatment as the operatic literature of Canada has produced'; 'as a conglomerate with a strong dramatic appeal and an ability to grip the spectator's attention, it is brilliant.'[1] If these accolades do nothing else, they prove that *Patria II* is viable theatre. They also suggest that Schafer's most ambitious work ranks with his best.

The idea of *Patria* grew out of the television production of *Loving* and occupied Schafer much of the time between 1966 and 1969, when he completed much of the music (including *Requiems, Gita,* and *Tibetan Book of the Dead*), sketched his theories of stagecraft, and wrote the librettos of parts ɪ and ɪɪ (synopses of which appear in appendix 5). *Patria ɪɪ: Requiems for the Party-Girl* was finished in 1972, *Patria ɪ: The Characteristics Man* in 1974. Schafer's original plan was to resolve the issues of both works in a *Patria ɪɪɪ,* but at present his vision recedes into a distant future *Patria vɪ.* Thus the plan of the whole can now only be guessed – even by the composer – and there could develop an indefinite sequence of unresolvabilities. But the two completed portions stand independently, and some general conclusions seem already determined. Schafer explains the plot himself:

Patria ɪ is about a displaced person in a new society and that person's problems. *Patria ɪɪ* is the story really of a woman in an unspecified locale, which we assume is a mental hospital, who is abandoned because there seems to be no way of communicating with her ... But the suggestion is that Ariadne, to the audience at least, is completely rational and all the people around her are the absurdities ... Ariadne's thread is the elucidation of the mystery of the labyrinth, and so what I had in mind ultimately was somehow to tie up the principal character of *Patria ɪ* and the principal character of *Patria ɪɪ* in a third section of the work.[2]

The principal characters, then, are everyman figures, non-particularized; their 'patria' or homeland is a menacing mob, an insane asylum. 'Broadly speaking,' Schafer adds, '*Patria* represents an anabasis, a departure from the world of reality, through the world of illusion and on up to a state of understanding, illumination or redemption.' The pattern, then, is a myth of descent, for which the story of Theseus and Ariadne in the labyrinth is a fitting symbol. (Coincidentally, another composer, Berio, has found it equally fitting in his *Laborintus ɪɪ,* a striking analogue to Schafer's work that incorporates texts of Ezra Pound.) The mute hero of *Patria ɪ,* D.P., is both Theseus and Minotaur, an immigrant in a hostile society, a rescuer turned attacker, who threatens Ariadne then saves her by committing suicide; Ariadne, held hostage by the desperate D.P. and liberated by his death, enacts in *Patria ɪɪ* her own descent into the labyrinthine insane asylum; in this context she too seems a guide, a Jungian anima figure – but she too kills herself and presumably enters yet another state in *Patria ɪɪɪ* (which will open with

La Testa d'Adriane). Thus the whole sequence promises a descent and return – or even perhaps a literal 'anabasis,' a journey to the interior for which there is no definite end but only deeper states of illusion. The events of *Patria*, then, form another psychic allegory like *Loving*, only far more complex. The identities of the *Patria* figures are more elusive, and the bilingualism of *Loving* has exploded in a Babel of remote tongues, not to mention an encyclopaedic collage of allusions both musical and literary. These allusions are tantalizing, yet difficult to coalesce into a pattern. Schafer not only severs the mythic elements from their narrative framework but fuses the labyrinth symbolism with the tale of Beauty and the Beast and tosses in teasing references to other sources. Furthermore, his myths appear in frustrated or ironically inverted form: his labyrinth has no exit; his beast remains a beast.

The underlying myth goes perhaps like this: Beauty-Ariadne is victim of the Beast-Minotaur, but she destroys him and escapes by guiding the hero Theseus (or the handsome prince trapped in Beast's body) through the labyrinth (or out of the enchanted castle). In Schafer's ironic version, victims male and female remain trapped in the maze – lunatic society or society of lunatics, both are equally confining – male and female remain separate, neither ego healed. In *Patria I*, Beast's comfortable castle-prison takes the form of North American society with its commercial comforts but without a plan. D.P., oppressed by the jolly mob, somehow recognizes Ariadne as a kindred spirit and tries to save her, but fails. In his kindly aspect, D.P. is known as 'Best,' but as Beast-Minotaur he returns the violence inflicted on him and takes her hostage for no apparent reason.

Facts surrounding Ariadne are obscure: at the party where she meets D.P. she is a mature woman who apparently kills herself; in the next scene, she is the young girl hostage and D.P. kills himself; in *Patria II* she is again mature, remembers the hostage incident, identifies one of the inmates as D.P., and again kills herself. Which suicide is 'real,' if either of them is (Ariadne sings her own requiem), never becomes clear. In *Patria II*, the castle of indulgence has become an insane asylum. The psychiatrists and nurses who give orders and shock treatments are simultaneously rescuers and attackers. Ariadne is both repelled and attracted by Beast, who practises witchcraft and threatens her with a broom but also plays Mozart on the piano (though the music gets hideously distorted). In the form of Nietzsche (the philosopher of the *Übermensch*, who ended his life insane) he represents the man of culture and outrageously inflated ego; in the form of Death, he represents the extinction of ego, terrifying but in the end attractive. Whether her suicide signifies mere negation, or something more positive as suggested in the *Tibetan Book of the Dead*, will perhaps emerge in *Patria III*.

This procedure poses dangers for composer as well as audience. Mythic archetypes, as McLuhan notes, are hard to distinguish from clichés; one critic complained, justly enough, that the psychology of *Patria II* is 'surprisingly basic,'[3] but he mistook its exaggerated incidents and caricatures for attempts at psychological penetration. (Schafer's preface compares *Patria I* to a comic strip, and *Patria II*, though more sombre, is similar in kind.)[4] More dangerously, the infinitely associative nature of the mythic imagination always threatens diffuseness, as Wagner discovered when he began unfolding his design backwards from *Götterdämmerung*. Without constraints of narrative, the danger increases, as witness many a medieval dream allegory or modern personal epic, like Pound's *Cantos*. The problem is doubly serious on stage, where a scene, though it may appear mysterious or episodical, must never appear superfluous. A few episodes of *Patria II* do not escape this danger and support one critic's reservations about 'structural sameness'[5] – but they are few, and fewer I think in *Patria I*.

As with *Loving*, Schafer worked out his stagecraft in an essay, 'The Theatre of Confluence,' before composing *Patria*. He first intended to have the two parts of *Patria* given 'coevally with two complete casts on two stages but in the same theatre,' but he could find no theatre adequate to the task. He did succeed, however, in heightening the stage interest and electronic technology of *Patria*, and he strove deliberately to keep music from swamping the other modes of expression, as it does in Wagnerian music drama. His aim in fusing the arts was to preserve a balance among them – not opera, but 'co-opera.' Still, his theory accepts hearing as the dominant sense, for if 'touch is the most intimate of the senses ... hearing is like touching at a distance.' For such a theatre, Schafer understood, realism is irrelevant: the violence of *Patria I* is the slapstick of comic strip or Punchinello; *Patria II* is more ambiguous because of its blacker mood and madhouse setting, but even there characters resemble Bedlamites of the Jacobean stage as much as bona fide lunatics. (Schafer's psychiatrist friend Peter Ostwald remarked to him how unusual it is for a woman to kill herself with a gun.) Schafer's theatrical writings repeatedly allude to the Russian director Meyerhold, Stanislavsky's rival, who insisted that in a theatrical performance the audience should not for a moment forget that they were in the theatre.

'The Theatre of Confluence,' in fact, manifests Schafer's eclectic rummaging for ideas from many masters of experimental stagecraft. Some he considers only to reject: the term 'total theatre' and most recent mixed-media pieces merely glut the senses 'to a point where discrete acts of discernment are impossible'; the Happening is non-repeatable and hence 'at variance with the fact of art'; chance 'promotes new modes of perceiving,' but leads only to 'boring chaos'; attempts to include the audience as part of the action threaten to vulgarize the artifact, sacrificing it 'to collective or herdesque whims' (though he does not rule out possibilities like an itinerant audience, which may emerge in future segments of *Patria*).

Remaining aloof from his audience and affirming 'the need for a strong-willed art,' Schafer prefers the resources of technological mobility. He wishes for the unbuilt theatre designed at the Bauhaus by Gropius for Erwin Piscator – a single space with movable walls and platforms capable of becoming proscenium stage, stage in the round, or circus amphitheatre, equipped with sound systems, lighting, projection booths, additional platforms, and areas for acting. He admires Oskar Schlemmer, another Bauhaus artist, for revealing the stage as three-dimensional space. (At Stratford the audience were perched high above the action on specially constructed bleachers, and some of the entrances were actually descents.) He respects the Brecht-Piscator agitprop movement for its creative fusion of movement, sound, and spectacle in simple propagandistic political skits (the political satire of *Patria i* reveals this influence). He cites Sergei Eisenstein on counterpointing the senses through the non-synchronization of, say, music and action (*Patria i* exploits this effect extensively).

Schafer not only melds this profusion of models into a coherent experience, but he sets it down in his own multimedia notation – musical, verbal, pictorial – so explicit that the score itself can be read as a virtually self-contained artifact (see page 177). Many stage works are enjoyed through recordings, but if *Patria* can be read like a picture book, then perhaps we possess a new genre Schafer never intended: closet opera. A whimsical spin-off from the literary-pictorial energy that created *Patria* took shape in 1976 as *Smoke: A Novel*, which provides a link between *Loving* and *Patria*, with some amusing sidelong glances at both.

In production, *Patria i* demands considerably larger forces than *Patria ii*. The thirty-two voice choir is matched by thirty-two individuals on stage, including the mute lead D.P., Ariadne young, and Ariadne mature.

Many of the smaller roles may be doubled, of course, but the impression of large crowds must prevail. The orchestra totals twenty-four players, dominated by the nine brass and three percussionists. This totals eighty-eight performing parts, not counting technicians. *Patria II* at Stratford required thirteen performers on stage with a nine-piece orchestra; the choral part, considerably smaller than in *Patria I*, was pre-recorded. Performance time is about ninety minutes for part I, eighty for part II.

Patria II provides maximum contrast to *Patria I* within the same genre; the two works are perfect complements for each other. Part I, with its male protagonist, is comic in tone, concentrating on satire of external society; D.P.'s mind emerges in the Diary segments but does not dominate. Part II, with its female protagonist, is darker, a psychodrama externalizing the inner substance of Ariadne's mind; the asylum inmates caricature the postures of the sane but do not dominate. In part I the violence is physical, sadistic; in part II the suffering is mental, masochistic. The musical interest of part I centres in the choruses, that of part II in the arias. The action of part I is mechanized, the scenic movement fluid, the language predominately English (though D.P. himself is mute); in part II the scenic movement is less disjunct, with festoons of incident freely draped over Ariadne's arias, and Ariadne's English is pitted helplessly against the impenetrable polyglot of her surroundings. In both works, however, the individuality of the lead character is overwhelmed by the grotesque, brutal multitude.

Where *Patria* as a whole might go from here can only be guessed, but a letter from the composer (20 June 1979) outlines some possibilities:

I've got folders for P 3, 4, 5, & 6 on my desk with progressively less and fuzzier contents. Titles (tentative): P 3 'Pieces' – the place where the pieces of P 1 & 2 begin to be put together again. P 4 'The Crown of Ariadne' – retelling of Theseus-Ariadne-Minotaur-labyrinth legend up to point where T enters labyrinth. Largely a piece for dancers with chorus speaking my invented Ectocretan language. P 5 'Theseus' set in the labyrinth explaining what happens when T (Nietzsche, Beast, D.P.) meets Minotaur ... P 6 no name yet: setting, in the labyrinth through which the public individually is made to pass. Totally new form of theatre. 'Pieces' also new form since it will be given outdoors like a county fair from 15 or 20 booths in which various bits will be presented continuously. Audience moves & puts the pieces together.

Since *Patria* already has a history of compromise with possibilities of production, there is no saying how closely such a scheme might be

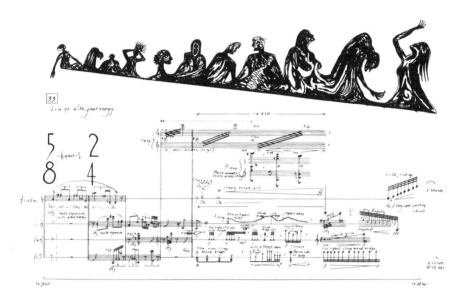

Patria II, page 48 of score

realized, as the enormities of Schafer's imagination struggle against the practical limits of human performance, theatrical space, and audience tolerance. The concomitant question of production as an integral six-part sequence seems for now barely thinkable, unless some new Prince Ludwig II should turn up in Canada. Stranger things have happened.

The investment of so much creative energy in a work like *Patria* is an audacious gamble. But Schafer's musical career has been until now a sequence of unlikely victories. His biggest gamble has already yielded a series of excellent shorter works plus two successful, fascinating, complementary, yet fully independent works of theatre, and the viability of one of these has been attested in performance. The final test of theatre, of course, must be the audience, and it may be that the stage is too social a medium for a quirky individualist like Schafer; but even if the *Patria* venture ultimately fails, its composer has already created enough music of value for more than one career. If it succeeds, Schafer will have achieved a position entirely his own in the history of musical theatre.

10

Epilogue (1979–)

Since 1979, Schafer's life, centring in Monteagle Valley, Ontario, has proceeded along lines already set down, his interests in certain areas intensifying in some surprising ways. If anything, these interests have become ever more entangled, so that separate categories are even harder to perceive than they were. But through all, the paradox of Schafer's position remains. He lives simultaneously in two worlds: the world of *Patria*, a private place of teasing symbolism and modernistic idiom, and the world of Monteagle Valley, a community of people living in a specific environment. These worlds are not separable: they interpenetrate, occupy the same space. Schafer's most recent work is often born of the contacts between them.

Much of Schafer's energy has been devoted to the *Patria* sequence. Not only has *Patria III* taken shape (including several new smaller works), but the whole of the sequence has expanded in his imagination to an enormous scale. Other works not directly connected with *Patria* share its tendency towards ritual, its inclusion of the performance environment and the audience itself within the concept of the work. *Music for Wilderness Lake* (1979) can be described as an environmental ritual, a genre which has grown to larger proportions in *The Princess of the Stars* (1981). Meanwhile, Schafer's environmental imaginings have produced interesting spin-offs in the form of sound sculpture, while his work on the libretto of *Patria* has led to a small but intriguing body of related literary work.

This book is not an appropriate place to detail Schafer's unfinished projects. Plans for *Patria* are still tentative. Nevertheless, the general outlines of *Patria III* are sufficiently clear to provide a context for the segments already made public. In Schafer's words,

Patria III is subtitled 'Pieces' and is to consist of 100 small vignettes for actors, dancers, musicians, and circus people, performing outdoors in booths, tents and mini-theatres like a village fair or carnival. Everything is fragmented in 'Pieces' including Theseus and Ariadne. Ariadne, for instance, appears as a disembodied head in an act run by an accordionist-magician (*La Testa d'Adriane*). In 'Pieces' the entire material of *Patria I and II* is literally pulverised .. until only the siftings remain, later to be mixed with catalytic elements that will bring about the myth-apotheosis of the works to follow ... While there are deep and disturbing currents in 'Pieces,' it will be attractive at the surface level. Certainly the audience should be amused; it will be a relief for them not to have to sit at attention and endure another 'major contribution to culture.'[1]

Besides *La Testa d'Ariadne*,[2] Schafer has produced six other separate segments of *Patria III*:

1 *Hear Me Out* (March 1979), a composition for four voices, contains neither definite pitches nor rhythms: it is a verbal composition playing on clichés of common speech.

2 *Gamelan* (March 1979), another composition for four voices, is a choral imitation of a Balinese gamelan ensemble, using the native pentatonic scale and taking for text the names of the five tones – *dong, deng, dung, dang, ding*. It may be performed by four voices of any type, solo or choral.

3 *Felix's Girls* (1979) is a setting of nine short texts by the Polish-Jewish immigrant poet Henry Felix, each of which describes a feminine character. The texts are broadly satirical, and Schafer's settings for vocal quartet (SATB) veer crazily from one idiom to another – Lutheran chorale, jazz, French folksong, scat singing, and so on. Some of the songs contain directions for stage action (in the Viennese waltz a waiter brings coffee).

4 *Wizard Oil and Indian Sagwa* (1981), for reader and solo clarinet, dramatizes a medicine show in which a huckster (the role created by bp Nichol) tries to sell bottles of a miraculous potion that will guarantee inspirational perception. His clarinet accompaniment was written for Robert Riseling. Costumed as an Indian chief with full headdress, he participates in the action, which concludes with both performers charging into the audience selling the bottles for one dollar each.

5 *Beauty and the Beast* (1981) was written for Maureen Forrester and the Orford Quartet, who gave the first performance. Described by the composer as an opera for solo voice, it enacts the fairy tale straightforwardly, the singer performing all the roles with the aid of masks.

6 *Situational Music for Brass Quintet* (1981), commissioned by the Canadian Brass and performed by them at the first Stratford Summer Music festival, was designed for outdoor performance in Stratford's City Hall Square. Through its eleven movements, the players disperse, appear on the rooftops of various surrounding buildings, then descend to lead the audience inside for the rest of the program.

One other work, *The Crown of Ariadne* (1979) for solo harp, is destined for *Patria IV*, also to be called *The Crown of Ariadne*. It is a suite consisting of a prelude and five dances, but its most striking feature is its incorporation of a large array of percussion instruments, all played by the harpist. The piece thus expands the colouristic resources of the solo harp immensely, calling for special effects (metal or wooden beaters, guitar pick, and so on), a pre-recorded part for harp with percussion in the last movement, plus cymbals and drums, triangles and bells, and (in one movement) ankle bells. A performance, therefore, is a *tour de force* of visual spectacle as well as virtuosity, even though the score makes no theatrical specifications. Judy Loman's performance of the premiere, wrote John Kraglund, drew 'the warmest reception any contemporary work has earned in many months.'[3]

In addition to these pieces, Schafer has made one other major extension of *Patria*: *The Princess of the Stars*, an eighty-minute outdoor pageant now designated as a prologue to the entire sequence. But this remarkable work is an outgrowth of the most important new development in Schafer's music since 1979, his increasing interest in environmental music.

It began in 1979 with *Music for Wilderness Lake*, written for a Canadian trombone ensemble called Sonaré. When Schafer moved with his wife, Jean, into their farmhouse outside Monteagle Valley, he was turning his back — and not just symbolically — on the urbanized and materialistic society around him, and on its concert habits. *No Longer Than Ten (10) Minutes* had attempted to sabotage the traditional concert; *In Search of Zoroaster* was a new performance ritual which rendered the audience unnecessary; *Music for Wilderness Lake* moves the performers themselves (with or without audience) out into the natural environment, which then becomes an intrinsic part of the composition. As Schafer writes in his score, his piece returns 'to an era when music took its bearings from the natural environment, a time when musicians played to the water and to the trees and then listened for them to play back to them.'

Given Schafer's soundscape theories, this development seems almost inevitable. Even so, *Music for Wilderness Lake* is a startling piece. It calls for twelve trombones, all distributed around the shoreline of a lake (for the performance, O'Grady Lake, an uninhabited lake about one kilometre in diameter not far from Schafer's home). The piece is in two parts, one performed at dawn, the other at dusk. It is at these times, Schafer notes, 'that the wind is slightest and refraction [of sound waves] is most apparent ... The multiple echoes around the lake were also interesting and they resulted not only from surrounding hills but also from various coverings of hardwood and evergreen trees.' He adds, 'late spring would be the ideal time for performance, for then the birds are at their singing peak.'

Since one's opportunity to attend such a performance is, to say the least, problematical, we are fortunate that the premiere, as well as its preparation, has been fully preserved on film by Fichman-Sweete Productions of Toronto. This film is faithful not just to the serious aspects of the piece but to the comic as well – trombonists in the underbrush, technicians in canoes, and Schafer giving cues with flags from a raft in the middle of the lake. Watching it, the audience feels less like a crowd of spectators than a gathering of individuals privileged to the sensations of the performers themselves. But still, seated most likely in a comfortable urban auditorium, the film viewers can never experience this work perfectly.

At the same time that Schafer was making this effort to explore his natural environment, he was not neglecting his social environment. As the neighbourhood musician, Schafer, soon after arriving in the area, organized a community choir in nearby Maynooth. For them – or rather, with them – he wrote *Jonah*, a straightforward liturgical drama on the biblical story. Unlike some of Schafer's theatrical pieces, *Jonah*, designed for performance by amateurs in a church, is eminently practical in its demands: the music is simple and accessible, the staging uncomplicated, the narrative clear. Much of the material, in fact, was developed through collaboration with the performers: dialogue was improvised, choir parts written or revised in rehearsal, and the role of the king of Ninevah wholly created by twelve-year-old Tony Fitzgerald, who acted it. The first performance, given in August 1979 at the Lutheran church in Maynooth, was a community effort involving about forty people. 'Considering that the total population of the Maynooth area is probably about 200,' Schafer observes in his note to the score, 'the per capita participation in this cultural endeavour probably exceeded the national average.'

The Princess of the Stars, however, is at present Schafer's most ambitious venture in environmental music. It is an eighty-minute ritual designed for a specific place and time: a wooded lake, in autumn, beginning exactly forty minutes before sunrise. The first performance took place at Heart Lake, north of Brampton, Ontario, on 26 September 1981, in pouring rain. (The repeat performance next morning was supplied with a more visible sunrise.)

Schafer's pageant enacts an original scenario patterned on Indian legends. It tells how the Princess (another metamorphosis of Ariadne) fell from the sky into the lake. Wolf comes to find her, gets help from the Dawn Birds, but is prevented from rescuing her by The Three-Horned Enemy, who holds her captive beneath the lake. A battle develops on the water, interrupted finally by the Sun Disc (sunrise), who drives The Three-Horned Enemy away, sets tasks for Wolf before he can release the Princess, and exhorts the Dawn Birds to cover the lake with ice and desist from singing until Wolf succeeds.

The action takes place entirely on the lake, the performers being moved about in canoes (several teams of muscular canoeists must be choreographed with diligence). After the audience has assembled – in an unfamiliar place in pitch darkness – they see a light at the far side of the lake moving slowly towards them. It is the Presenter (a role created by b.p. Nichol), who is required to explain the action, since the arias and choruses are performed entirely in a quasi-aboriginal language of Schafer's invention. Besides the Presenter, three other roles are performed by sound poets – Wolf, The Three-Horned Enemy, and the Sun Disc – while the Princess is sung by soprano. The six dancers playing the Dawn Birds all perform in separate canoes. Other forces – eight-voice chorus, seven winds, and four percussionists – are situated around the shore of the lake. The visual impact of all this, of course, is an important part of the pageant: most spectacular at the premiere was The Three-Horned Enemy, a sixteen-foot sculpture containing sound poet Steve McCaffery, mounted on a thirty-six-foot war canoe manoeuvred by nine paddlers.

For all this work's extravagance, Schafer sees its most radical innovation in its very demands upon the audience. The clichés of traditional concert presentation must themselves be broken down if new work is going to seem special. 'The big revolutions in musical history are changes of context more than changes of style,' he explains.

Like taking music out of the pastures and putting it into cathedrals. In *The Princess of the Stars* I've taken it out of the urban studio and put it back in the environment. A totally different kind of occasion results. New instruments are created, new kinds of performing, new relationships between performers and listeners. With *The Princess of the Stars*, instead of going to hear this thing on a full stomach at 8 p.m. and slouching out to the bar at the middle, you have to get up at 5 a.m. It takes a different kind of dedication.

What I am fighting against is the repeatability of art. Either art is a unique piece, an occasional piece, or else a piece submitted for reproduction and transportation. We have seen the growth of the last type in the last couple of centuries. It has led to the commodification of art. The work that sells the fastest and the most is the most successful.

In this piece, I am turning my back on this by producing a work for a particular occasion. There is no way this work could be done in Germany, Israel or New York City. It belongs to a certain lake in a certain part of Canada. It involves the notion of pilgrimage. You can't get it in your home on a video terminal.[3]

Meanwhile, Schafer has not turned his back on conventional performing situations, though he continues to modify them. On the same day as *The Princess of the Stars* premiere, the Orford Quartet in Boston introduced Schafer's *String Quartet No. 3*. In this ambitious work lasting almost half an hour, Schafer brings theatrical elements into the quartet more integrally than in *String Quartet No. 2*. The rhapsodic first movement begins with cello alone on stage (where the second quartet left off); the other players, situated in different parts of the auditorium, gradually converge on stage as the music converges. The second movement is energetic, reminiscent of the first quartet, and the players add shouts and other vocal effects synchronized with the musical gestures – as Schafer described it to me, 'rather like certain oriental gymnastic exercises.' The last movement is a long, slow unison, including microtones. Near the end, the first violin moves off stage and, while the others sustain an open fifth, he can be heard faintly, 'as if he were carrying the melody to another planet.' This piece, Schafer believes, 'is one of my best of recent years.'

One other work completes Schafer's catalogue of compositions through 1981. *The Garden of the Heart*, an extension of Schafer's earlier Persian interests, was composed for Maureen Forrester and the National Arts Centre Orchestra and performed by them on 6 May 1981. Taking his text from a passage describing the heart as an enclosed paradisal garden, Schafer spins out an expressive vocal line over an accompaniment in which every note the orchestra plays is drawn from the melody, sounded just before or just after the voice sings it. This device, suggested perhaps by the monophonic texture of Middle Eastern music, seems austere, but in effect it produces a score that may be fairly described as lush. Related to works like *Adieu, Robert Schumann* and *Hymn to Night*, it moves even farther towards unabashed romantic lyricism.

Throughout his career, Schafer has kept alive his interests in visual and literary media. In 1976, these interests combined in *Smoke: A Novel*, a narrative told in words and pictures, puzzles and concrete poems. It belongs to the recent mode of fictional experimentation, described by Richard Kostelanetz, which abandons 'lines of horizontal type – the fundamental convention of literature since Gutenberg – for other ways of populating the page.'[5] With further hindsight, *Smoke* may eventually be seen as a turning point in Schafer's career almost as important as *Loving*. Coinciding with his remarriage and move to Monteagle Valley, this little book seemed to release Schafer's multimedia talents and signalled the more celebratory tone of his most recent work.

From *Smoke*, two courses of exploration have diverged (though without losing touch with each other) in the visual and verbal directions. In 1979, the journal *Open Letter* devoted a special issue to Schafer containing, among other items, four new writings: 'The Listening Book,' 'Citycycles,' 'Ursound,' and, most impressive, 'Dicamus et Labyrinthos.' Subtitled 'A Philologist's Notebook,' this narrative purports to be the journal of a linguistic genius (not unlike Michael Ventris, decoder of the Linear B script) who gradually solves the mystery of ancient inscriptions in the Ectocretan language (another of Schafer's invented languages which will form the basis of *Patria IV*). Not surprisingly, the inscription concerns the story of Theseus and Ariadne. Dependent like *Smoke* on its graphic and typographic design, 'Dicamus et Labyrinthos' is in strictly literary terms a brilliant performance, mining the vein of ironic pseudo-scholarship associated with writers like Barth or Borges – and not unworthy of the comparison.

In the direction of visual expression, Schafer has most recently turned his attention from graphics to sound sculpture. This came about initially through his move to Monteagle Valley, for when he occupied his farm, he discovered the floors of the outbuildings littered with junk metal. One day, while he was cleaning his shed, his neighbour Elijah MacDonald stopped by and began to identify the relics: '"That's off a cream-separator ... this here's a binder guard ... look here! you've got a plate from a disc." I picked up the pieces and clanked them together dully, but then the horse-rake tooth (as Elijah called it) suddenly rang with a clear, bell-like tone. I must have had my hand exactly on a node.'[6] From this discovery sprang a whole series of sound sculptures built by Schafer, with help from friends, in his barn.

Viewers of Yehudi Menuhin's series for CBC television, 'The Music of Man,' will recall the fantastical contraption in Schafer's barn – festoons of wires and pipes and pieces of scrap metal and the remains of a piano – all set into motion by the composer and the distinguished violinist riding on a seesaw. Menuhin, a long-time supporter of Schafer's soundscape research, shares his concern with noise pollution and its consequences both to music and society in general. He was delighted with the sound sculpture as a foil to their televised conversation. 'What amuses me most,' comments Schafer, 'as I recall the marvellous day Menuhin and I spent together, is how this background of castoffs served as an accompaniment to a discussion about the future of music.'[7]

Today, Murray and Jean are securely ensconced in their rural home most of the year round. Schafer's removal to Monteagle Valley is often seen as a romantic gesture, and, seen from a distance, it does perhaps wear a pastoral aspect. But day-to-day living requires more than romantic gestures. Responsibilities frequently draw Schafer away from home. He supervises the preparation of new works, especially those with theatrical components like *Apocalypsis* or *The Princess of the Stars*. And he has accepted short-term teaching arrangements with several universities. At home, composing and writing are the chief tasks. But now there is a business to look after too, since he has established his own publishing company, Arcana Editions, to publish his works.

With her secretarial experience, Jean looks after the operation of Arcana Editions as well as Murray's correspondence. She finds time for the application of her hobby, calligraphy, in the preparation of scores for printing. And the tasks of running the household she and Murray do their best to divide equally. Murray describes it to me this way:

We garden, as you know, organically, and we do all the cultivation by hand. We also make enormous quantities of rhubarb, apple, and chokecherry wine. We also fix rooves, cut wood, clear trails in the bush – which usually amounts to about two hours' physical work per day, which we always perform together. The daily routine, since I seem to have gotten onto that, is that we get up about 8, make fires, have breakfast, then each go to our own rooms where we work until about 11:30 when we go outside and garden, cut wood (or whatever) – in the winter we ski – then eat lunch about 1:30. During the afternoon Jean usually works at her own projects, embroidery, quilting, handwork etc., and I compose or write until about 7:30. We have a late dinner about 8:30 and usually read

Murray and Jean Schafer in front of their log farmhouse, Monteagle Valley 1977

aloud to each other for a while afterwards. At the moment it is Fraser's *The Golden Bough* ...[8]

Country living for Schafer, a city-dweller until 1975, provides an ideal outlet for his polymorphous energies. Its effects on his most recent work seem wholly positive: if his preoccupation in *Patria I* and *Patria II* with moods of alienation or hysteria seemed more convincing than his promise of eventual reintegration, now, with *The Princess of the Stars* and related efforts, he has laid the foundation for a truly reaffirmative statement – on his own terms, of course.

As for his present way of life? 'The country is not paradise. It sets its own conditions. But it opens you up in a totally different way. I'm not moving back.'[9]

Notes

CHAPTER I

1 Letter to Wolfgang Bottenberg, 28 February 1980
2 Peter Such 'Murray Schafer' (Short titles refer to works listed in the bibliography.)
3 Schafer never uses Raymond, but he adopted the R. after he returned to Canada in 1961 and began to be confused with the Toronto-based electronic composer Myron Schaeffer.
4 Such 132
5 In the Ontario School system, students may take a diploma after grade twelve, or else continue to grade thirteen for an advanced diploma. At this time, the grade thirteen curriculum (equivalent to first-year university elsewhere) was standardized by the government, quite rigid, and culminated in province-wide examinations. This system has since been made more flexible, but grade thirteen survives.
6 *Harry Somers* (Toronto, University of Toronto Press 1975) 9 Cherney's remarks on musical taste in Toronto are applicable to Schafer's student years.
7 'Tributes on Weinzweig's 60th Birthday'
8 Ibid
9 Personal communication
10 Such 138
11 Letter to Dr Arnold Walter, 29 March 1968. See also Schafer's *Creative Music Education* 272–3. Properly, Schafer did qualify as an alumnus, even though he did not graduate.
   Concerning this incident, Richard Johnston has written the following to the author: 'That Murray Schafer is a creative genius and a significant

man of the theatre is evidenced in everything he does, including his telling of his eviction from the University of Toronto Choir which I conducted at that time. In those days I didn't know him for more than a student who didn't want to sing in that choir. Group discipline has to be maintained, and Murray is quite right in remembering that I flew into a rage at his continued reading of a book during rehearsal and kicked him out unceremoniously – although I did help him by holding the door open for him. I also recall stomping the seat out of a chair in the process.

'The next day Arnold Walter summoned me into his presence and invited me to add evidence to that of others, preparatory to the dismissal from the university of young Schafer. Dr Walter did not detail the others' evidence, but Schafer was seen no more and Walter never after had a good word to say for him.

'Much later Murray and I became good friends, and we developed a little act for public consumption: Murray refers to me as the person who had him kicked out of the University of Toronto – to which I gleefully agree and point out that it would now be my pleasure to engage him as a distinguished professor on my staff. Murray also asked for, and got, my support of his application to teach at Simon Fraser University.'

12 Personal communication
13 Keith Potter and John Shepherd 'Interview with Murray Schafer' 3
14 Gordon L. Tracy, review of *E.T.A. Hoffmann and Music* 403
15 Norbert Lynton *Paul Klee* (Secaucus, NJ, Castle Books, 2nd ed, 1975) 40
16 Dulan Barber 'Murray Schafer: A Discussion with Dulan Barber' 20
17 Gillian Naylor *The Bauhaus* (London, Studio Vista 1968) 55. See Schafer 'A Basic Course.' Schafer also has affinities with Itten's mystical philosophy, 'with its stress on personal salvation through a mystic communion with matter' (Naylor 66).
18 Schafer 'The Philosophy of Stereophony' 18
19 See Schafer 'The Theatre of Confluence (Notes in Advance of Action).' The best introduction to the *Totaltheater* is *The Theater of the Bauhaus*, ed Walter Gropius, trans Arthur S. Weinsinger (Middletown, Wesleyan University Press 1961).
20 Quoted in Schafer 'Music and the Iron Curtain' 411. Information for these three paragraphs also derives from Schafer's unpublished article 'A Balkan Diary.'
21 'R. Murray Schafer: A Portrait' 9
22 'Young Composers' Performances in Toronto 55
23 Potter and Shepherd 3–4
24 Letter to the author from Peter Racine Fricker, 27 March 1979
25 Schafer *British Composers in Interview* 137, 138–40

26 Potter and Shepherd 3
27 J. A. Westrup 'Editorial' 325
28 *Opera* 14, November 1963, 762
29 *The Testament of François Villon*, directed by Robert Hughes, has been recorded on Fantasy 12001.
30 *Ezra Pound and Music* 465
31 Ibid
32 Ibid
33 See the bibliography for reprints.
34 Quoted in Ralph Thomas 'Europe's All Right But He Likes It Here' *Toronto Daily Star* 26 January 1963
35 Program notes, Ten Centuries Concerts, 4 November 1962. Schafer writes about these events in 'Ten Centuries Concerts: A Recollection'
36 Program notes, Ten Centuries Concerts, 7 October 1962
37 Quoted in John Kraglund 'Composer Backs Appreciation' *Globe and Mail* (Toronto) 10 October 1962
38 Personal communication
39 'Music and Education' 5. The allusion is to Boris Berlin's 'Monkeys in the Trees,' a piano piece for beginners.
40 'The Graphics of Musical Thought' 109
41 Cf Andrée Désautels 'The History of Canadian Composition 1610–1967' in Arnold Walter, ed, *Aspects of Music in Canada* (Toronto, University of Toronto Press 1969) 137.
42 'Dream Opera on TV a Musical Nightmare' *Toronto Daily Star* 13 March 1967
43 'The Future for Music in Canada' 37
44 *The Public of the Music Theatre* 31
45 *Creative Music Education* 269–70
46 From Schafer's class notes
47 'Ear Soaks Up All Information' *Washington Sunday Star* 22 October 1967
48 *Creative Music Education* 267
49 Personal communication
50 'The Philosophy of Stereophony' 5
51 Potter and Shepherd 6
52 'Schafer Sees Music Reflecting Country's Characteristics' 7

CHAPTER 2

1 'R. Murray Schafer,' pamphlet from BMI Canada Limited (now P.R.O. Canada) 1975
2 Jacob Siskind 'R. Murray Schafer: Youth Music' 199

3 'Richard Wagner and R. Murray Schafer: Two Revolutionary and Religious Poets'

4 *E.T.A. Hoffmann and Music* 3–4. Where no confusion is possible, subsequent page references to this work are given in parentheses in the text of this section.

5 'R. Murray Schafer: A Portrait' 9

6 *Natural Supernaturalism: Tradition and Revolution in Romantic Literature* (New York, Norton 1971) 13

7 *Creative Music Education* 260; quoted in John Kraglund 'Lustro Wagnerian but Not in Length' *Globe and Mail* (Toronto) 31 May 1973

8 *Classic, Romantic and Modern* (New York, Doubleday Anchor 1961) 14–15

9 Ibid 63

10 *Creative Music Education* 233; 'Opera and Reform' 10

11 *Modern Painters* III iv 16

12 Review of Alwyn et al 151

13 Personal communication

14 *Ezra Pound and Music* 256–7

15 Hugh Kenner, quoted in Schafer 'Ezra Pound and Music' 21

16 Ibid 36

17 *Gaudier-Brzeska* (1916; Hessle, Marvell Press 1960) 87

18 *E.T.A. Hoffmann and Music* 155, 'Opera and Reform' 11

19 'The Theatre of Confluence (Notes in Advance of Action)' 39

20 See 'How to Read' *Literary Essays of Ezra Pound* ed T.S. Eliot (London, Faber 1954)

21 'The Theatre of Confluence' 37

22 'Ezra Pound and Music' 31; reiterated in *Ezra Pound and Music* 293. David Cope's is the first book on modern music to mention Pound's influence, though with little indication of his true importance; see *New Directions in Music* (Dubuque, Wm C. Brown, 2nd ed 1976) 199–202. See also my article 'Musical Neofism: Pound's Theory of Harmony in Context' *Mosaic* 13 (Fall/Winter 1980) 49–69.

23 'The Theatre of Confluence' 37

24 *E.T.A. Hoffmann and Music* 28. Cf Susanne K. Langer 'The Principle of Assimilation' *Feeling and Form* (New York, Scribner's 1953).

25 'Ezra Pound and Music' 21

26 'Poets as Composers,' unpublished radio script. This program, never produced, covered Pound, Gerard Manley Hopkins, Rabindranath Tagore, and García Lorca.

27 'Ear Soaks Up All Information' *Washington Sunday Star* 22 October 1967

28 'The Theatre of Confluence' 39–40

29 See Cope 146–7.
30 *Silence* (Cambridge, M.I.T. Press 1961) 17 and 129
31 *Creative Music Education* 232
32 *Silence* 12, 149
33 'R. Murray Schafer: A Portrait' 9
34 Dulan Barber 'Murray Schafer: A Discussion with Dulan Barber' 20
35 'The Theatre of Confluence' 35
36 *Silence* 149, 46
37 *Creative Music Education* 233
38 *A Year from Monday* (Middletown, Wesleyan University Press 1967) 42
39 *The Tuning of the World* 205. Subsequent page references to this work
   are given in parentheses in the text.
40 Cope 217–18
41 *Ezra Pound and Music* 317–18
42 *A Year from Monday* 125
43 'The Theatre of Confluence' 44
44 Cope 217
45 'Two Musicians in Fiction' 34
46 Quoted in Donald Mitchell *The Language of Modern Music* (London,
   Faber, 3rd ed 1976) 36–7
47 *Silence* 3
48 'Schafer's Morning Holds Audience Spellbound' *Montreal Star*, 26 February
   1971
49 Quoted in Elliott Schwartz *Electronic Music: A Listener's Guide* (New
   York, Praeger, rev ed 1975) 241
50 Keith Potter and John Shepherd 'Interview with Murray Schafer' 6
51 *Creative Music Education* 273. Subsequent page references to this work
   are given in parentheses in the text. *The New Approach to Music: Junior
   Division*,developed by the Ontario Institute for Studies in Education
   (Toronto, Holt, Rinehart, & Winston 1972), suggests something of Schafer's
   impact: 2 pages on 'Discovering Environmental Sounds' out of a total
   297.
52 Bennett Reimer *A Philosophy of Music Education* (Englewood Cliffs,
   Prentice-Hall 1970) 5
53 'New Approaches to Music Teaching' in Schwartz 183. This chapter includes
   some praise of Schafer's booklets.
54 Reimer 102
55 Ibid 128
56 Ibid 133
57 'R. Murray Schafer: A Portrait' 9. This is a debate of long standing in

Canadian music; see George A. Proctor *Canadian Music of the Twentieth Century* (Toronto, University of Toronto Press 1980) 19–21 and passim. Proctor sees growing trends towards romanticism and overt nationalism since 1960.

58 'The Limits of Nationalism in Canadian Music, 71. Subsequent page references to this work are given in parentheses in the text.
59 Potter and Shepherd 5
60 Ibid
61 'What Is This Article About?' 201
62 *The Public of the Music Theatre: Louis Riel: A Case Study* 18
63 Potter and Shepherd 6
64 'Schafer Sees Music Reflecting Country's Characteristics' 6
65 *The Vancouver Soundscape* (Vancouver, World Soundscape Project 1974) 32
66 'Schafer Sees Music Reflecting' 6–7

CHAPTER 3

1 Barry Edwards 'Discography' *Fugue* 2 (October 1977) 40
2 This harpsichord gesture reappears late in *Loving*; see below, page 212.
3 'Young Composers' Performances in Toronto' 55
4 Letter to John de Lancie, 7 November 1972
5 This song should be compared with the improvisation exercise on the same text described in *The Composer in the Classroom*. See *Creative Music Education* 41–7.

CHAPTER 4

1 Keith Potter and John Shepherd 'Interview with Murray Schafer' 4
2 'The Graphics of Musical Thought' 109
3 Potter and Shepherd 4
4 See above, page 67.
5 Unpublished radio script, '*U.S. Highball* by Harry Partch'
6 *The Tuning of the World* 80
7 '*U.S. Highball* by Harry Partch'
8 For the performance of 10, 11, and 12 November 1974, by Donald Bell, Simon Streatfeild, and the Vancouver Symphony Orchestra
9 Personal communication
10 Jackson House 'An Attack with Mallets on Steel Features 3rd Ten Centuries Concert' *Toronto Daily Star* 6 December 1965

11 *Prudentius* Loeb Classical Library (Cambridge, Harvard University Press
    1949) vol 2
12 Personal communication
13 Personal communication
14 Note in Schafer's private papers
15 *Twentieth Century Music* (New York, McGraw-Hill 1969) 228

CHAPTER 5

 1 'Notes for the Stage Work "Loving" (1965)' The composer's score includes
    the following dates: 'Quartet' (August 1964/February 1965); 'Modesty'
    (January 1965); 'Air Ishtar' (January 1965); 'Phantasmagoria' (February
    1965).
 2 Program notes for 'The Geography of Eros,' Ten Centuries Concerts
 3 Personal communication
 4 'Ezra Pound and Music' 40
 5 Aside from the added accordion part, the revision affected only the first
    seven scenes up to the end of Modesty's aria. In scene ii there are a few
    significant changes in the voice parts, and the accordion adds welcome sup-
    port to the end of the 'Quartet.' But the chief revisions occur in 'Modes-
    ty,' where the accompaniment, formerly assigned to live string quartet plus
    two pre-recorded quartets, is more economically rescored for live strings
    and accordion with no tape. The voice part is unchanged except for slight
    condensation near the end. Further revisions since the Melbourne recor-
    ding are noted in the published score: minor cuts or changes in the three
    subsequent arias.
 6 Program notes for 'The Geography of Eros'
 7 *E.T.A. Hoffmann and Music* 52–3
 8 'Notes for ... *Loving*' 24
 9 Ibid 23–4
10 'The Theatre of Confluence' 50
11 'Notes for ... *Loving*' 12. Similar in some respects is Harry Somers' allegor-
    ical opera *The Fool* (1953), in which the four characters represent four
    different persons, or four aspects of one person, or four aspects of society.
12 Program notes for 'The Geography of Eros'
13 'Notes for ... *Loving*' 12
14 Andrée Desautels 'The History of Canadian Composition 1610–1967'
    in Arnold Walter, ed *Aspects of Music in Canada* (Toronto, University of
    Toronto Press 1969) 138
15 'The Theatre of Confluence' 50; cf 'Notes for ... *Loving*' 21.

CHAPTER 6

1 Quoted in John Kraglund 'Lustro Wagnerian but not in length' *Globe and Mail* (Toronto) 31 May 1973
2 William Littler 'Murray Schafer's Lustro puts listener into orbit' *Toronto Star* 1 June 1973
3 Kraglund 'Lustro Wagnerian but not in length.' *Divan i Shams*, incidentally, was given its first performance by a student orchestra, the University of Toronto Symphony, conducted by Victor Feldbrill, on 12 April 1972.
4 Reuben Levy *An Introduction to Persian Literature* (New York, Columbia University Press 1969) 107. Rumi previously figured in Karol Szymanowski's *Third Symphony*, but there is no influence.
5 'A Middle-East Sound Diary' 24
6 Levy 103
7 Ezra Pound 'Canto 116'
8 'The Philosophy of Stereophony' 9, 18
9 Ibid 19. On the significance of Expo 67 to Canadian music, see George A. Proctor *Canadian Music of the Twentieth Century* (Toronto, University of Toronto Press 1980) ch 6. Proctor (page 168) mentions the National Film Board's popular Labyrinth exhibit, with music by Eldon Rathburn, which may have contributed to the symbolic labyrinth of Schafer's *Patria*, conceived at about this time.
10 Ibid 18
11 'The Sound Story Behind Taping of Lustro' CBC Radio Network Promotion, No. 176 (28 August 1973). The audio supervisor, Stanley Horobin, used ten technicians, an Ampex eight-track recorder, four Neve portable mixing consoles, four Dolby noise suppressors, four loudspeakers to monitor sound, about 25 high-quality condenser microphones, 14 clocks, and at least 6000 feet of cable to record the piece. The broadcast was first aired on 11 September 1973.
12 See Meyer 'Some Remarks on Value and Greatness in Music' in *Music, the Arts, and Ideas* (Chicago, University of Chicago Press 1967) 22–41; Kraglund 'Not absolutely boring, but close' *Globe and Mail* (Toronto) 11 February 1972.
13 *The Tuning of the World* 259
14 *E.T.A. Hoffmann and Music* 43
15 *The Tuning of the World* 171
16 Rueben Levy 107–8
17 See *The Tuning of the World* 170
18 'Song of Myself' No. 26

CHAPTER 7

1 *E.T.A. Hoffmann and Music* 3
2 Robert Sunter 'Lo, the Triceratops! Or Maybe It's Just Our Symphony Orchestra' *Vancouver Sun* 13 January 1967
3 Personal communications from the composer and Jack Behrens
4 Letter to Franz-Paul Decker, 27 September 1968
5 *Tuning of the World* 7; cf ibid 112
6 *Toronto Symphony News* March/April 1974, 4
7 Personal communication
8 'Provocateur in Sound'
9 William Littler, 'An Exciting Experiment Stuns Concert Audience' *Toronto Daily Star* 17 February 1971; cf John Kraglund 'Ten Minutes Tedious, Outlasts Some Listeners' *Globe and Mail* (Toronto) 17 February 1971.
10 *Silence* (Middletown, Wesleyan University Press 1973) 4
11 *Weinzweig, Gould, Schafer: Three Canadian String Quartets* (dissertation, Indiana 1976) 84. The following pages are indebted to Skelton's analysis.
12 Quoted in ibid, 96
13 *Tuning of the World* 113
14 Other similarities include the c–f axis in the opening cluster, the frustrated melody in the first section, and the improvised chromatic passage-work for massed strings. *Lustro* describes a similar threefold pattern.
15 'Schafer Sees Music Reflecting Country's Characteristics.' Anna Wyman has choreographed *North/White* as the ballet *Undercurrents* for the Anna Wyman Dance Theatre.
16 *Tuning of the World* 85
17 Ibid 81
18 Ibid 82. John Beckwith's *The Music Room* (1951) uses E♭-minor sonority in a comparable way.
19 Ibid 175–6
20 Ibid 227
21 John Weinzweig, founder of the Canadian League of Composers, hearing that Schafer had used the same bird call already used by himself, John Hawkins, and Norman Symonds, remarked, 'We've got to make this bird a member of the union.'

CHAPTER 8

1 'Notes sur "Requiems for the Party-Girl" de Schafer.' The translations are my own.

2 Quoted by Suzanne Ball 'Murray Schafer: Composer, Teacher and Author' 7
3 *Selected Essays* (London, Faber, 3rd ed 1951) 258
4 Verses 57 and 58 of the original are interchanged.
5 *The Tibetan Book of the Dead* ed W.Y. Evans-Wentz, with a preface by
   C.J. Jung (London, Oxford Univesity Press, 3rd ed 1957). The text in Schafer's score differs slightly from the passage on page 91; I have followed
   Schafer.
6 This is the French psychiatrist of *Patria II*; a translation of it can be found
   in the score, page 23, and one of the Arabic benediction page 32.
7 See above, page 72.
8 *Tuning of the World* 250–1; cf ibid 172; see also *E.T.A. Hoffmann and Music*
   7 and 157 and M.H. Abrams 'The Correspondent Breeze: A Romantic
   Metaphor' *Kenyon Review* 19 (1957) 113–30.
9 *Twentieth Century Music* (New York, McGraw-Hill 1969) 133
10 Ibid
11 *Creative Music Education* 261, 263
12 Ibid 262
13 John Kraglund, 'Concert Comments on Man's Injustice to Man' Toronto
   Globe and Mail 16 March 1965; Geoffrey Thomson 'Threnody Memorable
   Item in Lacklustre NAC Concert' *Ottawa Journal* 3 June 1970
14 Robert Sunter 'Youth Orchestra Presents Shocker' *Vancouver Sun*
   12 June 1967; Jacob Siskind 'R. Murray Schafer: Youth Music' 199
15 *Creative Music Education* 261
16 'Schafer's Threnody theme moves the concert' *Telegram* (Toronto) 26
   November 1969
17 'Edmund Waller' *Lives of the Poets* (London, Dent 1925) I 173
18 *Creative Music Education* 262
19 Irving Lowens 'The Coolidge Festival has promising start' *Washington
   Star* 31 October 1970
20 After the concert premiere in Ottawa with the National Arts Centre
   Orchestra (14 March 1978), Brian MacDonald beautifully choreographed
   Adieu, Robert Schumann as a ballet, and Maureen Forrester has performed it on stage with Les Grands Ballets Canadiens. Another ballet by Mac-
   Donald, 'Double Quartet,' fuses Schafer's first string quartet with Schub-
   ert's *Quartettsatz*.
21 'Your face so sweet and fair / lately in a dream I saw, / so mild and
   angel-like, / yet so pale, so full of pain. / And your lips, they alone are red; /
   but soon will death kiss them pale. / Out will go the heavenly light / that
   shines from your gentle eyes' (trans by George Bird and Richard Stokes, *The
   Fischer-Dieskau Book of Lieder* (London, Victor Gollancz 1976) 104).

22 Reginald Smith-Brindle *The New Music* (London, Oxford University Press 1975) ch 16

23 Admirers of the piece include former US president Richard Nixon, who, hearing a performance in Ottawa, remarked, 'You must have done it electronically. You must have some speakers hidden somewhere.' See 'Provocateur in Sound.'

24 See above, page 54.

25 The same painting inspired Gunther Schuller in his *Seven Studies after Sketches by Paul Klee.*

26 *Creative Music Education* 260

27 *Psalm* has been recorded in its 1975 version by Simon Streatfeild and the Vancouver Bach Choir (RCI 434); the published revision is considerably shorter, and for the *Apocalypsis* premiere Schafer authorized further cuts (page 6, bars 1–3; page 8, bars 4–7).

28 Compare Schafer's remarks in 'The Theatre of Confluence (Notes in Advance of Action)' 43.

29 'Zoroaster moving, at times just a laugh' *Globe and Mail* (Toronto) 14 May 1973

30 Yasna LVI, in *Sacred Texts of the East* ed F. Max Müller (Oxford 1887) vol 31, 296. 'Yasna' means 'psalm.'

31 The 'cosmic sound' is the hum of 60cps alternating current. See *Tuning of the World* 99: 'I have discovered that students find B natural much the easiest pitch to retain and to recall spontaneously. Also during meditation exercises, after the whole body has been relaxed and students are asked to sing the tone of "prime unity" ... B natural is more frequent than any other.' In Europe the pitch is G♯.

32 'A Middle-East Sound Diary' 21–2

33 Schafer cites the relevant volumes, but I have not traced sources for any more than a few passages. Information on Zoroastrianism is found in James Darmstetter's introduction to vol 4, especially ch 4, 'The Origin of the Avesta Religion.' See also Franz König, 'Zoroaster' and J. Duchesne-Guillemin 'Zorastrianism and Parsiism' in the *New Encyclopedia Britannica* (Chicago 1974).

34 The oratorio tradition has produced a handful of examples since part 3 of Handel's *Messiah*: Franz Schmidt's *Das Buch mit sieben Siegeln*, Vaughan Williams' *Sancta civitas*, and Domenick Argento's *Revelation of St John.*

35 'London Explodes in Spectacular Fashion' *Toronto Star* 1 December 1980

CHAPTER 9

1 Peter Gorner of the *Chicago Tribune* and Raymond Ericson of the *New York Times*, both quoted in MacMillan 'Yes! There *Is* Canadian Opera' 13; William Littler 'Powerful Evening of Musical Theatre by Stratford Group' *Toronto Star* 24 August 1972; John Kraglund 'Schafer's Patria II Has Strong Appeal' *Globe and Mail* (Toronto) 24 August 1972. Actually, the first performance of *Patria I* was heard in a version prepared for radio under the title *Dream Passage*, broadcast on 'CBC Tuesday Night' 27 May 1969.
2 Gareth Jacobs 'R. Murray Schafer, Sound Innovator' *Toronto Symphony News* March–April 1974, 4
3 Max Wyman 'Schafer Produces Enigmatic Work' *Vancouver Sun* 14 March 1969
4 A comic strip is 'an endless form in which a central character who never develops or ages goes through one adventure after another until the author himself collapses' (Northrop Frye *Anatomy of Criticism* (Princeton, Princeton University Press 1957) 186).
5 Littler 'Powerful Evening of Musical Theatre'
6 A striking analogue to the symbolism of this scene appears in the dream described in Wordsworth's *Prelude*, book 5, and analysed at length in W.H. Auden *The Enchafed Flood: The Romantic Iconography of the Sea* (New York, Vintage Books 1950).

CHAPTER 10

1 Personal communication, December 1981
2 See above, pages 153–4.
3 'Schafer Premiere Saves Concert' *Globe and Mail* (Toronto) 13 May 1979
4 Quoted in William Littler 'Composer Murray Schafer Takes His Music Outdoors' *Toronto Star* 19 September 1981
5 Introduction to *Breakthrough Fictioneers* (Vermont, Something Else Press 1973) xviii
6 'Bricolage: There's a Twang in Your Trash' 34
7 Ibid 37
8 Personal communication, April 1981
9 Quoted in Littler 'Composer Murray Schafer Takes His Music Outdoors'

Compositions by R. Murray Schafer

Entries provide the following information, where applicable: title (text), instrumentation, publisher, duration, and first performance (performers).

1952

Polytonality; pno
Berandol; 4'

1953

A Music Lesson; voice, pno
Berandol; 4'; Toronto 1958 (Phyllis Mailing, Murray Schafer)

Trio for Clarinet, Cello, and Piano
Not available; Toronto 1958 (Morris Eisenstadt, Ronald Laurie, Walter Ball); withdrawn

---

1954

Concerto for Harpsichord and Eight Wind Instruments; hpschd, 2 fl, ob, cl, bass cl, 2 bn, hn
CMC; 26'; Montreal 1958 (Kelsey Jones)

1956

Three Contemporaries; 3 songs, medium voice, pno
Berandol; 10'; Toronto 1958 (Phyllis Mailing, Weldon Kilburn)

Minnelieder; 13 songs, low voice, wind quintet
Berandol; 29'; London, Feb. 1960 (Dorothy Dorrow, in arr for wind octet)

1958

Kinderlieder; 9 songs, soprano, pno
Berandol; 17'; Toronto, Jan 1959 (Phyllis Mailing)

Sonatina for Flute and Harpsichord (or Piano)
Berandol; 7'; London 1959 (Celia Bizony, William Bennett)

1959

In Memoriam: Alberto Guerrero; str orch
CMC; 5'; Vancouver 1962 (John Avison, CBC Vancouver Cham Orch)

1960

Protest and Incarceration; 2 songs, mezzo, orch
CMC; 13'; Toronto, 10 Mar 1968 (Phyllis Mailing, J.-M. Beaudet, CBC Toronto Festival)

1961

Brébeuf; cantata for baritone and orch

Arcana; 26'; Toronto, 17 Nov 1966 (Cornelius Opthof, E. Mazzoleni, TSO)

The Judgement of Jael; cantata for soprano, mezzo, and orchestra
CMC; 22'; withdrawn

Partita for String Orchestra
CMC; 8'; 1963 (Gordon Macpherson, CBC Halifax Orch)

Dithyramb for String Orchestra
CMC; 18'; withdrawn

1962

Canzoni for Prisoners; full orch
Berandol; 19'; Montreal 1963 (Victor Feldbrill, MSO)

Five Studies on Texts by Prudentius; soprano, 4 fl
Berandol; 12'; Toronto 1963 (Mary Morrison, Robert Aitken prerecorded)

Four Songs on Texts of Tagore; choir (SA)
CMC; 11'

Opus One for Mixed Chorus; choir (SATB), tape
Not available; withdrawn

1963

Divisions for Baroque Trio; fl, ob, hpschd, tape
CMC; Montreal 1963 (Montreal Baroque Trio); withdrawn

The Geography of Eros; soprano, cham orch
Berandol; 10'; Toronto, 5 April 1964 (Mary Morrison); aria from *Loving*

Invertible Material for Orchestra; youth orch
Not available; Scarborough (Ont), 1961 (John Adaskin); withdrawn

Untitled Composition for Orchestra No. 1; full orch
Berandol; 5'; Toronto, 3 Nov 1966 (J.-M. Beaudet, TSO)

Untitled Composition for Orchestra No. 2; full orch
Berandol; 4'

1964

Statement in Blue; youth orch
Berandol; 5'; Toronto 1965 (Carol Burgar, Dufferin Heights Jr High School Orch)

1965

Loving; 4 voices, 2 actors, dancers, orch, tape
Berandol; 70'; Montreal, 24 May 1966 (Serge Garant, cond; Evelyn Maxwell, Huguette Tourangeau, Margo MacKinnon, Phyllis Mailing, singers; Marilyn Lightstone, Benoit Girard, actors)

Modesty; soprano, cham orch
Berandol; 7'; aria from *Loving*

Air Ishtar; soprano, cham orch
Berandol; 9'; aria from *Loving*

Vanity; soprano, cham orch
Berandol; 11'; aria from *Loving*

1966

Requiems for the Party-Girl; mezzo, cham orch
Berandol; 19'; Vancouver, 21 Nov 1968 (Phyllis Mailing, Vancouver Sym Cham Players); Fromm Music Foundation Award (1968); arias from *Patria II*.

Festival Music for Small Orchestra
CMC; 3'; Charlottetown Festival 1966 (John Fenwick); withdrawn

Sonorities for Brass Sextet;
brass sextet, tape
CMC; 12'; St John's, 1967 (Donald
Cook, St John's Brass Consort);
withdrawn

1967

Threnody; youth orch, choir,
speakers, tape
Berandol; 18'; Vancouver, 11 June
1967 (Simon Streatfeild,
Vancouver Jr Sym, West
Vancouver Secondary School
Choir)

Gita; choir (SATB), 3 tr, 3 hn, 3
trom, tuba, tape
Universal Ed; 14'; Tanglewood
Festival, 10 Aug 1967 (Iva Dee
Hiatt); portion of *Patria I*

Kaleidoscope; tape, 12'
Not available; created for film-
maker Morley Markson and the
Pavilion of Chemical Industries,
Montreal Expo 67

1968

Epitaph for Moonlight; choir
(SATB)

Berandol & Univeral Ed; 6';
Vancouver 1968 (Harold Ball,
Point Gray Secondary School
Choir); score also printed in *Ear
Cleaning* and *Creative Music
Education*

Son of Heldenleben; full orch,
tape
Universal Ed; 11'; Montreal, 13
Nov 1968 (Franz-Paul Decker,
MSO)

*From the Tibetan Book of the
Dead*; soprano, choir (SATB), fl, cl,
tape
Univeral Ed; 7'; Vancouver 1968
(Phyllis Mailing, Cortland
Hulberg, CBC Vancouver Cham
Singers); portion of *Patria II*

1969

Minimusic; any combination of
performers
Universal Ed; duration variable;
Maryland Summer School for the
Arts, Aug 1970

Dream Passage; mezzo, choir,
actors, dancers, cham orch,
tape
CBC Vancouver, 27 May 1969
(Phyllis Mailing, Norman Nelson,
Vancouver Sym Cham Players,
Univ of British Columbia Singers);
revised as *Patria II*

Yeow and Pax; choir (SATB),
organ, tape
Berandol, 7'

1970

String Quartet No. 1
Universal Ed; 17'; Vancouver, 16
July 1970 (Purcell Qt); Prix
Honegger (1980)

No Longer than Ten (10) Minutes;
full orch
Berandol; duration variable;
Toronto, 16 Nov 1971 (Victor
Feldbrill, TSO)

Sappho; mezzo, harp, pno, guitar,
perc
Washington, Library of Congress,
31 Oct 1970 (Phyllis Mailing);
withdrawn

Divan i Shams i Tabriz; full
orch, 7 voices, tape
Universal Ed; 23'; Toronto, 12 Apr
1972 (Victor Feldbrill, Univ of
Toronto Orch); part I of *Lustro*

*Music for the Morning of the
World*; soprano, tape
Universal Ed; 28'; Montreal, 25
Feb 1971 (Phyllis Mailing); part II
of *Lustro*

1971

In Search of Zoroaster; 150-voice
choir (SATB), perc
Berandol; 45'; Dartmouth
College, May 1973 (Paul R. Zeller,
Dartmouth Glee Club)

Enchantress; soprano, exotic fl, 8
vlc
Berandol; 13'; Vancouver, 21 Sep
1972 (Mary Morrison, Robert
Aitken, Vancouver Cello Club)

Okeanos; quad tape
On rental from Berandol; 90';
Simon Fraser Univ, March 1972;
composed in collaboration with
Bruce Davis and Brian Fawcett

*Miniwanka, or The Moments of
Water*; choir (SA or SATB)
Universal Ed; 4'; Toronto 1973
(Lloyd Bradshaw, Children's
Opera Chorus)

1972

Lustro; full orch, 8 voices,
tape
Universal Ed; 70'; Toronto, 31 May
1973 (Marius Constant, TSO);
triptych of *Divan i Shams i
Tabriz, Music for the Morning of*

the World, Beyond the Great Gate
of Light

Beyond the Great Gate of Light;
full orch, 8 voices, tape
Univeral Ed; 16'; part III of Lustro

Arcana; 14 songs, soprano, cham
orch (or full orch)
Universal Ed; 17'; Montreal International Competition, 1973

Patria II: Requiems for the
Party-Girl; mezzo, choir (SATB),
actors, dancers, cham orch,
tape
Berandol; 80'; Stratford (Ont),
23 Aug 1972 (Phyllis Mailing)

Psalm; choir (SATB), perc
Berandol; 8'; Vancouver, 1975
(Simon Streatfeild, Vancouver
Bach Choir); portion of
Apocalypsis

1973

East; full orch
Universal Ed; 9'; Bath (Eng), May
1973 (Mario Bernardi, NAC Orch)

North/White; full orch,
snowmobile
Universal Ed; 9'; Vancouver, 17
Aug 1973 (Kazuyoshi Akiyama,
National Youth Orch)

1974

Patria I: The Characteristics Man;
mezzo, choir (SATB), actors, cham
orch, tape
Berandol; 90'

1976

String Quartet No. 2 ('Waves')
Berandol; 19'; Vancouver, 24 Nov
1976 (Purcell Qt); Jules Leger Prize
(1978)

Train; youth orch
Berandol; 5'; Toronto 1979
(Shirley Sage, East York
Secondary School Orch)

Hymn to Night; soprano, full
orch, tape
Universal Ed; 16'; Toronto, 8 Jan
1978 (Riki Turofsky, CJRT Orch);
portion of Patria V

Adieu, Robert Schumann;
contralto, full orch, pno,
tape
Universal Ed; 16'; Ottawa, 14 Mar
1978 (Maureen Forrester, Mario
Bernardi, NAC Orch)

1977

Cortège; full orch
Universal Ed; 15'; Ottawa, 6 Dec
1977 (Mario Bernardi, NAC Orch)

La Testa d'Adriane; soprano, free-
bass accordion
Arcana; 14'; Toronto, 11 Mar 1978
(Mary Morrison, Joseph
Macerollo); score also printed in
R. Murray Schafer: A Collection
(Arcana); portion of *Patria III*

1978

Apocalypsis; 9 soloists, choirs (SA,
TB, 2 SATB, speech, boys), winds,
perc
Arcana; 120'; part I: 'John's
Vision,' part II: 'Credo'; London
(Ont), 28 Nov 1980 (Simon Streat-
feild, Deral Johnson, Brian
Jackson, Hugh Timmons, conds;
b.p. Nichol, Paul Dutton, Steve
McCaffery, University of Western
Ontario Orch and Choirs)

1979

The Crown of Ariadne; harp,
perc
Arcana; 20'; Toronto, 11 May 1979
(Judy Loman); portion of *Patria IV*

Music for Wilderness Lake; 12
trom, small lake
Arcana; 15'; O'Grady Lake (Ont),
26 Sep 1979 (members of Sonare)

Jonah; choir (SATB), actors,
children, fl, cl, organ, perc
Arcana; 40'; Maynooth (Ont), 29
Aug 1979 (Murray Schafer,
Maynooth Community Choir)

Hear Me Out; 4 voices
Arcana; Maynooth, July 1979
(Gloria Leveque, Mary and Terry
Wilton, Jean Schafer); portion of
Patria III

Felix's Girls; 9 songs, vocal
quartet or choir (SATB)
Arcana; 12'; Toronto, 26 Apr 1980
(Tapestry Singers)

Gamelan; 4 voices
Arcana; 3'

1980

Beauty and the Beast; contralto,
str qt
Montreal, 1 Apr 1981 (Maureen
Forrester, Orford Str Qt);
portion of *Patria III*

1981

Wizard Oil and Indian Sagwa;
speaker, cl
Arcana; 14'; Toronto, 28 Mar 1981
(b.p. Nichol, Robert Riseling);
portion of *Patria III*

The Garden of the Heart;
contralto, full orch
Arcana; 24'; Ottawa, May 1981
(Maureen Forrester, Mario
Bernardi, NAC Orch)

*Situational Music for Brass
Quintet*; brass quintet
Stratford, July 1981
(Canadian Brass)

String Quartet No. 3;
str qt
Boston, 26 Sept 1981
(Orford Str Qt)

The Princess of the Stars;
4 speakers, soprano, 6 dancers,
7 instruments, 4 percussion,
canoeists
Heart Lake, 26 Sept 1981

APPENDIX 2

Discography

TITLE, ARTISTS	RECORD NUMBER*
Adieu, Robert Schumann; Maureen Forrester, Mario Bernardi, NAC Orch	CBC BR SM-364
Arcana; Mary Morrison, Sydney Hodkinson	RCI 434 or ACM 3
The Crown of Ariadne; Judy Loman	Aquitaine MS 90570
East; Mario Bernardi, NAC Orch	RCI 434 or ACM 3
Epitaph for Moonlight; Elmer Iseler, Festival Singers	SM 274 or ACM 3
– John P. McDougall, Lawrence Park Collegiate Choir	Melbourne SMLP 4017
Hymn to Night; Riki Turofsky, Dwight Bennett, CBC Vancouver Chamber Orch	CBC BR SM-364
Loving; Mary Lou Fallis, Susan Gudgeon, Jean MacPhail, Kathy Terrell, Trudie MacLeod, Gilles Savard, Robert Aitken (cond)	Melbourne SMLP 4035/6
Miniwanka; John Washburn, Vancouver Bach Choir	RCI 434 or ACM 3
Minnelieder; Phyllis Mailing, Toronto Woodwind Quintet	RCA CC/CCS 1012 or ACM 3
Music for the Morning of the World; Kathy Terrell	Melbourne SMLP 4035/6

* Recordings labelled SM or RCI (Radio-Canada International) or ACM 3 (Anthology of Canadian Music, vol 3) are available only from CBC Merchandising. Those on Aquitaine, CRI, and Melbourne are distributed commercially.

The New Soundscape; a talk by Murray Schafer	Melbourne SMLP 4017
Okeanos; a 90-minute quadraphonic tape composition by Bruce Davis, Brian Fawcett, and R. Murray Schafer	On rental from Berandol
Psalm; Simon Streatfeild, Vancouver Bach Choir	RCI 434 or ACM 3
Quartet No. 1; Orford Quartet	Guilde internationale du disque SMS 2902
– Purcell Quartet	Melbourne SMLP 4026
– Purcell Quartet	ACM 3
Quartet No. 2 ('Waves'); Orford Quartet	Melbourne WRC 1-1120
– Purcell Quartet	ACM 3
Requiems for the Party-Girl; Phyllis Mailing	Melbourne SMLP 4026
– Phyllis Mailing, Serge Garant, Ensemble de la SMCQ	Musique d'aujourd'hui, vol 2. RCI 298-301 (Disc 299), or ACM 3
– Neva Pilgrim, Ralph Shapey, Contemporary Chamber Players of the University of Chicago	CRI (Composer's Recordings, Inc.) SD-245
Son of Heldenleben; Franz-Paul Decker, Montreal Sym Orch	Selectcc 15-101 or RCI 387 or ACM 3
Statement in Blue; John P. MacDougall, Lawrence Park Collegiate Orch	Melbourne SMLP 4017
La Testa d'Adriane; Mary Morrison, Joseph Macerollo	Melbourne SMLP 4034
Threnody; John P. MacDougall, Lawrence Park Collegiate Orch and Choir	Melbourne SMLP 4017
The Vancouver Soundscape	World Soundscape Document No 5. 2 discs plus booklet. Ensemble Productions, Ltd. (Vancouver), EPN 186

Synopsis of *Loving*

Unit 1 The stage at first suggests the Wagnerian subaqueous world of the psyche, set with bluish lights and 'fluid shapes drifting like seaweed.' On tape emerge whisperings in French and English, followed by the live quartet, singing. Motifs later to gain importance stand out from the texture, both words ('écoute,' 'Yes') and isolated phonemes ('t-t-t'). Schafer originally planned to have a taped chorus singing as the audience arrived and as it left, but now the score specifies a beginning 'almost below the level of conscious hearing.'

Units 2–4 The Voice of the Poet speaks, while the quartet, in unmetered and improvisatory style, echo and reinforce particular words (see example 5.1). As he continues, Lui (in mime) approaches Modesty, Vanity, and Ishtar in turn, each approach introducing phrases and sonorities associated with that character.

Unit 5 'Quartet.' The four singers depict the mysterious and still undifferentiated identity of Elle. The music is still inchoate in effect, but begins to take more definite shape. At first the voices move quite independently, then gradually begin to act more as a unit. Text and musical figures anticipate the four arias – 'Yes oh yes' (Eros), 'No' (Modesty), 'Miroir' (Vanity), blues singing and laughter (Ishtar). Orchestration preserves the sonorities associated with each character, rapidly shifting and superimposing them. In this number, Schafer specifies 106 still photographs, more or less erotic in content, projected in co-ordination with the music. Projections and music intercut with darkness and silence. At a musical climax, eighteen projections flash by rapidly: a sudden shot of Modesty, faceless, elicits a scream from the entire quartet.

Units 6–7 'Modesty.' Lui in dialogue projects a picture of woman's fear, the subject of Modesty's aria. Schafer's Modesty is the hysterical

1 *Loving*: scene 7, Modesty's aria: a/ page 66 of score; b/ pages 59–60

variety rather than the demure. She enters with a slow-motion scream
on the word 'afraid' (like 'No,' one of her key words). Her vocal line is no
less erratic than those of the other singers, but it tends to passages in
narrow intervals, as well as semitone glissandi and narrow fluctuations
of pitch (example 1), hinting sometimes at the all-interval row that
dominates the music of *Patria* (see example 8.1). Modesty is accompanied by a string quintet with double-bass, plus accordion. The strings
suggest a softer personality than the other characters, and there are no
tape cues; but Schafer's accompaniment is violent nonetheless, calling
for sustained dissonances, tremolos, pizzicati, and *col legno* and
behind-the-bridge effects, and avoiding any suggestion of cantabile. The
accordion provides sustaining power, rather like a small organ.

Units 8–10 'Air Ishtar.' Elle rejects this portrait of herself ('That's not
how it was at all') and describes herself as Ishtar, fertility goddess and
embodiment of sexual desire. The aria opens with vulgar laughter, but it
is interrupted by Lui and Elle, who, seated with mannequins at a
banquet table, simultaneously and bilingually recite a sensuous catalogue of foodstuffs to each other (see example 5.2). When the aria
resumes, Ishtar's sexiness emerges in a pastiche of jazz and *avant-garde*
improvisation, mixed with laughter, breathy sounds, and a variety of
non-singing effects (example 2a). During the aria, Elle and Lui dance
together, while Ishtar dances alone 'like a go-go dancer in a discotheque'
and at times makes love 'to the musicians or to their instruments.' The
accompaniment is a large ensemble of percussion oriented toward a
jazzband sound, with sizzle cymbals, bongos, and slap bass. These

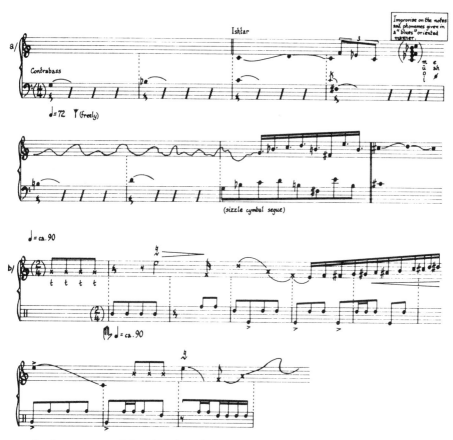

2 *Loving*: scene 9, Ishtar's aria: a/ pages 75–6 of score; b/ page 80

elements, however, never embarrass by departing too far from Schafer's usual idiom. Even the regular jazz beat appears and disappears within the unmetered texture, and at times becomes stylized in the voice (example 2b). A return to the jazz idiom near the end breaks into an indeterminate passage and leads into a climactic crescendo making effective use of the tape. The aria closes as it began, with vulgar laughter.

Unit 11 'Phantasmagoria.' In this short, vivid coda to 'Air Ishtar,' Lui pursues Elle among fantastically masked dancers; his pursuit suggests the male frenzy aroused by Ishtar. The only voices heard are male and female speaking voices on tape. The ensemble, in its first tutti since the

3 *Loving*: scene 14, Vanity's aria: a/ pages 131–2 of score; b/ pages 132–6

'Quartet,' dominates the opening, while electronic sounds take over the closing crescendo, the musical climax of the opera.

Units 12–15 'Vanity.' Vanity is the opposite extreme from Modesty, superior to sex rather than afraid of it, yet both are alike in repulsing the male (whereas Ishtar threatens to engulf him). For Vanity's character, Schafer cites Mallarmé's 'Hérodias,' whose excessive vanity 'has transformed a beautiful woman into a morbid narcissist who will not even let her handmaiden come near her' ('Notes for *Loving*' 13). He emphasizes her 'reptilian qualities' in the accompanying battery of plucked instruments – harpsichord, harp, mandolin, guitars (Spanish and electric), banjo, pizzicato strings, and percussion much reduced. Sonorities are abrupt, hard, brittle: 'in the higher extremes these sounds have a dazzling and severe quality ... underscoring Vanity's frigidity' ('Notes for *Loving*' 17–18). Perhaps because of the lack of resonance, this aria contains a higher proportion of metered writing (though it is still very free), typified by a nervous, jerky figure (example 3a).

Appropriately enough, Vanity has more words than any of the other characters, and her vocal line is more flamboyant and demanding, with rapid shifts from *Sprechgesang* to speech to screams, laughs, and a teasing cha-cha-cha (example 3b). As the aria ends on a welling up of instruments and taped voices, the Voice of the Poet breaks in dramatically at the peak of the crescendo, and the music subsides.

Units 16–17 'The Geography of Eros.' Eros's aria merges from spoken dialogue into singing. She seems to represent a proper balance between the three other faculties (these faculties bearing a remote resemblance to the Freudian superego, libido, and id, with Eros as the successfully integrated ego). Her line is slightly more sustained and lyrical than in the other arias, though it contains jazzy passages ('Sound, honey, sound'); but chiefly it is distinguished by the interaction of the live voice in duet with itself on tape. Eros is accompanied by predominantly bell-like sonorities, suggestive of psychic wholeness (Schafer associates bells with the Jungian mandala; see above, page 46): glockenspiel, vibraphone, celesta, tubular chimes, triangle, piano, harp. There are no strings. Eros seems at times a more restrained version of Ishtar, who is evoked in the drums that suddenly appear beneath the climactic word 'Love' near the end of the aria. Like Joyce's Molly Bloom, Eros ends on the word 'Yes.'

Units 18–19 The feeling of resolution (as opposed to climax) suggested by 'The Geography of Eros' is confirmed in the dialogue that follows:

ELLE Yes, I have a name.
LUI Je t'ai demandé ton nom, ton vrai nom de toi ...
ELLE When will your work be finished? I'd love to see it when it's finished. I hope you will let me see it. When I think about it, I am reminded so much of Botticelli.

The Botticelli allusion, linking with another near the beginning of the work (unit 4), brings the opera full circle. The full ensemble plays together for only the third time, but sotto voce, as the quartet and the Voice of the Poet combine in a texture reminiscent of the opening music.

Synopsis of *Apocalypsis*

Part I: 'John's Vision'

Apocalypsis begins while the audience is still gathering: six groups in different parts of the hall quietly recite passages from Isaiah and Joel foretelling doom. After a moment of darkness, seven torches are lit to reveal St John, there is a crash of waves on tape, and the instrumental groups burst out fortissimo.

1 *The Cosmic Christ.* As John chants 'In the midst of life I have had a vision,' the choirs enter one by one, the two mixed choirs in procession carrying 'chimes of light' (resonant metal bars twirled on sticks and illuminated). The Cosmic Christ appears suddenly, then gradually fades.

The high instruments, brass, and seven tam-tams (and later seven xylophones) move at different tempi, all multiples of seven, with internal rhythms playing on permutations of seven. This effect is visible in the score but chaotic to the ear. The choral chanting too uses variants of seven, not just in rhythmic patterns but in arrangements of seven vowels, or a seven-line text that dwindles from seven syllables to one. The chief aural experience, however, is of a series of non-synchronized crescendos and decrescendos. These too are based on seven: the underlying wave sound on tape swells for four minutes and fades for three, and all the other dynamic swells occur in proportions of 4:3 or 3:4, while the ratio of sound to silence within each part is the same.

2 *The Court of Heaven.* After these overlapping waves of sound, the second scene is static, thinner in texture, and formally symmetrical. As the men's choir chants and bows before the altar, lighting gradually reveals the four Living Creatures – sound poets (sopranos at the

premiere) fantastically costumed as eagle, lion, bull, and man, conventional emblems of the Gospels. At the exact mid-point, a flood of light reveals the Archangel Michael, who asks, 'Who is fit to open the scroll?' signalling the descent of the Book of Seven Seals.

In this symmetrical design, recalling the third of the *Prudentius Songs*, events are timed by two series of bells, twelve at thirty-five-second intervals in front, seven at sixty-second intervals in the rear. The men's choir alternates with instrumental groups at thirty-five-second intervals; the two overlapping mixed choirs time their chanting to the sevenfold bells. In the middle, the crescendo of the Living Creatures' 'Holy, holy, holy' is supported by twelve 'spirit catchers' (tubes spun overhead to produce a whirring sound).

3 *The Seven Seals*. The scene beginning the destruction is primarily spectacle. The Book consists of seven banners that unfurl at the command of one of the Living Creatures, accompanied by shouts and claps of thunder; each of the first four banners releases one of the four Horsemen (dancers) who pursues the choristers. This dance-pantomine continues through the fifth and sixth banners until Michael, at the mid-point of the section, interrupts the destruction until God's angels can set His seal on the Elect. While John declares 'I see angels as they pass amongst us,' the mixed choirs assemble at the front, while the Chorus of the Lost (speech chorus) flees through the hall howling in fear. This action is dominated by the sound and spectacle of seven pairs of flapping angel-wings (sections of roofing metal cut in the shape of wings and fastened high on columns around the hall). At the end of the scene, the benediction of the boys' choir leads directly into the following scene.

4 *Psalm*. The two mixed choirs at this point sing Schafer's earlier setting of Psalm 148 (see pages 163–4), a premonition of bliss in the midst of destruction. At the end the seventh banner unfurls, the choirs exit through clouds of smoke filling the front of the hall, and amid the masses of sound several players move about the hall ringing 'mandala bells' (small bells struck while twirling on a string, producing a Doppler effect).

5 *The Seven Trumpets*. The second approach to destruction, like the Seven Seals, is chiefly spectacle. The first five angels sound their trumpets (organ and brass sound twelve-second blasts at thirty-six-second intervals, building to a five-note cluster, over incantations in all choirs). At the fifth trumpet, locust dancers appear, costumed as John describes them with women's hair, fanged teeth, scaly bodies, and tails

like scorpions; their dance is punctuated rhythmically ($7'' \times 4, 6'' \times 5, 5''$ $\times 6, 4'' \times 7$) by the choirs and by the organ, which breaks into a cadenza leading to the sixth trumpet (the ominous F♯ is a flatted supertonic poised above the keynote F). This sets off seven claps of thunder; then, while the boys' choir sings its benediction, John takes a scroll from Michael and eats it in order to proclaim new prophecies. The last trumpet has yet to sound.

6 *The Battle Between Good and Evil.* Urged on by Michael, John evisions 'a woman adorned with the sun' and the overthrow of the dragon Satan. The Chorus of the Lost gradually assembles: 'They carry flags of different nations, with which they decorate the podium, ready for the Antichrist. Microphones are installed. Photographers are present.' The Antichrist arrives in military uniform and with maniacal energy extols patriotism, jet planes, computers, and the 'energy habit'; his speech is punctuated by six-note figures on six drums. (St John associates the mysterious number 666 with the Antichrist.) At the end, the woman adorned with the sun reappears transformed into the Whore of Babylon; accompanied by Middle Eastern instruments, she performs a belly-dance, while the crowd carouses.

7 *The Vision of the End.* Suddenly the Seventh Trumpet sounds (the keynote F), and a cry goes up while the boys' choir chants its benediction excitedly. Surrounded by darkness, John pronounces his vision of the white horse 'trampling the wine press of the passion and wrath of God Almighty.' Electronic tape returns for the first time since the beginning, though its earthly waves have become cathedral bells, ushering in a full tutti during the pouring of the seven Vials of Wrath (buckets full of nails, rivets, etc, poured from a height into saucers of resonant tin). As the Lost panic, the different choral groups enter with repeated incantations, mostly in groups of twelve; the crescendo, aided by the seven 'angels' wings,' gathers power until after the sixth vial has been poured, when there is a pause, a change of sonority. But this time the series is not interrupted: a fourfold instrumental gesture proclaims the seventh vial, and under the icon of the Cosmic Christ the Lost race out of the hall.

8 *Lament over Babylon and Transition to the New Kingdom.* Quiet returns with the benediction of the boys' choir, and the epilogue proceeds in twelve minutes of slow motion and darkness. From the back of the hall appears a lone, pathetic Old Woman dressed in peasant's garb, carrying a lamp, and wailing 'Babylon is fallen, now all is lost,' while John pronounces God's judgment. Then the alleluias begin: whispered at first, they evolve over measured strokes on six gongs into a

plainsong melody on F that begins in the men's choir and spreads among the others. Each choir as it takes up the chant lights candles and slowly makes its way out of the hall.

Part II: 'Credo'

Schafer's text for 'Credo' hymns an all-enveloping but solipsistic Deity. Adapted from Giordano Bruno, it is a litany of twelve statements, each beginning with the Invocation 'Lord God is Universe' and answered by Responses describing Infinity:

> Universe is all that exists.
> Universe is infinite in extent, immobile in time.
> Universe does not move, for there is nowhere that it is not already.
> Universe does not engender itself, for it is already all being.
> Universe is not corruptible, for there is no thing into which it can change itself.

The parallelism ensures one kind of consistency as the statements are distributed among the different voices and different choirs. The twelve sections begin softly and, supported only by tape, rise in gradual crescendo to the last; but within this plan each syllable of text has a predetermined shading:

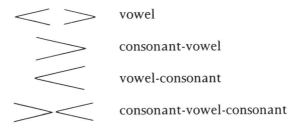

vowel

consonant-vowel

vowel-consonant

consonant-vowel-consonant

The twelvefold design invites serial treatment on several levels, and Schafer duly follows them out, unfolding various rotations symbolic of Eternity; but within these schemes he makes room for certain liberties. His heaven is orderly but not computer-generated. His twelve choirs (SATB) encircle the auditorium, each robed in colours of the twelve gems of John's heavenly city. Each section consists of a short, unharmonized Invocation, followed by a polyphonic Response.

section	1	2	3	4	5	6
tonic note:	C	G	D	A	E	B
duration:	3'30"	3'30"	3'30"	3'30"	3'30"	3'30"
		7'		7'		7'
invocation choirs:	1–6	2–7	3–8	4–9	5–10	6–11
	SA	S	T	AB	ST	B
response choirs:	1–12	1–12	1–12	1–12	1–12	1–12
	A	SA	TB	AB	ST	SAT

section	7	8	9	10	11	12	epilogue
tonic note:	F♯	C♯	A♭	E♭	B♭	F	C
duration:	3'50"	3'50"	4'00"	2'20"	2'10"	4'50"	4'00"
			14'			7'	
invocation choirs:	7–12	1, 8–12	1–2, 9–12	1–3, 10–12	1–4, 11–12	1–12	1–12
	S	SA	SB	A	B	SATB	SATB
response choirs:	4–9	1–3, 10–12	1–12	1, 3, 5, 7, 9, 11	2, 4, 6, 8, 10, 12	1–12	1–12
	SATB	SATB	SATB	SATB	SATB	SATB	SATB

1 *Apocalypsis*: part 2, 'Credo': durations and permutations of tonic notes and ensembles

Example 1 illustrates how the key centres of each section rotate upward from C through the circle of fifths, finally returning to C in the epilogue. The Invocations rotate around the hall from choir 1 to choir 6, from 2 to 7, from 3 to 8, and so on, to tutti in the last. The first six Responses are sung by one, two, or three parts in all twelve choirs; the last six are sung by four-part choirs variously distributed. The durations of the sections are based on seven-minute intervals: the first six sections are subdivided evenly, the last six sections unevenly, so that, overlapping, they become gradually shorter until the twelfth, which is five minutes long. In the four minute epilogue, the tape, which plays soft, filtered bell sounds throughout the piece (as in scene VII of part I), rises to a joyous, solemn peal over the final Amens.

2 *Apocalypsis*: part 2, 'Credo': a/ scale patterns; b/ Invocation 1; c/ Response 1, alto line; d/ harmonic outlines of Response 1; e/ melodic motif from Response 12

The tonal material in both Invocations and Responses derives from six six-note scales (example 2a) transposed successively to the twelve key centres. The original, a major scale lacking the fourth degree, appears in verse 1, then in verses 3, 6, and 12; the others successively alter one pitch (usually) of the original, distorting the diatonic quality and generating more dissonant textures until the diatonic original is restored at the end. The melodic material follows these scale patterns closely but not slavishly. The recurrent downward line of the Invocations (example 2b) is balanced by ascending lines in the Responses (example 2c), melodic figures that resemble Johannes Kepler's speculative 'music of the spheres' discussed in *The New Soundscape* (see *Creative Music Education* 132–3). The slow, rising patterns distributed in different rhythmic configurations among anywhere from twelve to thirty-six parts generate a recognizable harmonic swell within the stationary cluster of pitches that form each Response (example 2d). The general rhythms of the first six Responses remain the same, but in the last six they gather increasing momentum while maintaining the ascending contour (example 2e). In some verses the basic six-note series is extended to include other chromatic notes, bringing additional colouration to the harmonic and melodic material, but these extensions disturb the slowly unfolding design of the whole only slightly.

Synopsis of *Patria*

Patria I: *The Characteristics Man*

Units 1–3: *Patria I* opens with three tableaux punctuated by dissonant brass and truck engines on tape (most of the tape material derives from industrial noise): the first reveals D.P.'s suicide at the climax of the hostage-taking that ends the work; the second reveals Ariadne's suicide at the end of *Patria II*; the third returns in time to the Immigration Office where D.P. faces a twelve-foot-tall official dressed in gas-mask and goggles who shouts incomprehensibly through a loudhailer.

Units 4–5 The triple pillars of *Patria I* are three major choruses at beginning, middle, and end. The rugged ten-minute first chorus, sung in Italian, takes for text the inscription over the gates of Dante's Hell: 'Abandon all hope, ye who enter here'; but other texts sound in Morse code at various rates of augmentation in the instruments, creating a multiple overlay of nervous rhythms, fortissimo (the coded texts appear in Schafer's endnotes). Pitches are also determined by these texts, as in *Arcana* and *East*. There are seven messages, seven layers of sonority: choir, woodwinds, brass, strings, organ (aided by electric bass and guitar), percussion (sheets of steel, brake drums, etc), and tape (sounding 'One man's doom' at the longest augmentation using roars of industrial machinery).

Set against this din, the stage action is unperturbed. The crowd fill the stage, happiness prevails, a dwarf interchanges signs reading 'Patria' and 'Paradiso,' and D.P. makes his entrance, followed everywhere by a hand-held sign reading 'The Victim.' After the chorus, D.P. is interrogated by an employer, an intern, and a psychiatrist named Ovid Klein (his name ironically suggesting the shrinkage of mythic consciousness into modern psychiatry).

Unit 6 In this, the first of five 'Diary' sections, a speaking voice appears on tape (like the voice of the Poet in *Loving*) accompanied by accordion, strings, and Ariadne's voice, off-stage. Allusions to the labyrinth hint at subterranean links between D.P. and Ariadne. All the while, D.P.'s 'passport photos' (photos of Franz Kafka) appear on a screen. This Diary continues in units 15, 21, 26, and 32.

Units 7–9 A montage of scenes shows D.P. at work and play. Three workers in hard hats and carrying a toy drum force-march D.P. off to the factory – really an abattoir. There, in garish light, with stylized precision movements, some dismember animal carcasses suspended on a conveyer belt while others reassemble them. One of the carcasses is a woman with a bandaged head (Ariadne?). All line up for wages; D.P. is pushed to the front but misunderstands and receives nothing. The music is a *mélange* of speech chorus ('Give us this day our daily bread' in eleven languages), Morse code, anticipations of the *Gita* music, and industrial noises on tape, all alternating with ingenious treatment of the *Patria* series as a waltz tune.

Units 10–15 The paid workers drive off dreamily in large toy cars to the waltz, which merges into a bossa nova on the same serial tune, building in excitement as the stage fills with cars and balloons. Someone kicks D.P. in the back. Then, after interruption from the disc-jockey, Eddie le Chasseur, the speech chorus chants catchwords ('modern,' 'money,' 'speed') while Ovid Klein and the deposed dictator 'analyse' the human condition. New entertainment arrives in the form of Mimi Mippipo-poulos, a coloratura soprano, who sings music from Gounod's *Faust*. After the stage clears, D.P. undergoes 'Sensitivity Training': two hard hats return and beat him (waltz music).

Units 16–20 After the second Diary segment, D.P. tries to assist two deaf men gesturing in sign language; but the hard hats soon hustle him away to Language Class, conducted by Professor Knicker ('I speaking fourteen languages … und best from all iss English') – a broadly comic scene in which students have difficulty distinguishing oral from anal apertures; but the students grow menacing, assault Professor Knicker, and flee, leaving him alone with D.P.

As the violence erupts, the rhythmic speech of the classroom gives way to the second major chorus, 'An Assyrian Penitential Psalm,' which begins with unit 19 and extends as backdrop until unit 24. Dissonant and forbidding in the manner of *Gita*, this twelve-minute chorus would be a major work separated from its context. It is sung like *Gita* in an esoteric language, Assyrian, to a text not unlike an Old Testament lament, except that this Deity's commandments seem obscure ('The sins I have committed, I know not; the transgressions I have committed, I know not'). The choral writing, as in *Gita*, is rhythmically and tonally exacting, with each singer treated independently, and with some non-singing effects, including, at the end, stamping and clapping and the like from the on-stage actors. Unlike *Gita*, however, 'The Assyrian Penitential Psalm' shuns brass and tape, using instead strings with contact microphones, amplified percussion, and solo voices with loudhailers.

Units 21–6 After the third Diary segment (which interrupts the chorus for a minute), D.P. cowers to the side, while the stage again fills in a 'great Malthusian crescendo.' The crowd quickly becomes a mob. A speech in Spanish (from Ortega y Gasset's *Revolt of the Masses*) sounds over loudspeakers. The hard hats drag D.P. into the mob, which listens excitedly to the generalissimo, union leader, and disc-jockey (Eddie le Chasseur), then closes ranks in a marching phalanx. D.P. tries to join but, failing, waves a little flag pathetically in front of the marchers. Suddenly, the scene and the 'Penitential Psalm' are cut short by a siren (plus *Gita* fanfare in brass), the mob vanishes, and D.P. remains to face two outrageously farcical policemen who arrive on a tandem bicycle. Played by two contraltos, they sing snatches of Sappho to music borrowed from the *Fitzwilliam Virginal Book*. They leave D.P. hand-cuffed to a post, where he remains through the fourth Diary segment, a touching scene in which the young Ariadne enters with a candle, as if looking for something; she finds D.P., and, as the recorded voice addresses her, the mature Ariadne enters and takes the candle from her hand.

Units 27–32 Attention shifts to Ariadne, who first undergoes the analysis of Ovid Klein, then wins a prize from the insufferable Eddie le Chasseur. The prize is a party. This scene fuses the decadent jollity of the mob with its latent ferocity, two moods that have thus far alternated; and it brings together Ariadne and D.P. The music is another *mélange* of styles, dominated by a rock band with a driving but irregular beat. The rock singer Primavera Nicholson sings about double bubble gum. A futurist poet declaims. The Sapphic policemen dance provocatively to an Elizabethan fancy. Mimi Mippipopoulos returns with her Gounod. At the height of excitement, Ariadne suddenly produces a pistol; D.P. tries to stop her, but she shoots herself in the head. The attention of the party-goers, however, is deflected by a pornographic film, and the scene closes with the gently monotonous twelve-tone waltz. The last Diary segment is heard ('All that matters is the eternity of the stars ... Ariadne, do you hear?').

Unit 33 The third chorus, *Gita*, provides the background to the final action. The young girl Ariadne makes her way through the party debris, and there follow a few minutes of tender, hesitant dialogue; but suddenly D.P. seizes the girl as hostage, holding her at knifepoint. The crowd assembles, taking positions as in the opening tableau. Eddie le Chasseur taunts D.P. as 'Beast.' The girl breaks free. D.P. stabs himself in the stomach. (His suicide synchronizes with the recorded Schütz motet at the climactic moment of *Gita*.) As he slips to the ground he releases a muffled sob – his only sound through the entire work.

Patria II: *Requiems for the Party-Girl*

Units 1–2 Patria II opens with voices of German psychiatrists buzzing ominously on tape. Silhouettes reveal Ariadne undergoing a brain operation. A voice on tape (the Beast) calls to her.

Units 3–4 Ariadne sings her first three arias. Then the inmates appear, grotesquely deformed or wearing masks, walking backwards, sideways, or crawling. The choreography of all these massed scenes seeks to dislocate the time sense: sometimes 'there is no motion on stage, nothing to see or do but wait. At other times a whole universe of activity suddenly erupts and history is made in milliseconds.' Questioned, Ariadne recalls the Beast and the day she died.

Unit 5 The Tibetan Book of the Dead (see below, pages 148–9) recounts Ariadne's experience of afterlife. The action amid darkly coloured lighting creates an illusion of floating.

Units 6–9 After a benediction spoken in Arabic, Ariadne sings arias IV and V. She then opens her mouth and vomits insect bodies that turn into people: the inmates mime insect movements and sounds. It is not certain whether they respond to her speech or whether the audience sees them through her eyes (an Italian voice remarks, 'There are no real people here. They are all figments of each other's imagination'), but the fantasy identifies Ariadne's madness with her revulsion from other people. After a moment of nonsensical dialogue, Eddie le Chasseur enters with a tape recorder to interview Ariadne, but she screams into his microphone and the inmates jerk convulsively like marionettes (standard symbols of obsessive-compulsive behaviour).

Units 10–13 Ariadne sings aria VI as shadows loom behind her. As she is prepared for her bath, Nietzsche (Beast's alter ego) speaks to her briefly and the other inmates mime watery movements around her. Terrified, she thinks she is drowning but then calms down, humming 'I dream of Nietzsche with the light brown hair.' Water, as a German voice remarks, often signals a turning point in mental illness, but the voyage is abruptly cut short by the Serbo-Croatian nurse. This nurse, a threatening figure carrying keys and a flashlight in the next scene, stalks by Ariadne's bed. *Units 14–23*: After aria vii, sung from bed, begins the dream sequence, the longest action and dramatic centre of the piece. On a seashore, a fantastically costumed Arab alchemist presents Ariadne with a stone, which she promptly loses. This alchemical philosopher's stone, as Schafer's Jungian source makes clear, symbolizes the Self, whole, eternal, free from passions, indivisible (the score later alludes to Jung's treatise on alchemy, *Mysterium Conjunctionis*), while the seashore suggests the goal of a voyage through the depths, the safety of dry land; but the stone and desert-like shore also suggest the dessication of rationality.[6] This scene fades into a recollection of the party of *Patria 1*, the inmates in aristocratic finery holding picture frames before their faces, most prominent among them being Nietzsche. The nurse introduces her to Sigmund Freud, dressed as an Indian wise man, who pronounces a text from the *Isha-Upanishad* (the same used in *East*). As the party continues, the young girl Ariadne wanders about with a candle, which she hands to the mature Ariadne (as in *Patria 1*). Nietzsche then threatens her with a broom. Darkness. Best appears in a purple light. The young Ariadne approaches him. He turns. 'He has no face, just a formless, spongy substance, covered with worms.' He prepares to strike the girl with a knife. Darkness.

This vision of Death is in one sense the climax of the work, but the action moves on. Ariadne screams, chimes foreshadowing her requiem at the end, but she then recalls for her questioner the hostage incident: 'I couldn't remember whether I was dead and was dreaming I was alive, or was alive and was dreaming I was dead.' Nietzsche reappears, playing a toy piano (the music, a Mozart minuet, is performed by strings). Still recalling the hostage-taking, she is attracted to him, about to break the spell, even though his face is 'all misshapen ... like a strange growth,' but he fades back into cocktail party madness, plunging Ariadne into her next aria.

Units 25–32 Having sung aria viii, Ariadne receives a telephone call – a psychiatrist who offers advice in Danish and then hangs up. The inmates enter *en masse*, marching and declaiming on cue (a parody of the political mob of *Patria 1*). Nietzsche returns with his toy piano and, again practising witchcraft, delivers Ariadne to the labyrinth. Inmates walk through a series of corridors (projections) which shift unpredictably; Ariadne joins them, hounded by a crescendo of voices on tape, and grows more and more frantic. Silence. Shock treatment begins – an absurdly monstrous appliance, wheeled on stage by the nurse, the intern, and Eddie le Chasseur, sends the inmates into frenzies of speech and activity with deafening outbursts of speech on tape. Ariadne, as if running in slow motion through the uproar, cries 'I'm coming Beast ... wait for me.' Suddenly we hear again the choir and Ariadne in the climactic bars of the *Tibetan Book*, together with the speech of the Indian-Freud, then a low choral chant that continues under the subsequent arias. Ariadne reaches 'Omega ... the place.'

Units 33–5 Patria II closes with arias IX to XII in succession narrating (aided by projections) Ariadne's suicide and final requiems.

Bibliography

BOOKS BY MURRAY SCHAFER

British Composers in Interview 186pp. London, Faber 1963
Creative Music Education: A Handbook for the Modern Music Teacher
275pp. New York, Schirmer 1976. Collects pamphlets *The Composer in the
Classroom, Ear Cleaning, The New Soundscape, When Words Sing,
The Rhinoceros in the Classroom*
E.T.A Hoffmann and Music 202pp. Toronto, University of Toronto Press 1975.
Nire excerpts trans with commentary
Ezra Pound and Music 530pp. New York, New Directions; London, Faber 1977.
Pound's musical writings, edited with extensive commentary
The Tuning of the World 301pp. Toronto, McClelland and Stewart; New York,
Knopf 1977; 2nd ed., Philadelphia, University of Pennsylvania Press 1980.
Soundscape analysis.

PAMPHLETS BY MURRAY SCHAFER

The Book of Noise 31pp. Soundscape Document No 1. Vancouver, privately
printed 1970; 2d ed, Wellington (NZ), Price Milburn 1973. Soundscape
analysis
A Chaldean Inscription Unpaginated. Toronto, privately printed 1978; Ban-
croft, Arcana 1980. A typographical *jeu d'esprit*
The Composer in the Classroom 37pp. Toronto, Berandol 1965. Education
Ear Cleaning: Notes for an Experimental Music Course 46pp. Toronto,
Berandol 1967. Education
European Sound Diary Ed by Schafer. 104pp. Music of the Environment
Series No 3. Vancouver ARC Publications 1977. Soundscape
Five Village Soundscapes Ed by Schafer. 84pp. Music of the Environment
Series No 4. Vancouver, ARC Publications 1977. Soundscape

Music in the Cold Unpaginated. Toronto, privately printed 1977; Bancroft, Arcana 1980. Rpt in *Vanguard* (Apr 1977) by the Vancouver Art Gallery. Canadian music and culture

The Music of the Environment 35pp. No 1 of an Occasional Journal devoted to Soundscape Studies. Vienna, Universal Ed 1973. Rpt from an article in *Cultures* (Unesco) 1 i (1973)

The New Soundscape: A Handbook for the Modern Music Teacher 65pp. Soundscape Document No 3. Toronto, Berandol 1969. Education and soundscape

The Public of the Music Theatre: Louis Riel: A Case Study 32pp. Vienna, Universal Ed 1972. The impact of broadcasting on public reception of Harry Somers' *Louis Riel*

R. Murray Schafer: A Collection. Ed by b.p. Nichol and Steve McCaffery. 244pp. Bancroft, Arcana 1980. Originally appeared as special issue of *Open Letter* 4th series, 4 and 5 (Fall 1979)

The Rhinoceros in the Classroom 60pp. [London], Universal Ed 1975. Education

The Sixteen Scribes Bancroft, Arcana 1981. Calligraphic puzzle by Schafer and fifteen collaborators

Smoke: A Novel 73pp. Vancouver, privately printed 1976. Rpt as [Ariadne] *Exile* 4 iii–iv (1977) 167–242

A Survey of Community Noise By-Laws in Canada 186pp. Soundscape Document No 4. Vancouver, World Soundscape Project 1974

When Words Sing 50pp. Toronto, Berandol 1970. Education

PERIODICAL ARTICLES BY MURRAY SCHAFER

'Den akustica miljön' *Nutida Musik* 18, ii (1974–5) 34–5. In Swedish. Soundscape

'A Basic Course' *Source: Music of the Avant-Garde* 5 (Jan 1969) 44–7. Rev in *Rhinoceros in the Classroom*

'Bricolage: There's a Twang in Your Trash' *Music Educator's Journal* 66 (March 1980) 32–7. Sound sculpture

'The Canadian String Quartet' *Canadian Music Journal* 6 (Spring 1962) 29–30. Concert review

'Choral Conducting: An Interview' *Music Across Canada* 1 v (June 1963) 10–12. Interview with George Little and Elmer Iseler

'The City as a Sonic Sewer' *Vancouver Sun* 11 March 1969

'Cleaning the Lenses of Perception' *Artscanada* 122/123 (Oct 1968). Rev in *Rhinoceros in the Classroom*

'The Creative Process in Music' *Music Across Canada* 1 iv (May 1963) 14–17. Drawn from *British Composers in Interview*

'Discovering the Word's Soul' *Music Educator's Journal* 57 (Sep 1970) 31–2. Excerpt from *When Words Sing*

'Exploring the New Soundscape' *Unesco Courier* 29 (Nov 1976) 4–8

'Ezra Pound and Music' *Canadian Music Journal* 5 (Summer 1961) 15–43. Partly rpt in Walter Sutton, ed, *Ezra Pound: A Collection of Critical Essays* (Prentice-Hall 1963). Extract trans as 'Ezra Pound et la musique' *Les Cahiers de l'Herne* 7 (1965). Extract trans as 'Der absolute Rhythmus' in Eva Hesse, ed, *Ezra Pound: 22 Versuche über einen Dichter* (Frankfurt 1967)

'The Future for Music in Canada' *Transactions of the Royal Society of Canada* 5, series 4 (June 1967) 37–43. Rpt in *Musicanada* 7 (July 1967) 10–13. On music financing

'The Graphics of Musical Thought' In John Grayson, ed, *Sound Sculpture* (Vancouver: ARC, 1975) 98–125. Rpt in I. Bontinck and O. Brusatti, eds, *Festschrift Kurt Blaukopf* (Vienna, Universal Ed 1975) 120–40. On musical notation

'In Toronto' *Canadian Art* 80 (July 1962) 307. Concert review

'Lärmflut–eine Montage' *Musik und Bildung* 3 (July 1971) 333–6. In German. Soundscape

'The Limits of Nationalism in Canadian Music' *Tamarack Review* 18 (1961) 71–8

'A Middle-East Sound Diary' *Focus on Musicecology* 1 (1970) 20–5. Soundscape

'The Most Pressing Need for the Future in Music Education in the Schools' In *Music Education and the Canadians of Tomorrow* (Montreal, Proceedings of the Canadian Music Council, April 1968) 57–60. Education

'Music and Education' *Music Scene* 239/40 (Jan/March 1968) 5–6, 9–10. Rev in *Rhinoceros in the Classroom*

'Music and the Iron Curtain' *Queens Quarterly* 57 (1960) 407–14

'Notes for the Stage Work "Loving" (1965)' *The Canada Music Book/ Les Cahiers canadiens de musique* 8 (Spring 1974) 9–26

'Opera and Reform' *Opera Canada* 5 (Feb 1964) 10–11

'The Philosophy of Stereophony' *West-Coast Review* 1 (Winter 1967) 4–19. On media and acoustic space

'The Real Reason for Poor Mail Service' Toronto *Globe and Mail* 16 Sep 1978

Reviews of scores by Alwyn, Vaughan Williams, Rubbra, Walton *M.L.A. Notes* 17 (Dec 1959) 150–2

'Schafer Sees Music Reflecting Country's Characteristics' *Music Scene* 293 (Jan/Feb 1977) 6–7. Excerpt from broadcast talk on Canadian music

'Short History of Music in Canada' *Catalogue of Orchestral Music at the Canadian Music Centre* (Toronto, CMC 1963) v–x. Parallel text in French and English

'Ten Centuries Concerts: A Recollection' *Only Paper Today* 5 v (June 1978) 14–15

'The Theatre of Confluence (Notes in Advance of Action)' *The Canada Music Book/Les Cahiers canadiens de musique* 9 (Fall 1974) 33–52. Rpt in R. *Murray Schafer: A Collection.* On mixed-media stagecraft

'Thoughts on Music Education' *Canada Music Book* 5 ii (Fall 1971) 115–22. Rpt in *Australian Journal of Music Education* 10 (April 1972) 3–6. Paper presented at IMC Congress, Moscow, October 1971. Rev in *Rhinoceros in the Classroom*

'Threnody: A Religious Piece for Our Time' *Music: AGO/RCCO Magazine* 4 (May 1970) 33–5. Rpt in *Rhinoceros in the Classroom*

'Tributes on Weinzweig's 60th Birthday' *The Canada Music Book/Les Cahiers canadiens de musique* 6 (Spring/Summer 1973) 27

'Two Musicians in Fiction' *Canadian Music Journal* 4 (Spring 1960) 23–34. On Mann and Rolland

'What Is This Article About?' *Canadian Forum* 44 (Dec 1964) 201–2. About music financing

'Where Does It All Lead?' *Australian Journal of Music Education* 12 (April 1973) 3–5. Rpt in *Rhinoceros in the Classroom*

TRANSLATIONS OF BOOKS AND PAMPHLETS BY MURRAY SCHAFER

Le monde sonore. French trans of *The Tuning of the World* Paris, Editions Jean-Claude Lattès 1980

L'oreille pense: notes pour un cours de musique expérimentale French trans of *Ear Cleaning* Toronto, Berandol 1974

Die Schallwelt in der wir leben German trans of *The New Soundscape* Vienna, Univeral Ed 1971

Schöpferisches Musizieren German trans of *The Composer in the Classroom* Vienna, Universal Ed 1971

Schule des Hörens German trans of *Ear Cleaning* Vienna, Universal Ed 1972

Wann Worte klingen German trans of *When Words Sing* Vienna, Universal Ed 1972

Musik i Kylan Swedish trans of *Music in the Cold. Nutida Musik* 4 (1978) 22–25

Az új hangkép Hungarian trans of *The New Soundscape* Bucharest, Kriterion Könyvkiado 1977

Hallástisztítás Hungarian trans of *Ear Cleaning* Bucharest, Kriterion Könyvkiado 1977

Mikor a szavak énekelnek Hungarian trans of *When Words Sing* Bucharest, Kriterion Könyvkiado 1977

Zeneszerző az osztályban Hungarian trans of *The Composer in the Classroom* Bucharest, Kriterion Könyvkiado 1977

[Kyóshitsu no sai] Japanese trans of *The Rhinoceros in the Classroom*. *Humming* [sic] 5 (May 1978), 14–18, and in subsequent issues

FILMS ABOUT SCHAFER

Bing, Bang, Boom National Film Board of Canada, 1969. Directed by Joan Henson. Produced by Joseph Koenig. Award: American Film Festival. Schafer in grade seven classroom

Music for Wilderness Lake Fichman-Sweete Productions (Toronto) 1979. Produced and directed by Niv Fichman and Barbara Sweete. Performance of Schafer's piece at O'Grady Lake

SELECTED SECONDARY SOURCES

ANON 'Provocateur in Sound' *Time* (Can ed) (4 Sep 1972) 11

– 'R. Murray Schafer' Pamphlet from BMI Canada Ltd (now P.R.O. Canada) 1975

– 'R. Murray Schafer: A Portrait' *Musicanada* 23 (Oct 1969) 8–9

ADAMS, STEPHEN J. Review of *Ezra Pound and Music. Paideuma* 7 (Spring 1978) 327–32

BALL, SUZANNE 'Murray Schafer: Composer, Teacher and Author' *Music Scene* (May/June 1970) 7–8

BARBER, DULAN. 'Murray Schafer: A Discussion with Dulan Barber' *Times Educational Supplement* (London) (18 June 1971) 19–20

BATES, DUANE 'Murray Schafer Interviewed by Duane Bates' *Canadian Music Educator* 22 ii (Winter 1981) 7–13

BECKWITH, JOHN 'Young Composers' Performances in Toronto' *Canadian Music Journal* 2 iv (Summer 1958) 54–5. Earliest notice of Schafer's music

BEYER, ROBERT T. Review of *The Tuning of the World. The Sciences* 18 iv (April 1978) 20–2

BISSELL, KEITH. Review of four education pamphlets *The Canada Music Book/Les Cahiers canadiens de musique* 2 (Spring 1971) 192–4

CHUSID, HARVEY 'Astonishingly, People Go on Writing Operas' *Saturday Night* 89 iv (April 1974) 19–22. Partly on Schafer

COLGRASS, ULLA 'Murray Schafer' *Music Magazine* 3 i (Jan 1980) 16–23. Mainly on *Music for Wilderness Lake*

CREECH, GWENLYN 'Surviving *Apocalypsis*' *Music Magazine* 4 ii (March 1981) 11–13

EDWARDS, BARRY 'Composer of the Month: R. Murray Schafer' and review of *The Tuning of the World* and *Smoke: A Novel. Fugue* 2 ii (Oct 1977) 32–4 and 40–1. With critical discography

JACOBS, ARTHUR Review of *British Composers in Interview*. *Opera* 14 (Nov 1963) 762–3

JEFFERSON, MARGO Review of *The Tuning of the World*. *Newsweek* 90 (25 July 1977) 74

JONES, GAYNOR G. Review of *E.T.A. Hoffmann and Music*. *MLA Notes* 32 (June 1976) 757–9

KASEMETS, UDO 'Schafer, R. Murray' Keith MacMillan and John Beckwith, eds, *Contemporary Canadian Composers* Toronto, Oxford 1975, 199–205. French trans in Louise Laplante, ed, *Compositeurs canadiens contemporains* Montreal, Les Presses de l'Université du Québec, 1977

– 'Schafer, R(aymond) Murray' *Grove's Dictionary* 6th ed, London, Macmillan 1980

KRISTL, LJILJANA Review of *The Public of the Music Theatre*. *International Review of the Aesthetics and Sociology of Music* 4 (1973) 139–41

KROEGER, KARL Review of *The Composer in the Classroom*. *MLA Notes* 24 (Sep 1967) 50–1

– Review of *Ear Cleaning*. *MLA Notes* 26 (1969) 50–1

LONCHAMPT, JACQUES 'Les paysages sonores de Murray Schafer' *Le Monde* (24 Nov 1977). Review of *The Tuning of the World* (French trans)

LONGYEAR, R.M. Review of *E.T.A. Hoffmann and Music*. *Musical Quarterly* 62 (Apr 1976) 282–4

MACMILLAN, RICK 'Grand Apocalypse from an Ontario Farmhouse' *Fugue* 2 (Oct 1977) 6–9, 45. On *Apocalypsis* et al

– 'Yes! There *Is* Canadian Opera' *Opera Canada* 17 (May 1976) 12–13. Partly on Schafer

MATHER, BRUCE 'Notes sur "Requiems for the Party-Girl" de Schafer' *Les Cahiers canadiens de musique/Canada Music Book* 5 (Spring 1970) 91–7

MENUHIN, YEHUDI, AND CURTIS W. DAVIS *The Music of Man* New York, Methuen 1979. On soundscape and sound sculpture, 19–28

PORTER, PETER Review of *Ezra Pound and Music*. *New Statesman* 95 (17 Mar 1978) 368–70

POTTER, KEITH, AND JOHN SHEPHERD 'Interview with Murray Schafer' *Contact: Today's Music* 13 (Spring 1976) 3–10

REA, JOHN 'Richard Wagner and R. Murray Schafer: Two Revolutionary and Religious Poets' *The Canada Music Book/Les Cahiers canadiens de musique* 8 (Spring 1974) 37–51

SHAND, PATRICIA 'The Music of the Environment' *Canadian Music Educator* 15 (Winter 1974) 5–12. Rpt as 'The World Soundscape Project Studies Man's Relation to Sonic Environment' *Music Scene* 280 (Nov 1974) 6–7

SISKIND, JACOB 'R. Murray Schafer: Youth Music' *The Canada Music Book/ Les Cahiers canadiens de musique* 2 (Spring 1971) 199–200. Review of *Threnody* phonorecord

SKELTON, ROBERT *Weinzweig, Gould, Schafer: Three Canadian String Quartets* PHD dissertation, University of Indiana 1976. Analysis of *String Quartet No. 1* pp 84–108

SOKOLOV, R.A. Review of *The Tuning of the World. New York Times Book Review* (30 Oct 1977) 16

SUCH, PETER 'Murray Schafer' *Soundprints: Contemporary Composers* (Toronto, Clarke Irwin 1971) 126–61. Biography

TRACY, GORDON L. Review of *E.T.A. Hoffmann and Music. University of Toronto Quarterly,* 45 (Summer 1976) 403–4

TREMBLAY, GILES Review of *The Book of Noise. Canada Music Book* 2 (Spring 1971) 187–8

WESTRUP, J.A. 'Editorial' *Music and Letters* 44 (Oct 1963) 319–24. Review of *British Composers in Interview*

Index

Principal discussions of Schafer's works are printed in boldface type.

CANADIAN COMPOSERS SERIES

1 *Harry Somers* by Brian Cherney; Toronto, University of Toronto Press 1975
2 *Jean Papineau-Couture* par Louise Bail-Milot; Montréal, Les Editions Fides (à paraître)
3 *Barbara Pentland* by Sheila Eastman and Timothy J. McGee; Toronto, University of Toronto Press 1983
4 *R. Murray Schafer* by Stephen Adams; Toronto, University of Toronto Press 1983

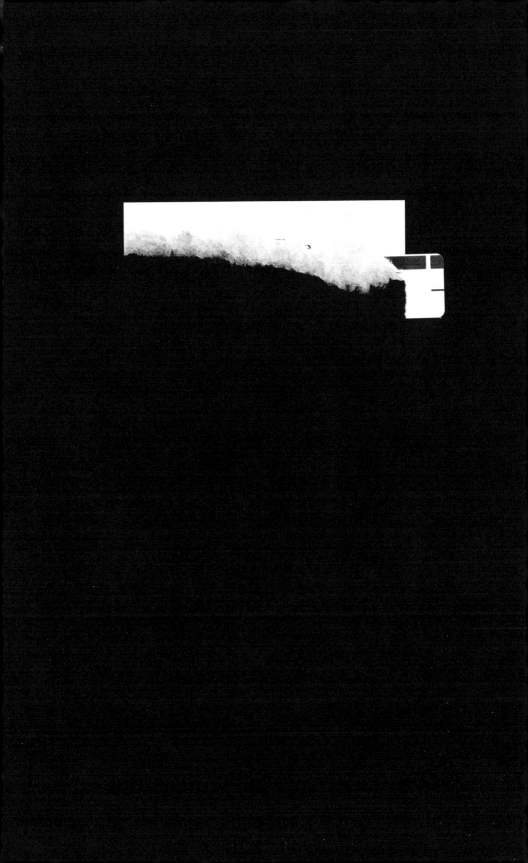